CULTURAL WORK

The great achievement of this collection is to bring together academics and cultural workers who can write eloquently about the vitally important but shamefully neglected topic of cultural work. The results are always interesting, often enlightening and sometimes brilliant.

David Hesmondhalgh, The Open University

Why do studies of film, popular music and television frequently talk about consumers rather than those who produce the work? And what do we actually know about those involved in the creative industries?

Cultural Work examines the conditions of the production of culture. It maps the changed character of work within the cultural and creative industries, examines the increasing diversity of cultural work and offers new methods for analyzing and thinking about cultural workplaces.

Cultural Work brings together a mixture of practitioners and scholars to think about the production of culture in an industrialized context: it includes those who began in the creative industries and now teach and study cultural practices, those who have left academia and are now involved in cultural production and those who maintain profiles as both educators and practitioners.

Cultural Work investigates previously unexplored aspects of the creative industries. Studying television, popular music, performance art, radio, film production and live performance, it offers occupational biographies, cultural histories, practitioners' evidence, and considerations of the economic environment, as well as new ways of observing and studying the cultural industries.

Contributors: Philip Auslander, Andrew Beck, Dina Berkeley, Shirley Dex, Sally Hibbin, Mike Jones, Cathy MacGregor, Graham Murdock, Robin Nelson, Yvonne Tasker, Steve Taylor, Jason Toynbee, Janet Willis.

Andrew Beck is head of Communication Culture and Media at Coventry University. He is co-author of *AS Communication Studies: The Essential Introduction*, also published by Routledge.

CULTURAL WORK

Understanding the cultural industries

Edited by Andrew Beck

Routledge
Taylor & Francis Group

LONDON AND NEW YORK

First published 2003
by Routledge
11 New Fetter Lane, London EC4P 4EE

Simultaneously published in the USA and Canada
by Routledge
29 West 35th Street, New York, NY 10001
Routledge is an imprint of the Taylor & Francis Group

© 2003 Taylor and Francis Books

Typeset in Garamond by
Wearset Ltd, Boldon, Tyne and Wear
Printed and bound in Great Britain by MPG Books Ltd, Bodmin

British Library Cataloguing in Publication Data
A catalogue record for this book is available from the British Library

Library of Congress Cataloging in Publication Data
Cultural work : understanding the cultural industries / edited by Andrew Beck.
p. cm.
Essays which had their origins in the cultural work conference that took
place at Coventry University in 1988.
Includes bibliographical references and index.
1. Performing arts–Congresses. I. Beck, Andrew, 1952–

PN1574 .C85 2002
791–dc21

2002068009

ISBN 0-415-28951-3 (hbk)
ISBN 0-415-28952-1 (pbk)

CONTENTS

CONTENTS

CONTRIBUTORS

Philip Auslander is Professor in the School of Literature, Communication and Culture at the Georgia Institute of Technology. He has contributed critical and theoretical writing on performance to such journals as *Art-Forum, Performance Research, Performing Arts Journal, TDR: The Journal of Performance Studies,* and *Theatre Journal.* His books include *Presence and Resistance: Postmodern and Cultural Politics in Contemporary American Performance* (University of Michigan Press, 1992), *From Acting to Performance: Essays in Modernism and Postmodernism* (Routledge, 1997) and *Liveness: Performance in a Mediatized Culture* (Routledge, 1999).

Andrew Beck is head of Communication, Culture and Media at Coventry University. He teaches about the communication and cultural industries and has research interests in the working conditions and the training of cultural workers. He is the co-author of *Communication Studies: the Essential Introduction* (Routledge, 2002).

Dina Berkeley is currently working at the Public Health Research Unit of the University of Hull, Humberside, evaluating the Hull and East Riding Health Action Zone. She is also visiting professor in the Department of Social and Clinical Psychology at the Aristotelian University of Thessaloniki. She has researched in the fields of organizational analysis, project management, information systems development, decision making, decision support systems, health care and health promotion systems, media culture and media organizations. She was one of the two principal investigators of the ESRC funded project, Study of Industrial Modes of Production of TV Drama. She is co-author of *Software Development Project Management: Process and Support* (Ellis Horwood/Simon and Schuster, 1990) and the managing editor of *Context-Sensitive Decision Support Systems* (Chapman & Hall, 1998).

Shirley Dex is an applied economist, currently Senior Research Associate at the Judge Institute for Management Studies at the University of Cambridge. Formerly she was Research Professor at the University of Essex and Reader in Economics at the University of Keele. Her research interests include flexible employment, women's employment, human resource management, equal opportunities policies, family-friendly employment policies and comparative studies of women in the labor market. She has worked with the British Film Institute on an ESRC Grant (R000 237131) analyzing a longitudinal panel data set of television production workers that is the basis of the chapter in this volume.

Sally Hibbin is founder member of Parallax Pictures and a founder and board member of the Film Consortium. Amongst the films she has produced are the BAFTA award winning *A Very British Coup* (1988), the Cannes Critics' Award winning and Felix European Film of the Year *Riff-Raff* (1991), the Cannes Jury Prize winning *Raining Stones* (1992), the Berlin Film Festival Critics' Award and Berlin Film Festival's Silver Bear award winning *Ladybird Ladybird* (1994), *i.d.* (1995), *Carla's Song* (1996) and *Dockers* (1999). She is an acknowledged authority on the Carry On and James Bond films.

Mike Jones was a member of British pop group Latin Quarter between 1983 and 1997. In that time the group had one hit single in Britain (*Radio Africa*, 1986) but enjoyed album and live success in Europe. Latin Quarter released four albums for major labels (Arista and RCA) and two for German independent labels (Verabra and SPV). Mike is now Course Director, MBA Music Industries, Institute of Popular Music, University of Liverpool.

Cathy MacGregor is Lecturer in Performance, University of Wolverhampton, and has worked as a performance artist creating work since 1996. Her research interests are contemporary performance, particularly the body in performance and sex in performance, and early modern performance practices. She has contributed to a number of books and journals, most recently "The Eye of the Storm: Edwarda and the Story of the Eye" in *The Beast at Heaven's Gate: Georges Bataille and the Politics of Transgression*, edited by Andrew Hussey and Malcolm Pollard (2000), Rodopi Press and "Show and Tell: Performing the Sexual Body" in *Live Display*, edited by Jim Drobnik and Jennifer Ficher (2000), University of Chicago Press. Among original work she has made are the performance projects *In the Factory of Infinite Vanity* (Coventry, 1998), *Catholic Sex* (Arizona, London, New York, 2000), and *Scarlett's Story Part One* (Nottingham, New York, Wolverhampton, 2001).

Graham Murdock is Reader in the Sociology of Culture at Loughborough University and Professor of Communication at the University of Bergen. He is internationally renowned for his work in the sociology of culture, particularly for his work in political economy. He has been visiting professor at the universities of California, Brussels, Leuven and Mexico City.

He is head of the Political Economy Section of the International Association of Media and Communication Research. Among his recent works are the two-volume collection *The Political Economy of the Media* (edited jointly with Peter Golding).

Robin Nelson is Professor and Head of Department of Contemporary Arts at The Manchester Metropolitan University. His interests span the contemporary arts and media and his broad-ranging cultural research is typically grounded in case studies. His most recent full-length account of television culture is published as *TV Drama in Transition* (Macmillan, 1997).

Yvonne Tasker is Chair of the Film and Television Studies sector, University of East Anglia. Her study of action films was published as *Spectacular Bodies: Gender, Genre and the Action Cinema* (Routledge, 1993). Amongst her other publications are *Working Girls: Gender and Sexuality in Popular Cinema* (Routledge, 1998) and *Fifty Contemporary Filmmakers* (Routledge, 2002). Her most recent publication is a monograph on *The Silence of the Lambs* (BFI, 2002).

Steve Taylor lectures in Radio Production at Thames Valley University. He has worked in the retail music industry and music radio since leaving school in 1987. He obtained both his BA in Communication Studies and his MA in Cultural Policy as a mature student. He has worked as a DJ for Kix 96 (in Coventry), Xfm (in London) and The Bear (in Stratford-upon-Avon). He continues to work as a radio and live DJ.

Jason Toynbee sang in bands for a number of years and is now Lecturer at the Institute of Popular Music, University of Liverpool. He is the author of *Making Popular Music: Musicians, Aesthetics and the Manufacture of Popular Music* (Arnold, 2000) and *Creating Problems: Social Authorship, Copyright and the Production of Culture* (Open University, 2001).

Janet Willis was Media Research Officer in the Center for Audience and Industry Research at the British Film Institute. Between 1994 and 1998 she worked on the ESRC-funded, longitudinal Television Industry Tracking Study, which examined the career histories and working conditions of a panel of television production workers. A co-authored book *Working in Television* (Oxford University Press) is forthcoming.

ACKNOWLEDGMENTS

This collection of essays had its origins in the *Cultural Work* conference that took place at Coventry University in 1998. Most of the chapters in this book first emerged in the form of papers given at that conference but they have all been extensively revised for publication. Some chapters have been specifically commissioned for this volume.

Amongst colleagues whose work does not appear in the present volume but whose arguments and representations at the *Cultural Work* conference inform this work, I would like to thank Terry Atkinson, Martin Barker, Mavis Bayton, Mark Fortier, David Hesmondhalgh, Patrick Keiller and Angela McRobbie.

Thanks are also due to Suzanne Perry for her work before, during and after the *Cultural Work* conference.

Acknowledgment is due to the *New Statesman* which published an earlier version of Sally Hibbin's chapter.

I'd like to thank Oliver Bennett and Jim McGuigan for staying with this publishing project as long as they have.

I began my own cultural work making music in Bedford in the 1960s with Paul Cummergen. Paul died in Swaziland in April 2001. I'd like to dedicate this work to his memory.

INTRODUCTION

Cultural work, cultural workplace – looking at the cultural industries

Andrew Beck

> Many books exist on film, recording, broadcasting and publishing yet few make reference to the working conditions and financial recompense available to the people working in these industries. Such issues have been absolutely central to the sociology of work in general, so why have they been marginalized in the study of *cultural* work?
>
> David Hesmondhalgh (in Curran, 2000: 113–14)

In recent times research into the cultural industries has tended to focus on either conditions of consumption and reception or on the changing character of both the structures of the cultural industries and the changing character of the national, transnational and global structures in which they function. *Cultural Work* is an ambitious book for, if nothing else, it seeks to return to work, to an examination of the conditions of the production of culture in a large range of arenas, to map the changed character of work within cultural industries, to examine the increasing diversity of cultural work and to suggest new perspectives and new methodologies (or, at the very least, new methodological imbrications) with which to interrogate changed worlds and changed work. All of *Cultural Work*'s authors are teachers, researchers or practitioners, workers in cultural industries. But even these distinctions are fluid and partial, for many of them have either moved from cultural practice to education and research or manage to maintain profiles as both educators and practitioners. In a very real sense the character of cultural work as it is perceived, constructed and practiced within the academy has also changed.

No one text about the cultural industries could achieve comprehensive coverage of every single industry or investigate every territory in which the cultural industries operate. For this reason *Cultural Work* focuses on neglected or under-theorized cultural industries, on the operation of the cultural industries in (mainly) Britain, and on neglected aspects of the cultural industries. In this way the contributions by Steve Taylor and Jason Toynbee can be seen as invitations to future study of neglected topics (creativity) or neglected industries (music radio). Further, this means that *Cultural Work* can embrace polemic in the form of Sally Hibbin's characterizations and prognostications for British film culture and Mike Jones's call to academics to re-think analyzing the popular music industry in terms of its being a workplace.

In terms of the book's structure I have avoided the temptation to group chapters in sections organized around crude industrial clusters; rather, I have sought to identify generic themes (conditions, practice, organization, representation). What I propose to do here is to guide you through the book's chapters whilst simultaneously sketching in some of the backdrop against which *Cultural Work* is set.

Conditions

Cultural Work has to be something more than a call to return to existing research traditions; before this new work begins it is vital that the changed and still changing character of the environment in which cultural work takes place is examined. The last twenty years have witnessed fundamental changes in the structures in which cultural work takes place. One of the most significant of these changes has been the governing role of marketizing and corporatizing dynamics. In the UK this has meant that the previously existing state sponsored or underwritten, or state sanctioned monopolistic or duopolistic, structures in which cultural work took place have been replaced by privatized or in-all-but-name privatized structures. This is where Graham Murdock comes in. Jim McGuigan has remarked that Murdock has a reputation for being able to "produce a diagnosis of current ills and to outline what should be done in a practical fashion" (McGuigan, 1997: 8). *Back To Work: Cultural Labor in Altered Times* is the keynote chapter of this book and sets the scene for all that follows. Murdock sets out to examine past, present and future in cultural production, to map those shifts which have occurred since sustained work on the cultural industries was last undertaken and to suggest the shape future research might take.

Murdock identifies the investing of as much money in marketing cultural products as in developing them as one of the key practices to understanding the contemporary production of culture. The manner in which marketing can accommodate its fiercest critics and absorb that criticism in a post-modern fashion was acutely satirized by the late Bill Hicks in his routine "Marketing & Advertising" (Hicks, 1997). In mid-performance, with no preamble, Hicks springs this on his audience: "By the way if anyone here's in marketing or advertising – kill yourself [. . .] No joke here – really seriously – kill yourself. You have no rationalization for what you do – you are Satan's little helpers – kill yourself, kill yourself, kill yourself." He then develops the satire in terms of how marketing can generate its own disarming auto-critique: "You know what bugs me though? Everyone here who's in marketing is now thinking the same thing – oh cool, Bill's going for that anti-marketing dollar – that's a huge market [. . .] Don't turn everything into a dollar sign, please. Woo – the plea for sanity dollar. *Huge* market. Look at our research" (ibid.). The awful power and position of marketing in contemporary cultural work casts a shadow over many of the accounts of work in the cultural industries in this collection.

Practice

An abiding problem when considering cultural work is the special status frequently accorded cultural workers. John Ruskin offered a characterization of this conception of the cultural worker, or Artist, as special:

> In general, the men who are employed in the Arts have freely chosen their profession, and suppose themselves to have special faculty for it [. . .] No one expects any honest or useful work of [the Artist]; but every one expects him to be ingenious. Originality, dexterity, invention, imagination, everything is asked of him except what alone is to be had for asking – honesty and sound work, and the due discharge of his [work].
> (Ruskin, quoted in Thomas, 1999: 479–80).

More recently Jamous and Peloille (1970) have characterized this specialness as the "mystery" all professions spin around themselves.

However, within the cultural industries the notion is endlessly reproduced that cultural work is special and mysterious and can only be undertaken by special and mysterious people (the ideology that cultural work (cf. Ruskin) isn't actually work). That sense of "mystery" is in many ways reinforced by novels and films which seek to demystify specific forms of cultural work in specific eras but which frequently end up functioning as *roman à clefs*. As such they expressly invite the audience to decode the text and to enter the magic circle of those who know the true identities of the disguised characters in such books or films. Any number of texts may be read in this fashion. J. B. Priestley's 1968 novel *The Image Men* features troubled comedian Lou Bracton who is modeled on the troubled comedian Tony Hancock. Elaine Jesmer's 1974 novel *Number One with a Bullet* features a troubled soul singer signed to a record label clearly modeled on Marvin Gaye and Tamla Motown. Ted Heller's 2001 novel *Slabrat* makes fascinating reading as much for its portrait of the thinly disguised Condé Naste organization as for its charting of the rise of its lead character Zachary Arlen Post. Sometimes (as in the 1985 film *Perfect*) the audience is tipped a huge wink to help decode the text: alongside John Travolta playing a pop journalist, Jann

Wenner essentially plays himself, editor of *Rolling Stone* magazine. The knowingness, the insider joke, doesn't always work; *Perfect* was classically judged by *Variety* magazine to be "Guilty of the sins it condemns – superficiality, manipulation and smugness." Finally, one could point to Bruce Wagner's novel *Force Majeur*, clearly a work which is informed by his experiences of working as screenwriter of *Nightmare on Elm Street Part Three: Dream Warriors* and *Scenes from the Class Struggle in Beverly Hills*, where the superficiality, manipulation and smugness of the movie business are satirized to the point of bitterness, at which point the novel breaks down into its bitter, fantasy conclusion.

In all of these fictionalized accounts of working in the cultural industries, insecurity features prominently. The popular musicians of Jason Toynbee's researches might only dream of such experiences of insecurity in that they perceive themselves as being outside of those formal work structures of the music (or any other) industry. Toynbee examines the ways in which those musicians understand their own creativity, how they form mutual support networks (in the absence of record company safety nets) and how the paraeconomics of such scenes are viewed by the music industry itself. Viewed from one perspective, this is labor at the margins; viewed from another, this is a last space of resistance.

Another space of resistance which cultural workers explore is performance. As questions about the primacy and authenticity of live (as opposed to mediatized) performance abound, Cathy MacGregor offers a timely survey of performance work over the last thirty years. No stranger to controversy herself (the British press widely reported the opposition of local would-be lapdancing club proprietors to her performance of *Scarlett's Story* at the Sensitive Skin festival in Nottingham in March 2001), MacGregor has been concerned in recent work to make performances out of the work available to women in the glamour and sex industries, and to make work which is informed by a sense of performance history. At the root of many of these performances are explorations of the performative character of so much cultural work.

Jason Toynbee and Cathy MacGregor have worked or still work as performers within the cultural industries. So too does Steve Taylor. His extensive experience of work as a radio DJ in independent local radio is relentlessly examined and theorized in his *"I Am What I Play": the Radio DJ as Cultural Arbiter and Negotiator*. Not only does Taylor analyze his own and others' experiences in British independent music radio, but he also moves toward depressing conclusions about the possibilities of new work being made in that sector. The DJs of Taylor's descriptions are subject to endless surveillance and interference, working as they do in an audience-focused and profit-sensitive industry. Quite possibly they aspire to the condition of Howard Becker's "integrated professionals." Whilst in some ways resembling the guys working the track at Ford or GM ("integrated professionals have the technical abilities, social skills, and conceptual apparatus necessary to make it easy to make art. Because they know, understand, and habitually use the conventions on which their world runs, they fit easily into all standard activities" (Becker, 1982: 229)), nonetheless radio DJs frequently lack the security of working in long-established industrial formations where at the very least conventions exist and are, generally speaking, adhered to. Becker concluded that the integrated professional "operate[d] within a shared tradition of problems and solutions" (ibid.: 230). You get the feeling that Taylor's DJs would relish such securities, all the better from which to work to connect with audiences.

Organization

Citing the 1983 first edition of Todd Gitlin's *Inside Prime Time*, Diana Crane proposed that "the television industry purveys a kind of recombinant culture in which new products are designed to imitate products that were successful in the past, by combining features from several such products or by using products that have been successful in other media" (Crane, 1992: 62). Dina Berkeley has researched the financial and cultural economies of television drama. In her chapter, she explores the tensions which emerge when creativity is perceived as a commodity, where cultural workers in television drama are caught between conceptions of the popular and the economic.

Television drama is the most expensive type of programming in Britain as well as the most creative product of the media industry. The industry prides itself for producing quality drama which will, in the first place, appeal to domestic audiences and, in the second place, to international markets. Achieving high quality invariably requires sustained investment in its production, both in terms of appropriate time and sufficient and sufficiently high quality resources being allocated to it. Unfortunately, economic and structural changes in the industry have stressed the need to produce drama with the lowest possible budgets in the least time possible. The commitment to produce high quality drama still exists in the British television industry but it often tends to get compromised by the economics that drive its production. Value and creativity, in this instance, become adversaries in the competition of what the final product will look like (as well as to whether it will even ever get produced).

Berkeley's chapter investigates the conflict between the concerns of a cultural economy and a financial economy as they manifest themselves in television drama production. It looks at how the concepts of creativity and value take on different meanings at the different levels of negotiation between the different agents involved, within the whole television drama production process, from the time an idea for a production is put forward to the time when the product itself becomes ready for distribution and transmission. It argues that the concept of value employed by the various decision-makers in the chain embodies a reification of the concept of creativity which is based on consensual notions about what would appeal to the audience that the particular broadcaster aims at, and the various potential markets the final product can appeal to. Creativity is seen as a commodity, required for the production of the product (measured in terms of audience ratings, good reviews, prestige). This tendency gives rise to risk aversion and conservatism toward innovation, as estimates of potential success (and, hence, commissioning) are based on the past successes of similar products. These act as reference points for assigning values to new ideas for television drama production.

The culture of uncertainty in the television industry doesn't just affect cultural workers in the workplace; it also produces a state of mind and being where security is sought after, worried about, lost, and mourned. Security may be achieved by all manner of means. Many working people rely on family for security and comfort. Family formation in contemporary cultural industries, with their fearful culture of presenteeism and structured over-work, is not so easily achieved or maintained. Indeed the problems facing women working in the cultural industries are as acute as ever. The film-maker Sarah Maldoror has stated that she is "one of those modern women who try to combine work and family life [and] this is a problem for me. Children need a home and a mother. That is why I try to prepare and edit my films in Paris during the long summer vacation" (quoted in Adair, 1999: 110). In *Mothers Returning to Television Production Work in a Changing Environment*, Janet Willis and Shirley Dex draw on research work into women working in the British television industry. In particular they address problems raised for women seeking to engage in both cultural and family work, and examine the extent to which changing industrial, structural and technological changes either help or hinder women seeking career breaks without having to sacrifice career progression.

This culture of uncertainty and lack of security clearly manifests itself in the material working conditions of workers in the cultural industries. Indeed it is unseemly to think about the end products of the cultural industries without thinking about the conditions in which those products are created. Underpinning any consideration of work in the cultural industries are the processes of casualization, of part-timism, of the destruction of career-building. Casualization's continuing ascendancy and the proliferation of part-time jobs has been wryly remarked upon by Stanley Aronowitz (in "The Last Good Job in America"): "the part-timers have little space for individual development or community participation. You may have heard the joke: the politician announces that the Clinton administration has created ten million jobs in its first four-year term." "Yeah," says the voter, "and I have three of them" (Aronowitz and Cutler, 1998: 213).

There exist many accounts – both fictional and factual – of the workings of the film industry. These range from the hysterical grandeur of Joseph L.

Mankiewicz's *The Barefoot Contessa* (1954) to the conscientious reportage of Lillian Ross's *Movie* (1953), from the kiss and tell of William Goldman's *Adventures in the Screen Trade* (1985) to the snort and tell of Peter Biskind's *Easy Riders, Raging Bulls* (1998). Such accounts can contribute to the processes of mystification referred to above. *Cultural Work* employs different insider knowledge to develop an account of contemporary film production. Sally Hibbin is a successful producer of films for theatrical and television release but is also a key player in the reconfigured market in which film production takes place in contemporary Britain. Not only does Hibbin detail the fragile character of contemporary film-making but she also develops her argument to point to what she terms "catastrophic cycles" in British film production.

Catastrophe is no stranger to the pop musician. Indeed it would appear to be an essential feature of popular musicians' working lives. In his account of his entry as a teenager into the late 1950s pop music world, Al Kooper admits, "We knew we were being ripped off, but our financial interests at such a formative age were strictly secondary" (Kooper and Edmonds, 1977: 22). Over a decade later the saxophonist Dick Heckstall-Smith described his situation at the end of more than thirty years as a professional musician: "I had no cash and nothing in the bank. Throughout my whole career in music [Alexis Korner's Blues Incorporated, the Graham Bond Organization, John Mayall's Bluesbreakers, Colosseum], not one of the bands I had ever been with had done more than pay the wages [. . .] So I went round to a local minicab firm and hired myself and my car to it for three weeks" (1989: 143). For all the promise of the bright lights of the pop business (and for all the ways in which pop musicians are capable of describing their being seduced by false promises with disarming humor) the predominant experience of the majority of pop music makers is failure.

Approaching failure in the popular music industry, Mike Jones has used his own experiences to investigate how and why most pop records fail to achieve the success they aim for. Jones is not concerned with soi-disant avant-garde musical products but rather popular musics which are conceived of as popular but which nonetheless fail to find their mass audiences. Methodologically speaking, Jones has moved outside the frameworks of media and cultural studies and has used Organizational Theory to explore and explain the phenomenon of the popular which fails to achieve popularity.

Jones's chapter examines the interactions between all of those groups that bear on the realization of compositions as recorded texts – where the context for this discussion is the twin statistics that only one in eight pop acts signed to major labels will make mass selling commodities and that the total of signed acts represents barely one percent of all pop acts existent at any one time.

Pop music making is not only cultural work, it is, apparently, very badly organized cultural work. Considered from this perspective he argues that it is Organizational Theory rather than media or cultural studies that offers the concepts and the potential of analytical insight to access the experience of attempting to make music that will become popular. Only record companies can address the mass market for popular musical products. The terms "music industry" and "record industry" are common currency in discussions about pop music, but rarely is the logic of pop as a creation of industrial production ever explored or discussed, whether by consumers or researchers.

Representation

Live performance is endlessly problematic. Steve O'Connor has asserted that it is "the 'live show' which seems to offer this unfalsifiably real, corporeal presence, for here – apparently – are to be found life, music, the body themselves, naked and intense, with no barrier or representation" (O'Connor, 1987: 131). It is also a site, particularly in popular music performance, that is endlessly prepared and rehearsed to the extent that "live" performance is frequently an attempt to reproduce the previously recorded. Philip Auslander returns to and builds upon notions first explored in "Liveness: Performance and the Anxiety of Simulation" (in Diamond, 1996), concluding there that "Cultural criticism must walk a tightrope between uncritical acceptance or cynical celebration of new technologies and cultural configurations on the one hand, and a nostalgic commitment to categories that are very nearly obsolete on the other" (ibid.: 210). Auslander here proposes a return to Benjamin to explore the character of the relationship between the live and the mediatized.

From here we turn to the workplace, both as an imagined and represented locus and as a prime location which increasingly casualized (or never fully established) cultural workers can only view from the margins. Yvonne Tasker explores ways in which a form of cultural work (the cinema) conceives of, constructs, and represents forms and loci of work itself, in this case the office in the film *Disclosure*. Tasker examines the way in which a changed work environment (in the form of, for example, the career aspirations of working women or the fears of redundancy in working men) impacts upon narrative and character construction and representation in *Disclosure*. Whatever else, *Disclosure* reflects an experience of work characterized by insecurity.

Lack of security in developing new television programs, the failure to be bold, is a feature of Murdock's general analysis of cultural work and of Berkeley's analysis of specific cultural work, television. The most frequent form this insecurity, this lack of confidence, takes is in sticking with tried and tested formulas, albeit in recombinant form. In the second edition of *Inside Prime Time* (1994) Todd Gitlin noted the emergence of this recombinant production ethic: "The safest, easiest formula is that nothing succeeds like success. Hits are so rare that executives think a blatant imitation stands a good chance of getting bigger numbers than a show that stands on its own" (Gitlin, 1994: 63). Later he observes that "The logic of maximizing the quick payoff has produced the very Hollywood hybrid, the recombinant form, which assumes that selected features of recent hits can be spliced together to make a eugenic success" (ibid.: 64). The American television industry experience pre-dates the British television industry experience, but the same motor now governs British television program development and production. In 2001 the British comedy scriptwriter Stan Hey lamented:

> The additional pressure today is that most of the companies don't have the time or the money to develop a situation comedy [...] In the old, pre-shareholder, pre-management consultant days, broadcasters threw cash at the development of a comedy, because one hit could become a rock in the schedule for years. [...] With investment minimized, producers look for short-cuts – smaller budgets, a known face, even if he or she can't act, and a set-up that resembles something that's already been successful.
>
> (Hey, 2001)

In one sense this picture of the glory days of British situation comedy is a nostalgia for an age that never existed. In the same way the hope and promise of, respectively, punk and "alternative comedy" have been endlessly valorized. Mike Barnes has characterized the late 1970s music scene as one where "rock's New Wave – and its fans – had spontaneously decided it was time to kill the kings; to destroy the hegemony enjoyed by redundant, bloated rock stars and replace it with [...] the democratization of the stage and the realization that grasping the means of production, at least in the music business, was something you could do, and now" (Barnes, 2000: 283). The aspiration retrospectively ascribed by Barnes to the heady days of punk recalls the hopelessly idealistic words of George Lucas at the time of *Easy Rider*'s release (1969). Heralding the arrival in town of the "Movie Brats" Lucas asserted: "The power is with the people now. The workers have the means of production" (Pollock, 1983: 246). It is patently obvious that punk, "alternative comedy" and the Movie Brats all failed to achieve their soi-disant revolutionary ambitions: those elements that could be absorbed were; those that couldn't be absorbed were discarded. Emasculated elements of punk and "alternative comedy" exist in various combinations and recombinations in today's pop music and television comedy. And the Movie Brats have taken over the film industry and effortlessly reproduce versions of those industrial practices and personnel they once sought to replace.

In Hollywood the notion of "high concept" is used as an industry-standard method of summarizing a film's content (frequently for pitching purposes), but it also functions as producers' index of audiences' capacity to only understand the most simple of film narratives. The devising of "high concept" has been attributed to Steven Spielberg: "If a person can tell me the idea in twenty-five words or less, it's going to make a pretty good movie. I like ideas, especially movie ideas, that you can hold in your hands" (Wyatt, 1994: 13). It is certainly true that all industries – and the cultural industries are no exception – have shorthand codes for communicating complex ideas quickly and efficiently within the industrial community. But the combined effect of Hollywood's reliance on "high concept" and on tried and tested films as the only guide to the devising of "new" films led producer Michael Philips to describe a Hollywood looking for films like "*Jaws* in Outer Space." He decried the process whereby the only projects that would get greenlighted were those that were built on "precedent and analogy" (Biskind, 1998: 404).

In the final chapter of *Cultural Work*, Robin Nelson investigates the ramifications for this kind of recombinant ethic as it may be found in British television drama design in an era when individuals are increasingly constructed as privatized consumers. Factor together the experiences, researches and observations of Berkeley, Gitlin, Hey, Murdock, and Nelson and what are we faced with? The sad conclusion that the possibilities of new cultural work are profoundly limited: instead of new work, we have merely the frenzy of the visibly recombinant.

References

Aaronowitz, S. and Cutler, J. (eds) (1998) *Post-work*, New York: Routledge.

Adair, G. (ed.) (1999) *Movies*, London: Penguin.

Barnes, M. (2000) *Captain Beefheart*, London: Quartet.

Becker, H. S. (1982) *Art Worlds*, Berkeley: University of California Press.

Biskind, P. (1998) *Easy Riders, Raging Bulls*, London: Bloomsbury.

Crane, D. (1992) *The Production of Culture: Media and the Urban Arts*, London: Sage.

Curran, J. (ed.) *Media Organizations in Society*, London: Arnold.

Diamond, E. (ed.) (1996) *Performance and Cultural Politics*, London: Routledge.

Gitlin, T. (1994) *Inside Prime Time*, New York: Pantheon.

Goldman, W. (1985) *Adventures in the Screen Trade*, London: Futura.

Heckstall-Smith, D. (1989) *The Safest Place in the World*, London: Quartet.

Heller, T. (2001) *Slabrat*, London: Abacus.

Hesmondhalgh, D. (2000) "Alternative Media, Alternative Texts? Rethinking democratization in the cultural industries," in *Media Organizations in Society*, J. Curran (ed.), London: Arnold.

Hey, S. (2001) "So What Now for the Great British Sitcom?," the *Independent Review*, 31 May, 4.

Hicks, B. (1997) *Arizona Bay*, Cambridge: Rykodisc.

Jamous, H. and Peloille, B. (1970) "Changes in the French University-Hospital System," in *Professions and Professionalization*, J. A. Jackson (ed.), Cambridge: Cambridge University Press.

Jesmer, E. (1974) *Number One with a Bullet*, London: Weidenfeld & Nicolson.

Kooper, A. and Edmonds, B. (1977) *Backstage Passes*, New York: Stein & Day.

McGuigan, J. (1997) *Cultural Methodologies*, Sage: London.

O'Connor, S. (1987) "The Flag on the Road," *New Formations*, 3, 129–37.

Pollock, D. (1983) *Skywalking: The Life and Films of George Lucas.* New York: Random House.

Priestley, J. B. (1968) *The Image Men*, London: Heinemann.

Ross, L. (1953) *Picture*, London: Penguin.

Thomas, K. (ed.) (1999) *The Oxford Book of Work*, Oxford: Oxford University Press.

Wagner, B. (1991) *Force Majeure*, London: Abacus.

Wyatt, J. (1994) *High Concept: Movies and Marketing in Hollywood*, Texas: University of Austin Press.

Part I

CONDITIONS

In recent times there has been surprisingly little sustained research on the changing character of work in the cultural industries. Attention in media and cultural studies has tended to be directed toward questions of consumption and response, while political economy has concentrated on mapping basic changes in the overall structure of capitalism and corporate and governmental responses to them, leaving the everyday practice of cultural production as something of a black box.

Cultural Work is one marker of a wider recognition that it is time to reopen this box and "get back to work." But this cannot be a simple resumption of currents of research already established. The period 1990 to 2000 has also seen a series of fundamental and continuing shifts in the environment in which cultural production takes place. These shifts include: a basic rebalancing of the relations between private and public enterprise; a shift in the bases and forms of public investment and support for cultural activity; the emergence of new kinds of cultural enterprise; the uneven consolidation of global markets; further moves toward concentration and the extension of corporate reach; and the development of new technologies of production and distribution. These developments pose new challenges, both for the questions we ask and the ways we seek to answer them.

Graham Murdock's keynote chapter sets out, therefore, to do three things: first, to map these shifts; second, to explore the ways they are reorganizing the conditions of contemporary cultural work; and third, to suggest an agenda for future research.

1

BACK TO WORK

Cultural labor in altered times

Graham Murdock

Over the last two decades the cultural industries have increasingly moved to the center of political debates about the transformation of contemporary capitalism. They are frequently celebrated as a "multi-million pound growing force" (Department of Culture, Media and Sport, 2001: 1) and assigned a pivotal role in economic regeneration. Here, for example, is Chris Smith, the Minister responsible for overseeing cultural enterprise in the United Kingdom's first New Labour government (1997–2001):

> During the past few years in Britain we have seen an incredible flower-
> ing of the creative industries: [. . .] that rely on [. . .] creative talent
> for their added value. [. . .] They earn more revenue at home and
> abroad than the whole of manufacturing industry. And the sheer
> scale of these figures tells us something about the great sea-change
> that has occurred in the British economy over the last twenty years.
> (Smith, 1998: 31)

Anyone looking to media and cultural studies for relevant information and analyses over that period, however, would have found only a comparatively slim body of relevant research. Attention has been largely focused elsewhere.

When, in 1968, Roland Barthes declared the "death of the author" and anointed the reader as the true originator of the meanings generated by cultural artifacts (Barthes, 1977: 148) he found a ready audience among scholars who had gravitated to the emerging field of cultural studies with the intention of rescuing popular creativity from the condescension of orthodox cultural critics. This emphasis on the "symbolic work of everyday life" (Willis, 1990) pursued through reading, viewing, shopping and DIY culture, was given an added push by the increasing valorization of consumption as a pivotal site of identity formation. Its conceptual attractions were further reinforced by its methodological convenience. Conversations with consumers are generally easier to arrange than interviews with company executives and stressed professionals, and observing the rituals of clubbing,

15

or even a night of family television viewing, is likely to pose fewer problems of access than sustained observations of work in recording studios or board-room meetings. In the resulting accounts of audience activity, cultural workers appeared, at best, as ghosts at a feast of creative labor, organized elsewhere. While the agency of consumers was dissected in detail and often celebrated, the agency of cultural producers was denied or ignored (Garnham, 2000: 98). And when production was considered, attention was directed to the social and cultural margins rather than to the "centers of professional and specialized cultural production" (Born, 2000: 406).

Recently, however, there have been signs of a shift with researchers in media and cultural studies returning to work as a necessary focus of study: "Those who once talked about texts, readings and resistance have started to think about institutions, industry and policy in a much more pragmatic manner" (Oswell, 1998: 93). This research is still strongly influenced by the dominant structures of attention in media and cultural studies with journalism, television, and the music industry attracting the lion's share of attention, leaving other significant areas of cultural production, such as novel writing, relatively neglected. But it is an important beginning. Analytically "It is currently fashionable [. . .] to claim that the economic is embedded in the cultural. This claim is true enough, but it tells only part of the story. The other part resides in the complementary claim that the cultural is embedded in the economic; and never has this been more the case than in contemporary capitalism" (Scott, 2000: ix).

Some commentators picture public meanings continually traveling round a circuit in which production and consumption both offer pit stops for refueling and modifications. For the purposes of analysis, they argue, it doesn't matter at which point you enter this circuit since it can only be understood as an integrated system. This position has been forcefully put by Paul du Gay and his colleagues in their account of the life and times of the Sony Walkman. They envisage cultural artifacts moving within a "circuit of culture" made up of inter-linked processes of representation, identity, production, consumption, and regulation and insist that "you have to go the whole way round before your study is complete" (du Gay *et al.*, 1997: 4). At first sight, this is an attractive solution to the difficulties presented by the notion of determination and its long association with models of relatively rigid relations between a productive base and a cultural superstructure. Any attempt to trace the career of cultural objects that claims to be comprehensive must integrate multiple moments and levels of economic, social, and symbolic activity. However, an analysis that sees production and consumption as mutually constitutive still has to specify "the nature, strength, direction and duration" of their interrelations. "Mutuality does not mean equal influence" (Mosco, 1996: 5–6). Because "production is processually and temporally prior to consumption" (Born, 2000: 406) it remains determinant in Raymond Williams's revised sense of exerting pressures and setting limits

16

on interpretation and use. This is why exploring the dynamics that are currently reshaping the professional production of public culture is an essential first step to understanding the symbolic textures of everyday life. Studying cultural work is at the heart of this enterprise since it is precisely at the points where creative agency rubs up against structural pressures, organizational strategies and occupational formations that the cultural sites, experiences, and meanings offered to the public are shaped in decisive ways.

Despite the general dearth of work on cultural labor in media and cultural studies, there is a range of resources we can call upon in embarking on this enterprise. Some have been developed against the grain of fashion in cultural analysis, others have been produced by scholars in other areas, notably political economy, sociology, economics, cultural and economic geography, and anthropology. In the space available here, I simply want to draw up a preliminary inventory of these resources and point to some of the key issues that are emerging as foci for research and debate.

We can distinguish six main currents of relevant research and theorizing:

1   analyses of the general shifts currently taking place in the dynamics of contemporary capitalism and their implications for the organization of cultural production.
2   attempts to map the structure and operations of the contemporary cultural industries as a whole or particular sectors within them. These have come from a variety of disciplinary perspectives, including: economists interested in investment opportunities (e.g. Vogel, 2000) or business economics (Caves, 2000); economic geographers concerned with the spatial distribution of production (e.g. Scott, 2000); and sociologists and political economists wanting to trace the connections between industrial organization and cultural diversity (e.g. Flichy, 1980; Gitlin, 1983).
3   studies of organizational structures and market strategies of the major corporations and public organizations involved in cultural production. Examples here include Bill Ryan's work on corporate forms of cultural production (1991) and Tom Burns's case study of the BBC (1977).
4   research on the organization of cultural occupations or occupational segments using interviews or questionnaires to construct cross-sectional snapshots of particular groups of workers at a particular moment in time (e.g. Tunstall, 1964; 1971).
5   in contrast, research on the careers pursued by cultural workers follows cohorts through time, using personal interviews or questionnaires to examine patterns of entry, advancement, situational experience, and drop-out (e.g. McRobbie, 1998; Paterson, Dex, and Willis [2003]). Alternatively, analysts may use the "found" materials in biographies to construct accounts of career dynamics (e.g. Toynbee, 2000).
6   finally, there is a range of ethnographic studies that employ direct

observation of specific cultural projects (such as the making of a film or a television play) or sites of production (such as newsrooms or recording studios) to examine how external pressures and internal power plays organize creativity and shape the diversity and style of public expression in particular circumstances.

Although these various traditions of analysis work at very different levels of generality they should be seen not as self-enclosed domains of study, but as a set of Chinese boxes. The aim must always be "to range from the most impersonal and remote transformations to the most intimate features of the human self – and to see the relations between the two" (Mills, 1970: 14).

Capitalisms: political economies of transition

In his influential model of "fields," Pierre Bourdieu (1993) envisages particular sectors of cultural production, such as the music or television industries, as fields of play on which the various actors (corporations, regulatory bodies, star players, consumer groups, professional organizations, and trade unions) are engaged in a permanent struggle to maintain or advance their position and alter the rules of the game to their advantage. Within these fields, particular organizations operate as micro-fields, with their own continuing contests for internal position. Consequently, as he argues, in his recent work on journalism in France, "to try and understand what journalists are able to do, you have to keep in mind first, the relative position of the particular news medium [within the field of news production] and second, the positions occupied by journalists themselves within the space occupied by their respective newspapers or networks" (Bourdieu, 1998: 40). Work on the logics of cultural enterprise and the organization of cultural production has a lot to say about these two interlocking fields of external and internal contest and their consequences for the diversity of cultural production. However, Bourdieu is also careful to point out that all cultural fields are embedded in the meta field of economic relations as a whole, and that shifts at this level can re-order sub-fields and alter their dynamics in important ways. Consequently, as a first step we need to examine competing models of shifts in contemporary capitalism as a general system and identify both the problems they pose and the opportunities they open up for key players in the field of cultural production.

There is now universal agreement that contemporary capitalism either has moved, or is in the process of moving, from its "classical" state, based on the manufacture of material goods, to a new condition. But there is fierce disagreement about the defining features and dynamics of this emerging formation. One influential body of work identifies it as a shift from Fordism, centered around the mass production and consumption of standardized

18

goods, to Post-Fordism, based on flexible specialization and niche markets (see Amin, 1994). However, as critics have pointed out, this binary opposition draws altogether too sharp a distinction between past and present and pays too little attention to uneven development (Hesmondhalgh, 1996). Consequently, in recent years attention has shifted to models that focus on the networks and flows made possible by innovations in communications technology (notably computerization, broadband cable systems, and geostationary satellites) and argue that in the new social order, the old, heavy, production of material goods is being replaced at the center of economic activity by the weightless, liquid, movements of information, images, and experiences creating what Lash and Urry call "economies of signs and space" (1994). This general argument has been pursued with particular vigor by Manuel Castells, who proposes that the organizational focus of activity within this informational and communications-based capitalism is shifting from firms to the business projects based around networks of shifting alliances and partnerships (Castells, 2000: 11). This fits the move from in-house to independent production in the British television industry in the 1990s and the new contractual relations between majors and independents in the record industry rather neatly. But does it illuminate the central tendencies in the cultural industries as a whole at the present time? I would argue that it doesn't.

In advancing his model, Castells is at pains to point out that it "is still in its exploratory stage" and should be read "as a work in progress" (Castells, 2000: 6). His characterization may turn out to be correct but, for now, it remains a possible destination rather than a general condition. If we want to make sense of how changes in the dynamics of capitalism have affected the organization of the cultural industries over the last two decades, we need to begin with a process that is already both well advanced and ubiquitous — marketization.

I am using the term "marketization" here to describe all those shifts in public policy that have had the effect, first, of enlarging the scope of market relations and the degrees of operational freedom allowed to corporations and, second, of confirming market measurements of success as the yardsticks against which all institutions are judged, including those still formally in the public sector. As I have argued elsewhere, for analytical purposes it is useful to distinguish four main aspects of this general process (Murdock, 2000).

Privatization. The disposal of public assets to private investors and the consequent conversion of the organization into a profit-seeking corporation, as in the sale of TF1, formerly France's leading public service terrestrial television channel.

Liberalization. The introduction of competition into markets which were formerly dominated either by a single supplier (as in the case of British television before the launch of ITV) or by two or three large concerns (as with the BBC/ITV duopoly before the roll-out of cable and satellite services).

The re-orientation of regulatory regimes to give corporations increased scope for maneuver. Examples include: the relaxation of rules governing the degree of concentration allowed in media markets and the loosening of restrictions on cross-media ownership; the weakening of labor laws; moves away from hands-on to "light touch" regulation and greater reliance on self-regulation by the industries themselves; and the dilution of public interest requirements. The net effect of these changes is to shift the center of regulatory gravity from the defense of the public interest (however defined) to the promotion of corporate interests.

Corporatization. Moves to encourage or impel public organizations to act as though they were commercial corporations. Examples include: the conversion of Television New Zealand into a State Owned Enterprise with a statutory duty to return a surplus to the Treasury; the BBC's increasing involvement in commercial enterprises and public–private partnerships; and the introduction of internal markets in service provision, as in the BBC Producer Choice initiative.

The period 1980 through 2000 has seen variants of these four processes become increasingly pervasive across the major capitalist economies. Taken together, they have precipitated a fundamental shift in the historic bargain struck between public and corporate interests during the high tide of Welfare Capitalism between 1950 and 1980, increasing both the size of the market sector and its competitive advantages.

This process of marketization has been further extended and accelerated by two other shifts.

The first is the continuing movement from analog to digital forms of coding and communication. By allowing all forms of expression – voice, music, still and moving images, texts, and data – to be produced, stored, and distributed in a single, universal, language of 0's and 1's, this simple shift has given additional impetus to the growing integration between the cultural industries, the computing industry, and the telecommunications industry. When charting this process, however, it is vital to avoid technological determinism in all its forms. It is not the new machines themselves that are restructuring cultural production but the ways corporations are choosing to deploy them.

The second shift is the emergence of a new global economic playing field. Capitalism has always aspired to global reach. The passage of time may have consigned many of the predictions that Marx and Engels made in the *Communist Manifesto* to the history of ideas, but one projection now jumps off the page with renewed force and relevance. As they sat down to write, the profits from Britain's early adventures in mercantile *capitalism* were already helping to underwrite the rise of industrial capitalism, and they saw very clearly that this emerging system's never-ending search for new markets would prompt it to expand over the whole surface of the globe. It must nestle everywhere, settle everywhere, establish connections everywhere. In place of the old local and national seclusion and self-sufficiency, we have inter-course in every direction ... And as in material, so also in intellec-tual production [. . .] it compels [all countries] to introduce what it calls civilization into their midst [. . .] In a word, it creates a world after its own image.

(Marx and Engels, 1968: 38–9)

The previous gap between this prediction and the realities of the global eco-nomic system is rapidly closing now as the scale, scope, and speed of marketization intensifies on a daily basis. Between 1980 and 2000 the world's three most populous nations, which for most of the post-War period had barricaded themselves against the full force of marketization to varying degrees, have increasingly adopted its core procedures and goals. In China, Deng set in motion an ambitious program of internal economic restructur-ing opening new "doors" to the West. In India, which had emphasized self-sufficiency and state direction of the economy since independence, Rajiv Gandhi's initial moves toward marketization were extended. And most spec-tacularly of all, the collapse of the Soviet Union opened the way for the rapid growth of marketization in Russia and the former "Eastern Bloc."

This massive extension of Western capitalism's potential geographical reach has been accompanied, first, by significant increases in the range of activities opened to marketization, as governments around the world have embraced market logics and structures either voluntarily or as a condition of securing an international loan and, second, by the progressive reduction in the gap between decisions taken in one place and consequences felt else-where, as a result of the new international communications infrastructure built around satellite systems and high speed computer networks.

This market-led mobilization of the potentials opened up by new media technologies coupled with the increased geographical, social, and ideological reach of market logics generally, has had three major impacts on the field of cultural production.

Concentration. First, and most obviously, it has accelerated the long-standing trend toward concentration of ownership in the cultural industries (see Barnouw, 1997) and facilitated the emergence of a new type of corpor-ate actor, the multi-media global conglomerate operating across the whole range of "old" and "new" media sectors. The company formed by the merger between Time-Warner (the world's largest concentration of print and audio-visual interests) and AOL (the leading Internet Service Provider) is prototypical. This increasing convergence of ownership is bringing new players into the cultural field, many of them from business cultures built around the construction and operation of machines, infrastructures, and operating software rather than cultural products. In the longer term, this may mean that the cultural industries become more like other industries in their organization and operating logics. This is particularly likely if, as many commentators argue, industries operating in other sectors are themselves becoming more dependent on the manipulation of information and symbols. The immense efforts devoted to the protection and extension of corporate brands by companies like McDonald's suggest that this is indeed the case.

Casualization. The second impact has been on the organization of labor markets within the cultural industries as corporations have sought to cut costs by shifting workers from secure employment to freelance contracts and making more use of part-time and casualized labor, hiring people "just-in-time" to meet particular production needs and then returning them to the reserve army of cultural labor.

Commodification. The third effect of the extension of marketization has been to pull more and more forms of cultural experience into the orbit of the price mechanism. This is most obvious in the case of television services where subscription channels and pay-per-view opportunities have now established themselves alongside the traditional advertising supported channels and public services funded out of taxation. These are not simply different ways of paying for a service. They mobilize different moralities of exchange and entail different relations between producers and consumers.

Installing ability to pay as the primary means of regulating access to "premium" cultural goods reinforces the already unequal distribution of cultural choices and consolidates the relative exclusion of those on low incomes. At the same time, by giving more prominence to modes of address organized around appeals to consumers, it further erodes rhetorics of citizenship. Audiences are encouraged to think of themselves as actors in the marketplace, with entitlements to maximize their choices and pleasures, rather than as members of moral and political communities with responsibilities for the well-being of others. The pursuit of private interests takes precedence over commitment to the public good.

The celebration of paying customers and the eclipse of the citizen shifts the conditions of cultural production, placing added emphasis on satisfying existing demands and tastes.

It is important to remember, however, that these broad-brush characterizations do not necessarily apply to every sector of the cultural industries to the same degree. "Despite the growing intersections, crossovers and convergences, they are composed of a set of distinct production pathways" (Lacroix and Tremblay, 1997: 51). Consequently, to understand their impact we need to look at the "specific historical and structural conditions confronting cultural workers [. . .] within particular sectors" (Ryan, 1991: 265). This is the second necessary level of analysis.

Fields: mapping the cultural industries

There are a number of cross-cutting divisions that can be used to generate classifications and comparisons of different sectors within the cultural industries. I want to draw attention to four that have featured particularly prominently in research and debate.

Artifacts and flows

In a pioneering work published in 1980, Patrice Flichy distinguished between two main logics of cultural production which he called "publishing" and "flow." Publishing sectors, he argued, are in the business of producing artifacts or events that can be sold directly to customers. Examples include books, records, and films. In contrast, flow sectors such as broadcasting are organized around the provision of a continuous sequence of output. Consequently, their principal product is the schedule rather than the individual program.

This is a serviceable distinction but becomes more useful if we redefine the central terms so that publishing refers to the production of one-off events or artifacts (such as literary novels or single television plays) and flow to the production of continuous sequences of material – serial and genre fictions, soap operas, weekly magazines, records designed to become hits. It was precisely the relentless seriality of flow production that led Adorno and Horkheimer to equate the industrialization of cultural production with the standardization of the cultural product. For them: "one should understand 'industry' in the strict sense of the term. It refers to the standardization of the object itself – for example, the standardization of the Western, well-known to all movie-goers" (quoted in Lacroix and Tremblay, 1997: 42).

In other words, the more closely cultural production resembled the conditions of assembly-line manufacture (the locus classicus for their image of "industry") the more likely it was to cater for already embedded tastes and work with well-established generic formulas. Conversely, according to this argument, truly "creative" production that reflects the unique personal vision of the author and is prepared to break generic rules and disregard prevailing fashions is more likely to be found in unique events or artifacts.

This view that artists are inner-directed while commercial producers are other-directed is firmly anchored in German Romanticism. Here, for example, is Marx contrasting the true "authorship" of Milton with the purely economic motivations of the serial writer: "Milton produced *Paradise Lost* for the same reason that a silk-worm produces silk. It was an activity of his nature. [. . .] But the literary proletarian of Leipzig, who fabricates books under the direction of his publisher [. . .] his product [. . .] comes into being only for the purposes of increasing capital" (Marx, 1969: 401).

In his travels around England in search of the authors of the pulp fictions of the 1950s and 1960s, Steve Holland discovered a modern day "literary proletarian" living in a cellar in Soho, supported very frugally by his publisher: "The writer sat on a stiff kitchen chair at a small kitchen table, centered under a naked electric light bulb. [. . .] He sat at that table from morning to night, tapping timidly away at an old typewriter [. . .] 70,000 words a week, ten thousand words a day" (Holland, 1993: 69).

These simple overlapping oppositions between creativity and commerce, artists and hacks, integrity and "selling out," have been vigorously deconstructed by critics arguing for the aesthetic value of selected examples of serial and mass production. Analytically, however, we still need to ask whether the generic mix promoted by serial production oriented toward maximizing audiences (whether mass or niche) can also guarantee to maximize diversity of expression, or whether there are significant areas of experience that cannot be spoken, shown or sung about within these familiar cultural forms or which can only be represented in particular ways and from particular perspectives. Arguably, it is more useful analytically to see commercial imperatives setting limits to public expression through the selection of genres and expressive styles that are seen to be marketable.

The distinction between publishing and flow production is also helpful in identifying a major division in the security and continuity of employment enjoyed by cultural workers in different sectors of the cultural industries. The need to maintain the continuous flow required to fill a daily newspaper or television schedule or a weekly change of program at cinemas has traditionally given key workers in these industries relative security of employment. This has been particularly true of craft occupations where a decision to withdraw labor could bring production to a halt. In contrast, cultural sectors based on publishing have been characterized by chronic insecurity and discontinuity of employment. The major American publisher Doubleday, for example, only publishes one in 15,000 of the unsolicited novels it receives, while a recent study of 2,000 visual artists in the United States showed that their median earnings of $3,000 a year fell some way short of the $9,500 they spent on average on materials (Fletcher, 2001: 30). In these circumstances, cultural workers have no choice but to supplement their income by doing other jobs which may or may not be in the cultural industries.

The coupling of production technologies which have made traditional craft skills redundant with the move toward out-sourcing and casualization, has moved many workers in flow sectors toward the insecurities familiar within publishing sectors.

Centers and peripheries

Another widely used method for segmenting the cultural industries has been to distinguish between the major centers of production owned by the big

conglomerates and independent producers coming up from the street constantly balancing expressive integrity against a precarious and uncertain
living. Again, this opposition owes more to romanticism than sustained
analysis. As writers on the music industry have argued for some time, independents have always acted as cost-free research and development agents for
the majors, identifying rising musical trends and new market niches. In
recent years this relation has been cemented by various kinds of licensing
and partnership deals as the majors have signed up independents operating
in markets that seem to "have legs." These alliances make it less and less
useful to draw a meaningful distinction between the two (see Negus, 1992).
A parallel process has occurred in the British television industry where the
number of independent production companies has steadily declined and the
major players have been increasingly incorporated into large, often vertically
integrated, broadcasting companies.

As David Hesmondhalgh has rightly pointed out, much of the analysis in
this area tends to approach the situation from the point of view of "the issue
of consumer choice" and says "very little indeed about the status and rewards
available for musicians working for independents" (Hesmondhalgh, 1998:
271). Recent research on workers in the fashion design and television production sectors strips away any lingering romanticism attaching to the image of
"independence" and highlights the high levels of self-exploitation involved in
trying to go it alone or negotiate successfully with major purchasers of talent
and services (see McRobbie, 1998; Ursell, 1998). By absorbing many of "the
costs and uncertainties" previously carried by larger companies, independents
have allowed the majors to cut their operating costs substantially (Ursell,
1998: 151). From this perspective, independents are in the vanguard of casualization, insecurity, and the accelerated turnover of personnel, rather than
expressive diversity. The pursuit of cost savings and the emerging contractual
relations between majors and independents also have important implications
for the spatial organization of cultural production.

Networks and locations

Specific forms of cultural activity have traditionally clustered in particular
areas. The American film industry's migration to Hollywood and the
importance of the Tin Pan Alley district of New York and of Nashville and
Chicago in the history of popular song writing, are perhaps the best known
examples. If the theorists of global networks as the key organizing principle
of the new capitalism are correct, however, one might expect place to give
way to space.

The new communication networks certainly allow for more effective co-
ordination of dispersed sites of activity. A call made to a corporate customer
service line can be answered in Delhi as easily as in Basildon, software design
can be organized as effectively in Bangalore as in Silicon Valley, and digital

effects can be designed, inputted, and transmitted back as efficiently in London as in Hollywood. There is no doubt that these new global putting-out systems will grow in importance as production budgets follow the talent and the cost savings wherever they are located. However, recent research in economic geography has also shown that despite this trend "cultural-product industries" still "materialize on the landscape in the form of dense spatial agglomerations" (Scott, 2000: ix). Examples include Alan Scott's work on the American film and music industries and Matthew Zook's work on Internet content generation (Scott, 2000; Zook, 2000). The concentration of US commercial Net site production in three main regions – San Francisco, Los Angeles, and New York – is particularly telling given the widespread belief that the Internet marks the final end of the tyranny of location. The reasons for the resilience of place in the age of cyberspace are not hard to find. As cultural production moves more toward project-based alliances and as freelance work becomes the norm, so command of social capital becomes an even more important resource in securing entrees, opportunities, and advancement. Who you know is as significant as what you know. "Parents, siblings-in-law, ex-spouses, neighbors, tennis partners – any or all of these may assist your career" or facilitate a productive alliance (Tunstall, 2001: 3). Networking is central to these exchanges of debts and favors but it requires concerted socializing. Text messaging is no substitute for hospitality and conversation and this can only be done by "being there" at the center of the new webs of influence as they move between clubs, launches, private viewings, restaurants, and dinner parties.

In addition to facilitating contacts with potential employers, agents, patrons, and collaborators, being in the "right place at the right time" also offers cultural workers access to a pool of potential customers. This is particularly important for those who sell direct to the public. As Judith Blau's survey of cultural activity in the 125 largest metropolitan areas in the United States shows, artists gravitate toward locations that already have sizeable artists' colonies since this "simultaneously means networks of information," support and promotion and a ready-made market for their work stimulated by the flurry of activity around galleries and local publicity (Blau, 1989: 159).

Commercial enterprise and public service

In most democracies for most of the twentieth century, the field of cultural production was split between a private sector funded out of customer payments and/or advertising revenues and a public sector supported out of local and national taxation. On the one side stood the cinemas, bookshops, record stores, dance halls, popular magazines, and commercial broadcasters. On the other stood the museums, public libraries, national art galleries, subsidized theaters, and public broadcasters. The primary purpose of commercial cultural enterprise was to retain, reproduce, and increase market share and to maximize profits. The principal aim of the subsidized sector was to address "market failures" by producing and distributing forms of cultural expression that were unlikely to survive in the marketplace but which were judged to be essential to the maintenance of a diverse communal culture and the exercise of rational citizenship.

It is easy to dismiss these subsidized interventions as cultural protectionism, subsidizing the tastes and judgments of the relatively affluent and well educated out of the taxes of the poor, and to condemn their efforts to reach a wider audience as paternalistic imposition. But this characterization is altogether too simple. It misses the contested character of publicly subsidized culture. There were continual struggles over which books should be displayed on the shelves of public libraries, whose art should be shown in galleries, whose voices and whose music should be heard on radio, and whose images and representations should be shown on television. There was a broadly based consensus on the general aim of public service but no agreement about how best to translate these intentions into concrete practices of preservation, subsidy, and display. It was precisely these continuing arguments that gave the public sector its distinctive pattern of diversity and differentiated it from the range of production supported by commercial enterprise.

Corporatization, in all its variants, erodes this distinctiveness by increasing the public sector's reliance on income raised in the marketplace and by installing market rhetorics and logics at the heart of decision-making. As a consequence, public organizations increasingly adopt strategies developed in the corporate sector.

Corporations: strategies and controls

The dispersal and re-composition of cultural production does not lessen the power and reach of the major multi-media conglomerates. Rather, it invests their control over the central channels of distribution with even greater significance. They become the impresarios of public culture, selecting and sifting ideas and projects offered from a variety of sources and distributing the favored few across a range of media and in variety of forms. Reducing the risks of this enterprise requires strategies that maximize the value of each product. This can be done in several ways; six have assumed particular significance in recent years:

1   using *consumer research* more intensively in the design and development of products. Hollywood film-makers and advertising agencies have long used public previews of initial ideas and intended releases to iron out problems of audience understanding and pleasure, often altering the initial product in line with audience comments. Similarly, the US networks employ pilot shows of prospective television series to assess audience reactions before committing themselves to a full production run.

As market competition intensifies, so these techniques of pre-testing, designed to fit the product as closely as possible to popular tastes, are now being much more extensively used in the British television industry where they were previously regarded with distaste as pre-empting the producer's creative control. The British Film Institute study that tracked more than 4,000 television production workers over the four years between 1994 and 1998 found that 37 percent had developed or adjusted a program as a result of audience research or focus group evaluations (British Film Institute, 1998: ii). Nor is this strategy confined to commercial producers. Faced with a declining share of the audience and intensified competition, BBC television executives employed focus groups "as a disciplinary tool [to] chastise producers for failing to meet what were described as audience wants, but which more accurately involved charges of failing to match the genres and successes of the competition" (Born, 2000: 415).

2   *branding* organizations more assertively in order to transfer the symbolic capital accruing from past reputation from one arena to another is a second risk-reducing strategy. In the same way as McDonalds's 2001 launch of a chain of hotels using its familiar logo and corporate colors, the BBC's transfer of its brand from broadcasting to the Internet has helped to make its public websites among the most visited in Europe.

3   a third strategy is to extend the market reach of a product by developing a range of associated *merchandise* that repackages it for distribution in other media (moving between books, films, and computer games, for example, or between consumer magazines and television programs) or by franchising the use of the characters, name or settings on a range of other products, a strategy used very successfully by Disney and Warner Brothers, both of whom have chains of shops selling products based on their cartoon characters.

4   exploiting the sales possibilities of *formats* as well as finished products.

5   investing as heavily in *marketing* products as in producing them.

6   vigorously defending *intellectual property rights* against unlicensed copying by consumers and efforts by production personnel to secure a greater share of the returns accruing to extended uses. Within the television industry, for example, this has prompted repeated struggles over the size of the "residuals" paid to actors and writers when a production is transferred to new formats (such as CD-ROM) or sold in new markets, and over who should own the rights to exploit a program's market potential after its initial screening – the independent production house that made it or the broadcasting organization that commissioned it and paid for it.

Taken together, these strategies are more likely to increase plurality rather than diversity. There may be more cultural products in circulation but they are more likely to be variants or spin-offs of a limited set of master templates.

Analyzing the growing reach of the major culture-producing corporations, and the seemingly relentless onward march of commodification, it is
tempting to lapse back into a diffuse pessimism, a stance that the Left has
always found oddly comforting. However, this ignores the counter trends
that are also evident. Saying that commodity relations are important or even
primary does not mean that "we can ignore the existence of other sorts of
relations" (Carrier, 1992: 203). A public culture based around publicly
funded facilities may be losing its former purchase on the centers of national
life and being progressively suffused by the logic of market competition, but
it has not yet disappeared. Nor is it likely to. As entry to more and more
cultural domains becomes conditional on consumers' ability to pay, and as
those people on low incomes find themselves excluded from pleasures they
previously enjoyed, the maintenance of a cultural commons offering full and
equal participation to all is likely to become more sensitive as a political
issue rather than less.

Added to which, "haunting the commodity and the market are non commodity production and non market exchange" (Gibson-Graham, 1996:
244). Despite the rapid commercialization of the Internet and the growth of
subscription services, many sites still operate as gift economies, in which
people offer material not in exchange for payments but in the expectation
that others will reciprocate by providing their own material. In fact, precisely because of its relative openness and horizontal configuration, the Net
is rapidly becoming the primary site of an intensifying struggle between
three cultural economies and their associated moralities of exchange:

1 commercial transactions regulated through the price system and the rigorous enforcements of intellectual property rights;
2 the "free" distribution of public cultural goods on the grounds that they
   have already been paid for out of public monies (MIT's 2001 decision to
   offer its academic course materials over the Web, in direct competition
   with the commercially based distance learning initiatives being
   launched by other major universities around the world, is a particularly
   interesting instance of this conflict between the morality of commodities and the morality of public goods);
3 gift relations based on the reciprocal exchange and pooling of services
   and information.

These three co-existing and competing systems of exchange have major
implications for the future organization of cultural labor, for the structure of
occupational reward systems, and for the sustainability of working careers in
cultural production. To understand their implications, however, we need to
examine the way these structures are already changing.

Occupations: hierarchies and solidarities

In his overview of the recent reorganization of culture-producing occupations, Jeremy Tunstall identifies three main periods. In the first, which lasted from the beginnings of the modern cultural industries at the end of the eighteenth century, through to the early 1950s, he argues that cultural work was characterized by strong vertical divisions between a small elite of stars (leading newspaper columnists, best-selling novelists, celebrated actors) who had reached the top of their respective occupational ladders and who were able to command substantial salaries, and the mass of routine cultural workers and craft operatives who labored for comparatively modest returns and whose positions were often provisional and insecure. In contrast, he argues, the period between 1950 and 1980 was characterized by strong horizontal forms of occupation organization as trade unions (and, to a lesser extent, professional bodies) were able to exercise varying degrees of control over entry to occupation, to negotiate and enforce minimum conditions of work, and to link basic salaries to agreed rates of remuneration. From 1980 onwards, however, he sees the re-emergence of vertical forms of organization together with an increasing polarization in rewards between the top and bottom echelons of cultural occupations. Between 1994 and 1998, for example, the proportion of television workers earning over £50,000 a year more than doubled, from 10 percent to 21 percent, while 23 percent earned less than £20,000 in 1998 (Paterson and Willis, 1999: 19). The gap between the top and bottom of the income scale for writers (who were members of the Society of Authors) is even steeper. In 2000, only 7 percent were earning over £50,000 a year and almost half were earning less than £5,000 (Ezard, 2000: 5). Arguably this pattern has always been characteristic of the publishing sectors of the cultural industries but, as we noted earlier, there is evidence that their conditions of work are now becoming generalized across the cultural industries as a whole.

A number of authors, perhaps the majority, have always found it difficult to live off their earnings from writing and most have supplemented their income by doing other jobs. This movement between creative projects and supplementary employment seems to be increasing among television workers, particularly among those working on a freelance basis. In the same way that authors have often turned their hand to advertising copywriting or magazine features, television workers are now expected to be multi-skilled and to be able to move between broadcasting, corporate video, and multimedia production. If these trends continue, "in the future, much television will be produced by fewer people doing more" (Thynne, 2000: 81). Some commentators see an even bleaker future for employment in television in the longer term, arguing that once the impact of digital technologies feeds through into all the areas of production "the bulk of program origination" is likely to "revolve around small teams of computer-literate newcomers" and most of the present workforce will be rendered redundant (Ursell, 1998: 151).

The drive to create a more "flexible" workforce that has accompanied the marketization process (and the consequent push to reduce production costs and maximize the value of labor inputs) has also had a profound impact on career patterns.

Careers: trajectories and insecurities

The moves toward outsourcing production, relying more on freelance labor, and assembling teams on a project-by-project basis, have combined to make careers in the cultural industries less secure and predictable and, as we noted earlier, more dependent on social connections. The increasing supply of young aspirants looking for a foot in the door and willing to work for no pay or a minimal wage has also reinforced the field's long-standing youth bias, while the difficulties of juggling a career with a family in a situation where an increasing number of women workers find themselves outside the safety net provided by in-house agreements has both shortened and fractured female careers. Recent evidence for the television industry suggests that "there appears to be a substantial outflow [of cultural workers] in mid career, people in their thirties or forties" (Tunstall, 2001: 5). Similarly, "although women working in the [. . .] industry have made considerable advances (at the level of either producer or director aged 40 or under) they are still the most likely group to be freelance" and therefore the group most vulnerable to contractions and shifts in the commissioning process (Paterson and Willis, 1999: 19). As one analyst pessimistically concluded: "If our working practices continue unregulated, our workforce will be increasingly made up of people who are under 35, male, childless, white [. . .] In a cultural industry, this is disastrous" for diversity of vision and expression (Thynne, 2000: 65).

The study of cultural economies, corporate strategies, occupational structures, and career trajectories tells us much about the ways in which the cultural industries are organized and how the conditions under which cultural products are made are changing, and how these shifts might impact on the diversity of cultural outputs, but they don't tell us much about how specific artifacts are shaped by the daily play of decision, negotiations, and power. To fully understand the connections between the organization of cultural work and the style and content of particular artifacts, we need to explore how the general trends and forces we have outlined here shape the everyday life of particular projects.

Productions: creativity, collaboration, and control

All sites of cultural production are fields of contest in which participants with differing stakes and resources jockey for position and advantage. As Joseph Turow notes, in the introduction to his study of the production on medical drama series on American television: "Telling stories on television is, above all, a game of power . . . One need only sit in the offices of TV producers [. . .] watch the actors, writers, directors, casting directors, consultants, network executives, production crews, and public relations personnel move through the day. Doing that, one feels the competitive tension in the talk, sees it in the place of work" (Turow, 1989: xiii).

Analysts have explored these games of power from two main vantage points. The first focuses on the clashes between creative personnel and executives. The second has examined the tensions between individualism and collective labor in the production process.

The supposed contradiction between creativity and control, expressivity and accountancy, is a central theme in cultural workers' accounts of their situation. As noted earlier, these definitions of the situation are rooted in deeply romantic conceptions of the artist's expressive capacities and rights. The tension between creativity and commerce is felt particularly acutely in advertising, where artistic talent is harnessed directly to the business of selling. As Janice Hirota notes, advertising artists see themselves as a group apart and "their work roles and partnerships as oases in the bureaucratic desert [and] because 'creativity' is antithetical to the rationalizing thrust of the modern workplace, [they] must continually lay claim to their distinctive occupational identity, principally by appearing 'creative'" (Hirota, 1995: 334–5). To this end they set their own schedules, dress as they wish, and express their opinions openly, a habit that often leads them to be excluded from meetings with clients. In contrast to the account executives whose role is to represent the agency to the client and speak up for the client's requirements within the agency, creative staff see themselves primarily as artists and a number will harbor ambitions to follow the well-trodden path into feature film production. In this context, the client's requests may appear as unwanted interference in the development of a campaign that will serve as a valuable shop window for their talents. The result is an uneasy *ménage à trois*. As one copywriter noted, talking about the agency's visual artists, "we've got common enemies – the account men in the agency, and the client" (Tunstall, 1964: 60).

The same theme runs through the accounts that television writers give of their work, though here the "good old days" when television was a writer's medium and executives respected authorial intentions are frequently contrasted unfavorably with the new climate of bean-counting ushered in by marketization. As Lawrence Marks and Maurice Gran, two of Britain's most successful scriptwriters, have complained in today's television industry: "The power the creative staff once had has been usurped by legions of lawyers, accountants, business-affairs executives. They apply to the production of television the same discipline they would apply to the production of biscuits" (Marks and Gran, 1997: 23).

These felt oppositions between creativity and accountancy, personal auto-nomy and bureaucratic routine, have a long history in the professional ideo-logies of cultural production. However, ethnographies of creative practice have comprehensively discredited romanticized images of the lone artist or author struggling to realize his or her unique vision. They have convincingly demonstrated that under modern conditions of production it "has become increasingly impossible to produce a cultural artifact alone without the intervention, assistance, guidance, collaboration or hindrance of other people" (Negus and Pickering, 2000: 271). This position was forcefully advanced by Howard Becker, an ethnographic sociologist and accomplished jazz performer, on the basis of his reflections on his own creative career:

> Maybe the years I spent playing the piano in taverns in Chicago and elsewhere led me to [treat] art as the work some people do, and [to be] more concerned with patterns of cooperation among the people who make the works than with the works themselves or with those conventionally defined as creators. [. . .] That has inevitably meant treating art as not so very different from other kinds of work, and treating people defined as artists as not so very different from other kinds of worker, especially the other workers who participate in the making of art works.
>
> (Becker, 1982: ix–x)

For some cultural workers, particularly those who think of themselves as "authors," being part of a chain of production cuts against the grain, as Ger-maine Greer discovered when she set out to make a program about the Psalms for the BBC:

> One of the joys of being a writer is that if you stick to your last, which is your text, you are entirely responsible for the quality of your work [. . .] Writing text for moving pictures is different . . . The writer produces a treatment, and then a script, which is then rewritten by the director, and rewritten again by the author-presenter, and the whole shebang is then disposed of by a galaxy of uncontrollable events as hours of location filming and endless pieces to camera process from can to cutting room floor.
>
> (Greer, 2001: 5)

Research has shown that Becker's insistence on the sociality of cultural labor holds not only for the more obviously collectivized sites of production, such as television or recording studios, but also for fine art and high fashion. Following Marcel Duchamp's celebrated 1917 decision to submit a ready-made male urinal to a sculpture exhibition on the grounds that if he, as an artist, defined it as art then it was art, modern aesthetics has accepted selection as well as execution as valid proof of artistic status. It is no longer necessary to be able to make an object or an installation. It is enough to imagine it and leave the mundane business of production to others. As Angela McRobbie has shown, fashion designers are inclined to define themselves as entrepreneurs of style, image and "look" and to delegate the realization of their creations to machinists (McRobbie, 1998). With the application of digital technologies to an ever-widening range of cultural production, from altered photographs to sampled sounds, the aesthetics of selection and re-combination look set to become more central to cultural practice.

Exploring the relationships between shifts in the array of available cultural forms, altered conditions of cultural production, and the reorganization of cultural careers, presents cultural analysis with its most testing challenge but also its best chance to construct a more comprehensive account of the changing relations between occupational biographies and cultural histories, creative practices and economic dynamics.

References

Amin, Ash (1994) *Post-Fordism: A Reader*, Oxford: Blackwell.

Barnouw, Erik *et al.* (1997) *Conglomerates and the Media*, New York: The New Press.

Barthes, Roland (1977) "The Death of the Author," in *Image/Music/Text*, Roland Barthes, London: Fontana Press.

Becker, Howard S. (1982) *Art Worlds*, Berkeley: University of California Press.

Blau, Judith R. (1989) *The Shape of Culture: A Study of Contemporary Cultural Patterns in the United States*, Cambridge: Cambridge University Press.

Born, Georgia (2000) "Inside television: television studies and the sociology of culture," *Screen*, 41, 4, Winter, 404–24.

Bourdieu, Pierre (1993) *The Field of Cultural Production: Essays on Art and Literature*, Oxford: Polity Press.

Bourdieu, Pierre (1998) *On Television and Journalism*, London: Pluto Press.

British Film Institute (1998) *Television Industry Tracking Study: Second Interim Report*, London: BFI.

Burns, Tom (1977) *The BBC: Public Institution and Private World*, London: Macmillan.

Carrier, J. G. (1992) "Occidentalism: the world turned upside down," *American Ethnologist*, 19, 2, 195–212.

Castells, Manuel (2000) "Materials for an explanatory theory of the network society," *British Journal of Sociology*, 51, 1, 5–24.

Caves, Richard (2000) *Creative Industries: Contracts Between Arts and Commerce*, London: Harvard University Press.

Department for Culture, Media and Sport (2001) "Creative Industries 'A Multi-Billion Pound Growing Force,'" London, Department for Culture, Media and Sport, Press Release, 13 March, p. 1.

Du Gay, Paul, Hall, Stuart, Jones, Linda, MacKay, Hugh and Negus, Keith (1997) *Doing Cultural Studies: The Story of the Sony Walkman*, London: Sage Publications.

Ezard, John (2000) "Only one author in seven can afford to live on their writing, survey shows," the *Guardian*, 22 June, p. 5

Fletcher, Winston (2001) "A little humdrum something to stagnate your creative juices," *The Times Higher Education Supplement*, 4 May, p. 30.

Flichy, Patrice (1980) *Les Industries de l'imaginaire: une analyse economique des media*, Grenoble: Presses Universitaires de Grenoble [second edition 1991].

Garnham, Nicholas (2000) *Emancipation, the Media, and Modernity: Arguments About the Media and Social Theory*, Oxford: Oxford University Press.

Gibson-Graham, J. K. (1996) *The End of Capitalism (As We Knew It): A Feminist Critique of Political Economy*, Oxford: Blackwell.

Gitlin, Todd (1983) *Inside Prime Time*, New York: Pantheon Books.

Greer, Germaine (2001) "In the beginning was the script," the *Guardian Saturday Review*, 5 May, p. 5.

Hesmondhalgh, David (1996) "Flexibility, post-Fordism and the music industries," *Media, Culture and Society*, 18, 469–88.

Hesmondhalgh, David (1998) "Post-punk's attempt to democratise the music industry: the success and failure of Rough Trade," *Popular Music*, 16, 3, 255–74.

Holland, Steve (1993) *The Mushroom Jungle: A History of Postwar Paperback Publishing*, Westbury, Wiltshire: ZEON Books.

Lacroix, Jean-Guy and Tremblay, Gaetan (1997) "Trend Report: The 'Information Society' and cultural industries today," *Current Sociology*, 45, 4, October, 1–128.

Lash, Scott and Urry, John (1994) *Economies of Signs and Space*, London: Sage Publications.

McRobbie, Angela (1998) *British Fashion Design: Rag Trade or Image Industry?*, London: Routledge.

Marks, Lawrence and Gran, Maurice (1997) "Comedy of errors blights television," the *Guardian*, 23 August, p. 23.

Marx, Karl (1969) *Theories of Surplus Value: Part One*, London: Lawrence and Wishart.

Marx, Karl and Engels, Frederick (1968) *Selected Works in One Volume*, London: Lawrence and Wishart.

Mills, C. Wright (1970) *The Sociological Imagination*, Harmondsworth: Penguin Books.

Mosco, Vincent (1996) *The Political Economy of Communication: Rethinking and Renewal*, London: Sage Publications.

Murdock, Graham (2000) "Digital Futures: European Television in the Age of Convergence," in *Television Across Europe: A Comparative Introduction*, Jan Weiten, Graham Murdock and Peter Dahlgren (eds), London: Sage Publications, 35–57.

Negus, K. (1992) *Producing Pop: Culture and Conflict in the Popular Music Industry*, London: Arnold.

Negus, Keith and Pickering, Michael (2000) "Creativity and cultural production," *Cultural Policy*, 6, 2, 259–82.

Oswell, David (1998) "Review," *Screen*, 39, 1, 93–9.

Paterson, Richard and Willis, Janet (1999) "Working daze," *Broadcast*, 21 May, 19.

Paterson, Richard, Dex, Shirley and Willis, Janet (2003) *Working in Television*, Oxford: Oxford University Press.

Ryan, Bill (1991) *Making Capital From Culture: The Corporate Form of Capitalist Cultural Production*, New York: Walter de Gruyter.

Scott, Alan (2000) *The Cultural Economy of Cities*, London: Sage Publications.

Smith, Chris (1998) *Creative Britain*, London: Faber and Faber.

Thynne, Lizzie (2000) "Women in television in the multi-channel age," *Feminist Review*, 64, 65–82.

Toynbee, Jason (2000) *Making Popular Music: Musicians, Aesthetics and the Manufacture of Popular Music*, London: Arnold.

Tunstall, Jeremy (1964) *The Advertising Man in London Advertising Agencies*, London: Chapman Hall.

Tunstall, Jeremy (1971) *Journalists at Work: Their News Organisations, News Sources and Competitor Colleagues*, London: Constable.

Tunstall, Jeremy (2001) "Introduction," in *Media Occupations and Professions: A Reader*, Jeremy Tunstall (ed.), Oxford: Oxford University Press, pp. 1–22.

Turow, Joseph (1989) *Playing Doctor: Television, Storytelling, and Medical Power*, New York: Oxford University Press.

UNESCO (1982) *Cultural Industries: A Challenge for the Future of Culture*, Paris: UNESCO.

Ursell, Gillian (1998) "Labour flexibility in the UK commercial television sector," *Media, Culture and Society*, 20, 1, 129–53.

Ursell, Gillian (2000) "Television production: issues of exploitation, commodification and subjectivity in UK television labour markets," *Media, Culture and Society*, 22, 805–25.

Vogel, Harold L. (2000) *Entertainment Industry Economics: A Guide for Financial Analysis* (2nd edition), Cambridge: Cambridge University Press.

Willis, Paul (1990) *Common Culture: Symbolic Work at Play in the Cultures of the Young*, Milton Keynes: Open University Press.

Zook, Matthew A. (2000) "The web of production: the economic geography of commercial Internet content production in the United States," *Environment and Planning A*, 32, 411–26.

Part II

PRACTICE

It is often assumed that cultural work is special work, that the trials and tribulations which affect workers in less spectacular industries do not affect cultural workers. One of the key aims of the chapters in this part is to demonstrate that cultural work is, above all else, work. The chapters in this section focus on working practices in a range of cultural industries: popular music, music radio, and performance.

While Lash and Urry have argued that other sectors now aspire to the ever increasing flexibility of cultural industry labor markets, Sparks (1994) has suggested that independent television production in Britain constitutes a "harsh new world" of chronic underemployment and uncertainty. However, what marks out popular music making is the sheer size of its "tank" (Miège, 1989) of labor waiting to be recruited. Neither amateurs nor professionals, music makers in a variety of genres linger at the margins of the music industry, unsure about whether and when they will "make it." This characteristic of the musical labor market has a number of causes: low cost entry into production, continuing traditions of collective practice, a series of "proto-markets" in the form of small-scale gigs and clubs, a bohemian ethos by dint of which long periods of unemployment yield an accretion of status. No doubt we have an excessive form of exploitation here which enables record companies to cherry pick talent and to force down the cost of first record contracts. Yet the culture of economic failure at the margins of the industry also has something of a resistance to it: if musicians keep on producing for little money then they may not be working at all. Rather, what's at stake is creativity envisaged as mutual endeavor. Jason Toynbee's chapter examines the economy of creativity in popular music making.

Cathy MacGregor's chapter draws on her work as both educator and performance artist to offer a survey of performance work between 1970 and 2000 in general and of the 1990s in particular. Focusing on performance artists' use of the body to make challenging work, her chapter brings a welcome focus to the very materiality of cultural work. In a similar vein,

Steve Taylor draws on his experience as both radio disc jockey and educator. He examines the conditions under which DJs work in an industry where tendencies identified by Murdock in his keynote chapter – in particular the concentration of ownership – impact on music radio's cultural workers. His conclusions in respect of listener choice both echoes Murdock's and foreshadows Nelson's pessimism about a recombinant cultural menu (in Chapter 11).

References

Lash, S. and Urry, J. (1994) *Economies of Sign and Space*, London: Sage.

Miège, B. (1989) *The Capitalization of Cultural Production*, New York: International General.

Sparks, C. (1994) "Independent Production: Unions and Casualization," in S. Hood (ed.) *Behind the Screens: The Structure of British Broadcasting in the 1990s*, London: Lawrence & Wishart.

2

FINGERS TO THE BONE OR SPACED OUT ON CREATIVITY?

Labor process and ideology in the production of pop

Jason Toynbee

It is a commonplace that labor practises in the cultural industries do not conform to the routines which are typical of work in the modern capitalist economy. On the one hand, cultural goods are made and sold for profit on a mass scale like any other kind of commodity. On the other, special qualities of creativity are attributed to the process of production and to the core workers who make cultural goods – musicians, actors, dancers, script writers, and so on. As the old song goes, "there's no business like show business." Raymond Williams couches it in rather different terms, but comes to a similar conclusion about the distinctiveness of cultural production:

> [T]he general productive order, throughout the centuries of the development of capitalism, has been predominantly defined by the market, and "cultural production" . . . has been increasingly assimilated to its terms, yet any full identity between cultural production and general production has been to an important extent resisted, one of the forms of this resistance being the distinctions between "artisan," "craftsman" [sic], and "artist," and in an important related form the distinction between "objects of utility" and "objects of art."
>
> (1981: 50)

In what follows we will explore some implications of these asymmetric relations of production which Williams identifies by examining popular music.

Pop makes a useful case study for two main reasons. First, an unassimilated form of production seems to have persisted in a stronger form here than in other cultural industries such as film or television which have tended to be relatively integrated and bureaucratic. Music making, conversely, has always been a relatively autonomous activity taking place beyond the

39

supervision of the firm for the most part. Arguably this tendency toward autonomy has become more pronounced in recent years. Second, we should note a powerful countervailing tendency in the shape of an increasingly concentrated record industry (Burnett, 1996). Because record companies control commissioning, marketing, and distribution functions, they exert a powerful grip on production. Not only is it the case that without a record deal musicians cannot reach a significant public, but for those musicians who do sign contracts, labor market conditions remain highly uncertain. Music-makers are constantly being "dropped" by record and publishing companies. This is an industry which generates failure (Jones, 1998, 2002).

Taken together, these two sets of factors (limited institutional autonomy and intense market regulation) suggest that popular music displays in an acute form the sort of contradictions found in all cultural work under capitalism. Over the course of the chapter we will examine them in detail. Actually, there is a larger argument lurking here, namely that in negotiating these contradictions musicians demonstrate a form of exemplary social agency. Creativity in popular music is not just an ideological construction, I want to suggest, but also a form of democratic practice.

What is creativity?

Because the notion of creativity is crucial to the present argument, we ought to ask what it consists in. However, even posing this question is difficult in media and cultural studies, mainly because of the influence of post-structuralist critique of authorship. (Clearly there are other reasons why the concept of creativity has been avoided in the field. One is the "turn to the audience" over the last twenty years (itself fed by anti-authorship critique) at the expense of studies of media production. Another is that for those researchers who have dealt with production on a critical basis the urgent problem has been to trace the dimensions of the gathering commodification of culture, an issue which I discuss toward the end of this chapter. For two exceptions to this trend see Petrie (1991) and Tulloch (1990).) Perhaps the best known and most concise example of this critique is the essay, "The Death of the Author" by Roland Barthes (1977). We can usefully begin by examining it.

"The Death of the Author" is a polemical piece. Barthes attacks the prevailing doctrine of expression in the literary world, that is the idea that the author translates internal aesthetic intuition into external symbolic form (Barthes, 1977: 146). This Romantic concept of creativity depends on the myth of a powerful and self-sufficient subject who can make great work with nothing more than his own imaginative resources – an "Author-God" (ibid.). (I use the gendered pronoun "he" intentionally. The romantic conception of the author is unequivocally masculine.) Barthes' point is that it is the archive of writings already done, not the author's genius, which provides the material of texts. I think this position has much to recommend it. But the problem is it does not explain enough. For if texts are indeed "a tissue of quotations" (ibid.) the question is, what does it mean to quote? Barthes gestures at an answer when he adopts the term "scriptor" to refer to writers of modern texts. The scriptor simply traces out language, "language which ceaselessly calls into question all origins" (ibid.). Yet this is not really a satisfactory formulation either. For scriptors surely do more than trace; they select, combine, and inflect components from a cultural tradition which has, if not origins, then precisely a history. Writers also finish texts. I mean by this that they package or frame them so as to make them fit for public display. In other words, the function which Barthes calls "scriptor" actually involves making a whole series of decisions about how to select and organize found textual materials and then present the result to an audience. Added together, this is a substantial amount of work.

If Barthes' scriptor is too shadowy a figure to be of help in understanding the design of texts (including musical texts) then we need a different approach, one which focuses on the processive dimension of making culture I have just outlined. The sociologist Howard Becker's (1982) theory of the "editorial moment" does just that. Becker begins from the premise that it is "choices which give the work its final shape" (Becker, 1982: 194). Crucially, artists work through a set of alternatives in the process of creation. We can find evidence of such alternatives in the successive sketches, drafts (or demo tapes) which are produced and then discarded. These hint at the "areas of choice the artist was aware of" (ibid.: 199).

Becker suggests that artists refer to the conventions of their particular art world when they make choices. However, it is difficult to identify such conventions because most producers cannot articulate them, and instead use an "undefinable but perfectly reliable standard like 'it swings' or 'it works'" (ibid.: 200). What gives these precepts coherence is actually their orientation toward the audience. As Becker puts it, "[d]uring the editorial moment all the elements of an art world come to bear on the mind of the person making the choice, who imagines the potential responses to what is being done and makes the next choices accordingly" (ibid.: 201).

Becker's "editorial moment" sheds light on the selective nature of creativity and its orientation toward audience effect, aspects which have long been recognized, if not theorized, by art makers (see, for example, Poe, 1976 [1846]). However, the concept provides few clues as to where alternative choices come from. Because conventions and the way that artists perceive them are undefinable, we are left with a creative "black box" – and an analytical impasse. To go beyond this we need somehow to combine a sociological approach to the practice of the artist with an understanding of how symbolic materials, idioms, and rules become available to her concretely and historically. The work of Pierre Bourdieu

(1993, 1996) offers a way forward here. For Bourdieu cultural production occurs at the intersection of "habitus," the set of structuring dispositions acquired by the artist over the life course, and the "field of cultural production," that is the rules and hierarchies which govern an art world. According to the way habitus meets field, the artist selects "possibles" from a range of many such possibles. These are rather like Becker's "alternatives," in other words they are choices which might be made at a given moment. However, Bourdieu goes further than Becker by explaining how possibles arise. He suggests they come from the "field of works" or historical fund of work done and techniques used in a particular cultural domain (Bourdieu, 1993: 176–83).

In the case of popular music I want to suggest that possibles are nothing less than *voices*, or sound-images. A short and necessarily incomplete list of voice types might include instrumental and vocal timbres, beats, genres, riffs, song forms, snatches of melody and characteristic chord changes, not to mention tropes of performance like the soul singer's melisma, metal guitarist's "hammer on" or the "cross fade" performed by a DJ. Voices have something in common with the heteroglot utterances which Bakhtin (1981) identifies in the novel. However, because music tends to have multiple strands running in parallel and also many parameters, it is difficult to identify the equivalent of a discrete, syntagmatic unit of discourse like the utterance. Rather, the coherence of what are often polyphonic voices derives from their double aspect of site (physical or textual point of origin) and sound (particular sonic-syntactic qualities). It is the loose–tight link between the two aspects which enables the initial identification, but also subsequent recombination, of voices. A medium scale voice which shows these characteristics of site–sound articulation quite clearly is "the quaver off beat, hi-hat lick used in disco and house." A more local one would be "Tori Amos's breathy yodel." A really large voice is "thirty two bar, AABA 'standard' song form."

Voices are identified in the audition of the music-maker. Actually, we might say that the main role of the musician is as primary listener, someone who listens ahead. Most voices will be obvious and immediately recognizable. Where the music-maker's creativity applies is in the selection, editing, and combination of voices. Elsewhere I have proposed a model for dealing with these issues called the "radius of creativity" (Toynbee, 2000). Here I simply want to highlight the limited but profoundly social nature of this process of creation. It is *limited* because, as we have seen, music-makers are constrained both by habitus, that is their own custom, taste, and ways of hearing, and by field, in other words the rules of the genre in which they work. Crucially, there tends to be convergence between these two sets of constraints since habitus disposes one toward taking a given position in the field. As a result, selection and combination of voices are generally predictable. Yet, at the same, time they are never absolutely determined. For there will always be a lack of fit between habitus and field which enables the selection of some unlikely possibilities.

Creativity in popular music is then *social* because voices are shared between music-makers and audience in widely recognizable structures. As a result, change occurs – the new is created – in two ways. First, musicians have to show audiences how different combinations and inflections of voice are, after all, coherent voices. In other words, musicians perform new voices, frame them, and present them to the public. Second, because of the limited nature of creativity, change is rarely accomplished by a single musician or group. Rather, it tends to take the form of a string of incremental innovations made by many different music-makers within a genre. To put it another way, transformations in style are the cumulative effect of small creative acts occurring across a social network of production.

We can call this limited and incremental mode of creativity, "social authorship." Historically, it has taken shape over several stages in popular music history, from the emergence of jazz and collective improvisation in the 1920s (Schuller, 1986; Ogren, 1989), through the development of the large, peripatetic swing band in the 1930s (Collier, 1989; Simon, 1981), to the return to small group recording units in post-War rhythm and blues and rock and roll (George, 1988; Gillett, 1983). In the rock era of the 1960s and after, social authorship assumed a rather different character as music-makers, still mainly organized in groups, came to be treated as artists (Straw, 1990; Kealy, 1990). Most recently in rap (Toop, 1991), but especially electronic dance music (see below), the organization of creativity in pop has changed yet again, taking on a more diffuse and anonymous character.

Despite the manifest differences between these successive forms of social authorship, there are continuous strands running through them all, namely a high degree of interaction and mutuality between members of the production unit, a blurring of distinctions between composition and performance, and the ceding of control of creative functions to musicians themselves. Arguably, such continuities in music-making have been more important than radical change in the history of pop. In the next section we will investigate these continuities at three key moments: in swing, rock, and contemporary electronic dance music.

Social authorship and institutional autonomy

The limited autonomy which is a basic condition of social authorship in pop has not been *won* in a struggle for creative freedom (as suggested in the mythology of jazz and rock) so much as *institutionalized* through the historical development of markets and media. Swing provides the best early example of this process. The ascendancy of the swing band in American pop from 1935 to 1945 depended partly on the fact that it could be "plugged into" a range of music disseminating channels. Concerts might be heard on radio via the live "hook up" (Lees, 1987), or bands could broadcast directly from the studio. Radio networks also recorded swing bands on "transcription discs" for later rediffusion by local stations (Collier, 1989: 67). By the end of the 1930s, with economic recovery from the Depression underway, record sales were also booming. They reached fifty million in 1939. John Collier estimates that 85 percent of this total were swing sides (ibid.: 257). Lastly, the film industry hired swing bands. Over the summer of 1941, eleven of them were filming in Hollywood studios (Simon, 1981: 67).

Although media performance and recording became increasingly important, the primary market for the swing orchestras nonetheless remained the dance hall circuit. As a result, bands toured constantly, either in particular territories like the South West (Driggs, 1959), or, in the case of "name" bands such as Benny Goodman's, across the whole United States (Rollini, 1987). It was this continuing importance of live performance together with demand for music from a variety of media which gave swing bands a degree of autonomy. Quite simply, they were able to sell their services directly to several buyers and so avoid dependence on any single one.

The mobility and autonomy of the bands was mirrored in the way they made music. They needed to be self-sufficient innovators, capable of generating new performances on the move. Most used a standard repertoire of pop tunes, or, in the terminology set out just now, voice-forms from the field of works. Social authorship then took a number of guises; first, and most obviously, in the arrangements which provided distinctive shape and color to the work of the wind sections. Books of arrangements were sometimes commissioned from professional specialists. But the leading bands tended to have arrangers among their own ranks – people like Sy Oliver in the Jimmie Lunceford Orchestra, Fletcher Henderson in his own band (Henderson also supplied arrangements to Benny Goodman), Mary Lou Williams in the Clouds of Joy, Gil Evans in the Claude Thornhill Orchestra (Simon, 1981; Rollini, 1987; Collier, 1989). A different method was adopted by the early Count Basie Orchestra, where the wind players worked up "head" arrangements collectively (Carr *et al.*, 1987: 31).

This points to a further aspect of social authorship within the swing bands, the mutual interaction of all players in the ensemble so as to produce "swing." Charles Keil (1994) suggests that swing is that sense of forward propulsion yielded by the regular four–four walking bass line and accompanying drum taps of the jazz rhythm section. On the one hand, it is a product of regularity and evenness of pulse. On the other, it derives from slight temporal discrepancies between drummer and bass player. Keil's point is that we are dealing here with a process of psychosomatic interaction between players rather than a formal syntax. Moreover, this is a process of considerable complexity in that it involves all group members, including "soloists whose placement of notes may be just as important to process as the contributions of any rhythm section member" (Keil, 1994: 66). (Keil's

44

examples are drawn from modern jazz but his argument can be applied to swing just as to the later form.)

How might we summarize the form of social authorship which emerged in swing? Clearly, the interplay of voices on a mutual basis was crucial. So too was reliance on the relatively anonymous arrangement. In this context even "heroic," improvising soloists took on a social role, contributing to and feeding off the collective groove. Finally, such shared authorship of the band's total sound was as much a matter of the performance of that sound as of its prior design. The kind of collective self-sufficiency that resulted from these approaches to music-making then enabled the swing bands to tour incessantly while also managing to record, make broadcast performances, and even appear in films.

If we jump twenty years now and examine rock music as it was developing in the work of the Beatles during the early 1960s, some surprising similarities with swing can be detected. I say "surprising" because accounts of the formation of rock by musician-*auteurs* have tended to deny continuities with earlier pop mainstreams like swing. John Lennon, for example, proposed an authentic lineage of folk expressionism which ran from the blues through rock'n'roll to his own work (Wenner, 1973: 14, 44–5). Yet when they started performing, the Beatles were precisely arrangers of the texts of others – especially rhythm and blues tunes from America. Moreover, it was the sound of beat music, just like the sound of swing, which was all important. In both cases we hear the re-voicing of an inherited repertoire rather than "original" expression. The difference is that in the case of early rock, since they were located outside the musical culture which had produced R and B, the bands were forced to *translate* the repertoire. Specifically, they changed arrangements to suit the guitar group format. This resulted in a simplification of the sophisticated productions they were trying to copy (Moore, 1993).

As for pattern of work, there were parallels here too. By February 1963 when the Beatles recorded their first album, *Please Please Me*, the group had been playing live almost every night for the previous three years. The hectic pace of live performance only abated slightly over the next two years, which meant that recording had to be squeezed in during tours. *Please Please Me* was actually recorded in less than ten hours during a day taken out of a tour of Britain. As composition of original songs became more important, this too was accommodated in the touring regime. "She Loves You" was written in a Newcastle hotel room, while Lennon and McCartney wrote the lyrics of "All My Loving" on a tour bus, and the group then worked out the music at the ballroom before the evening gig. "From Me to You" was another band bus composition (Lewisohn, 1994; McDonald, 1995).

What seems extraordinary in hindsight is the casual mode of authorship which the Beatles adopted at this stage in their career. While working as peripatetic performers, very much like the swing musicians of the previous

generation, they were also able to produce large numbers of new compositions. Just as important, the Beatles enshrined this regime of "banal creativity" in their public discourse. The sardonic, work-a-day pronouncements
made by the group at press calls or interviews always emphasized the ordi-
nariness of what they did.

After 1965, however, we can detect a change. Simon Frith (1983) has
shown how the values of the middle-class folk revival movement in America
were imported into the emerging rock formation. During the mid-1960s,
musicians in Britain and America increasingly came to see themselves as
artists. Frith links this ideological shift to changes in the means of production:

> [A]s recording studios and devices got more sophisticated, as musi-
> cians got more time and money to indulge themselves, as the indus-
> try began to care about the album as a medium, musicians got a
> chance to experiment with their music away from the immediate
> relationship with an audience, away from the constant beat of
> dancing feet.
>
> (1983: 74)

The double-sidedness of rock authorship is crucial here. On the one hand,
new material practices (most importantly multi-track recording) enabled a
radical blurring of the craft division of labor which marked earlier forms of
pop, a division between writing, arranging, performing, and technical functions (Kealy, 1990). On the other hand, these changes in the means of production corresponded with the new ideology of direct expression, according
to which the artist should control the whole music-making process from
start to finish.

The interlacing of ideological and material aspects in rock authorship
makes it a difficult mode to evaluate. Certainly substantial changes did
occur in the way popular music was produced in the age of high rock (say,
from 1967 to 1978). But just as certainly, the expressionist rhetoric of rock
musicians and critics has led to an overemphasis on heroic genius and given
the impression of a complete rupture with past forms of popular music-
making. In fact we can note both continuities and variations in social
authorship in the high rock era.

The most important continuity is in the type of production unit, namely
the peripatetic band of musicians. Rock and swing are both premised on a
strong collective input from band members to the total sound of the ensemble. In both genres the instrumental virtuosity of individual players is
important, but takes the form of dialogic exchange with the ensemble
sound. Both rock and swing bands are also mobile and adaptable, being able
to record and perform in different media.

However, there are also significant variations between forms of social authorship in the two genres. Rock bands are small, mostly between three and five in number, and authorship functions are therefore much more strongly concentrated in individual group members. Indeed it is often just one or two key members who receive most of the creative credit, particularly for song writing. This factor is connected with a second key difference in social authorship in rock: the importance of the record–song text. In swing, bands took songs which were effectively blank stock and stamped their particular arrangements and sonority onto them. The results could then be duplicated in real time performance through a number of different media – dance hall, radio, recording, film soundtrack. However, in rock, song and sound are produced together through the medium of sequential multi-track recording (Théberge, 1989; Gracyk, 1996). The initial song concept has only a tenuous existence as a "demo." The full form is precisely the recording whose shape is achieved partly through a collective process of trial and error by players, but also by the design work of the producer. (As in the case of the swing arranger, the producer might come from within the ranks of the band or be hired in from outside.) Rock recordings are large productions in which multi-track recording yields a three-dimensional, "virtual textural space" (Moore, 1993: 106). The very sophistication of such recordings means that bands then have to work out a stripped down version of the original record text for use in live performance.

We might say, therefore, that the social authorship of high rock differs from that of swing in at least three ways: in its dependence on songs generated by band members, in the "through-composition" of songs from initial conception to recording, and in the cult of original expression which accompanies this whole process. In the electronic dance music which has developed, first in Britain and then across Europe, since the end of the 1980s, certain of these tendencies have been intensified. But in other respects there has been a return to earlier forms of social authorship. We will examine these changes next.

Rock's mythology of original expression has tended to downplay the voiced nature of the music. The individuality and distinctiveness of a particular band or artist is emphasized instead. In one sense this is an accurate picture of rock authorship. As Will Straw (1990, 1993) has pointed out, the slow speed of change in album rock in the 1970s was premised on the long careers of a relatively small group of star performers. There was little aesthetic reflexivity here. Musicians did not tend to consider their work in relation to historical development of the rock style. Of course in practice musicians utilized a whole rock vocabulary; it is just that this was naturalized and treated as a mere *means* of expression.

Conversely, in the dance music scene which developed in the wake of the 1988 "acid house" movement in the United Kingdom, citation of voices has become a major creative trope. (Information for the following passage on dance music (unless otherwise shown by a reference) comes from personal, if intermittent, observation in clubs since 1990, the UK music journals *Music Week*, *DJ*, and *Mixmag*, and interviews with dance music-makers, especially house DJ and producer Kevin Mason in 1993–4 and drum and bass duo The Guardians of Dalliance in 1999.) There are at least two forms of citation. First, music-makers use sampling technology to quote from dance music's past – mainly from funk and disco – so as to evoke a strong sense of historical field. Second, and more generally, music-makers work within evolving generic conventions. The voicedness of the genre (its particular sounds and beats) becomes, in effect, the object of the music-maker's practice; the aim is to inflect common generic materials, "turning" them through a few degrees. This is associated with a decline in the significance of the author as a public figure. Producers of dance music are just that, relatively anonymous figures who often change their *noms de disque* with each record release (Hesmondhalgh, 1998). This rejection of the cult of personality in dance music has something to do with its avowed functionality: dance records should make people dance, not divert attention from the dance floor toward the figure of the author. In some ways, then, dance producers are more like the members of a swing band than rock musicians. Rather than belonging to a band, though, producers are affiliated to a genre with its particular sound and groove (house, garage, drum and bass, techno, and so on).

Another parallel between music-making in the pre-rock era and in the dance scene can be found in the latter's two stage song-performance system. Dance producers generate music texts (called "tunes") which are pressed up on 12" vinyl, and then "played out" in dance clubs by disc jockeys (DJs) as part of a long continuous mix of many such tunes (Rietveld, 1998). This latter function is no mere technical operation but a fully creative one depending on the selection of record-voices as well as various kinds of "beat-editing" or mixing *between* records. In effect, DJs perform new music and present it to the public – a key aspect of social authorship as I suggested at the start of the chapter. This sequential division of labor between conception and performance has something in common with that found in Tin Pan Alley. In both cases tunes (in the old music industry these took the commodity form of sheet music) require "finishing" by performers. Of course dance music can be disseminated in other ways than by the club DJ, particularly through the radio and compilation CDs. Still, the primary market is always the dance club. It is only after DJ approval and dance floor success that a record may be commercially exploited elsewhere.

The producer/DJ split represents a significant step down from the total authorship of rock where the album, unlike the 12" single, is offered to the public expressly as a completed text. Further, rock bands always play live as well as making records, and thus maintain the ideal of direct, authentic communication with the audience. If this suggests that authorial power is fragmented in dance music, then in another respect the trend has actually been toward *more* concentrated control over creativity. The rock band consisted of three, four or five members, but dance music producers most often work on their own or in duos. As in the case of rock, the reduction in size of the production unit has been enabled by new technology, first sequencers which allow the pre-programmed triggering of synthesizers and samplers, and more recently music production software like Cubase and Cakewalk which runs on personal computers (Théberge, 1997). With the arrival of these systems at the turn of the 1980s, one more element is added to music-making: the graphic inscription of music. Now music event information can be read from the screen, usually in matrix form with the horizontal axis indexing time elapsed (measured by bars, beats, and micro-beats) and the vertical axis showing the incidence of musical events at any given moment along the time line.

The degree of control which individual dance music producers can thus exert over the placement of musical voices in virtual time and space has certainly given them the potential to be self-sufficient as creators. But does this mean that dance music-makers are no longer *social* authors? I would argue strongly that they continue to be so. In the first place, producers and DJs, like all popular musicians, use possibles from the field of works to create the new. In the case of dance music these voices derive from genre, a collection of conventions, traits, and intensities shared between music-makers and audience. For dance musicians it is genre, rather than one's own *oeuvre* as in rock, which provides the continuities through which the new is formed.

Second, music-makers interact across genre networks consisting of record labels and shops, radio programs and stations, clubs and DJs. Often producer and DJ roles are combined to enable more effective networking. Perhaps most significant of all, though, the club itself is a network in which feedback between DJ and dancers is at a premium. Indeed, it is the extreme sociality of dance music as a cultural industry system which yields such a high rate of innovation within it. Small changes in voicing – organization of beats, timbre or tone color – are almost immediately endorsed or refused by dance floor crowds. This information is then fed back to record companies and producers through DJ reaction sheets and the index of record sales. In an important sense, then, dance music-making represents a more collective form of production than that found in rock. It has a relatively flat and democratic structure with a strong feedback mechanism. As a result, music-makers are more like delegates subject to instant recall than rock stars whose purported role as representatives of a community of dissident youth has always been more notional than actual anyway.

I want now to return to the three defining characteristics of social authorship set out at the beginning of this section: interaction and mutuality between musicians, the imbrication of composition and performance, and the ceding of control of production to musicians. The question is, how are we to evaluate developments in each of these areas across the different conjunctures in popular music we have been examining? On the evidence presented so far it is tempting to present a "Whig view" of history. It might look like this: in swing, the band was a relatively autonomous unit and musicians worked together collectively to produce a total band sound. However, innovation was slow and swing sonority quickly ossified. In rock, individual musicians and bands did create their own styles. But this was at the cost of the author–star cult and remoteness from the audience. Unlike the two earlier forms, in electronic dance music there seems to be a happy combination of high innovation and mutuality – both between music-makers themselves, and between music-makers and audience.

The trouble is, though, such a thesis seems unfeasibly optimistic. The music industry is, after all, a capitalist industry whose function is to make a profit. And if it licenses a certain amount of institutional autonomy, accommodation between social authorship and capital is surely a contradiction in terms. In the introduction to the chapter I pointed to the tension in popular music between the promise of creative autonomy for music-makers and the threat of commodification. Now I want to examine a more critical approach to music-making which concentrates precisely on that threat. The aim is to see what light such an approach might cast on the story of creative empowerment in pop set out above.

The bleak view: creativity and commodification

As Nicholas Garnham points out, "*{i}t is cultural distribution, not cultural production, that is the key locus of power and profit*. It is access to distribution which is the key to cultural plurality. The cultural process is as much, if not more, about creating audiences or publics as it is about creating cultural artifacts or performances" (1990: 161–2, original emphasis). In the case of the music industry these observations have important implications. For if there is, as I have suggested, little direct control of production, then there is certainly evidence of increasing concentration and integration at the level of distribution (Burnett, 1996). David Hesmondhalgh (1996) argues that it is this factor, rather than the supposed "flexibility" of the music industry with its independent record companies and accessible studios (Lash and Urry, 1994: 119–20), which has the most significant impact on what sort of music is made and who gets to make it.

According to Mike Jones (1998 and this volume, Chapter 8) record companies exert pressure on musicians precisely through their control of access to publics and audiences. A basic industrial condition is that huge numbers of musicians aspire to "make it," but only a tiny number succeed. Success does not come about through raw talent rising to the top though. As Jones puts it, "[c]ommodification [of pop acts] . . . is clearly not a neutral process (a gate that either opens or fails to open), it is an active transformational one" (Jones, 2002: 149). What Jones means is that managers and record companies mold artists in the image of the successful pop commodity, an image which is arbitrary and remote from the artists' own conceptions. Most of all, such preparation for stardom involves the constant anticipation of success and the development of a "buzz" of excitement around an act. Not only is this profoundly alienating for musicians in many cases, it also gives them a false sense of the likelihood of success.

In fact, as Jones points out, the music industry generates failure rather than success. The huge number of people who aspire to become successful pop musicians is drastically reduced through a brutal process of market elimination. Even an act which has reached the stage of signing a contract with a major record company remains constantly at risk. What happens is that record companies operate a covert system of "prioritization," under which allocation of resources for promotion will vary according to how record company personnel assess "the likely fortunes of their signed acts" at any moment (ibid.). Often an act will struggle desperately to cope with falling support, and members will argue among themselves, and with managers, friends, and supporters so that "[b]y the time the axe falls and the record company drops them they are exhausted and confused" (ibid.).

Now I would certainly agree with Jones that this system is in the interest of capital. It reflects the need of the music industry to maintain a "fish tank" or "reservoir of workers ready to work without the need to pay them wages" (Miège, 1989: 30). Bernard Miège (1989) argues that such a reservoir is required in the cultural industries because of the market conditions which prevail there; namely, demand uncertainty combined with a high rate of innovation. With a tank, intermediaries select those cultural workers who look likely to succeed, always in the knowledge that contracts can be terminated and new artists selected. As Jones documents, these conditions are found in their most acute form in the music industry where there is a particularly large tank from which a relatively low number of artists are selected.

In my view such an analysis of the music industry is not only accurate, it is indispensable. But it is at the same time a partial view. What's missing here is the enormous labor supply *push*, the fact that countless musicians want to make music. Jones, of course, considers this desire to be cruelly exploited by the music industry. Success is a lure which sooner or later breaks musicians on the rock of disappointment. It seems to me, though, that young musicians are considerably more robust and realistic than Jones suggests. If it is necessary to believe passionately in one's own star quality in order to be plucked from the tank, it is also the case that such a belief represents a strategy or performance. Only the seriously deluded believe in the "right to stardom."

This brings us to the nub of the issue. Popular music production is a form of capitalist enterprise in which money and labor are conjoined so as to produce star-commodities. Yet it also constitutes a creative arena in which people come together on a mutual basis to make symbolic artifacts.

Certainly these two zones are imbricated. But it is wrong to see the latter simply as a function of the former. In fact, as I have been arguing, the most significant aspect of popular music-making is precisely how *little* musicians are controlled by and oriented toward the record industry – not how much. We can attribute this partly to demand uncertainty and partly to the sheer accessibility of "the tank." Because of the comparatively low cost of entering production (in a local band or as a bedroom producer), and the small amount of cultural capital required (mainly self-taught skills), few potential musicians exclude themselves. Not only this; at an early stage musicians are able to enter local proto-markets – pub back rooms, small clubs, and so on. (Increasingly proto-markets are assuming a virtual form as acts distribute their music by uploading onto the World Wide Web.)

Exchange does go on in proto-markets. People buy and sell records and they pay to go to gigs or to enter clubs. But what defines the proto-market is that music-making cannot be explained solely by economic factors. Musicians produce and perform to small audiences for the love of it, for the esteem and also, of course, because they hope to be recruited by the music industry. What's more, creativity and innovation tend to be privileged here. The very weakness of the imperative to accumulate in the proto-market facilitates a strange mixture of experiment, hybridity, and parochialism. For the music industry this presents real difficulties. Intermediaries concerned with recruitment (artist and repertoire personnel) have not only to deal with an oversupply of artists, but also a bewildering array of trends and potential dead ends.

It is true that the music industry copes with this situation. What we have here is a system of "outworking," whereby musicians carry the burden of buying their own equipment, of writing and rehearsing, and then absorbing the risks of an uncertain (proto-)market until the unlikely event that they are recruited by a record company. As Mike Jones points out, in this situation record companies simply have to ensure they have backed a sufficient (always small) number of those artists who finally achieve success in the market.

But just how terrible is this situation? In an important sense musicians in proto-markets, or even in tiers further up the scale of commodification, are not workers in the conventional sense. As part of the reservoir of labor they are implicated in the production of musical commodities. But at the same time they are also creative agents who gladly give the products of their labor for free. In this sense they resist capital by refusing the calculus of equivalence and instead extravagantly expend their own resources in a kind of potlatch. I am suggesting, then, that there is a profound ambivalence about creativity in popular music. On the one hand, music-makers are exploited and ensnared in strategies of accumulation. On the other hand, they are exemplary agents who make gifts for others, possibly beautiful gifts. (Analogs for "beautiful" in the critical discourse of popular music include the epithets "swinging," "funky," "wicked," "rocking," and "bad.") My point is that both conditions pertain. What is more, musicians experience expectation and disappointment very much according to their trajectory in the career hierarchy, that is to say down below in the tank, ascending, attaining stardom, falling back, or indeed in any position between.

Conclusion

In this chapter we have examined aspects of that asymmetry, identified by Raymond Williams (1981), between capitalist production in general and social relations in the cultural industries. This asymmetry derives from the widely-held belief (held by industries, audiences, and producers) that making culture depends on special powers of creativity which cannot be routinized. The question then arises as to what creativity might actually consist in. In popular music-making, its most significant aspect, *contra* the romantic conception of authorship, is its limited and social character. Such a form of creativity might be called social authorship. We can trace the vicissitudes of social authorship as it has developed over the twentieth century. Arguably, there has been a benign shift toward a *more* socialized form of music-making. However, this shift has been partly obscured by the cult of expression and individual genius which accompanied the emergence of rock music in the late 1960s.

Now, though, in the new networks of dance music there seems to have been a return to certain pre-rock values. Above all, there is strong feedback from audiences to music-makers and strong connectivity between music-makers within genre. At the same time there is a high rate of innovation. In other words creativity is intense, and also intensely shared. Of course such an optimistic image becomes tarnished when we consider how creativity is commodified by the record industry, and the endemic failure amongst musicians that results. However, in the end, this should not prevent us from recognizing the significance of creativity in pop. Making music, in all its contradictions, offers an example of the virus-like persistence of mutual and democratic practice within capitalism. As such it offers the possibility of hope for the future.

References

Bakhtin, M. (1981) *The Dialogic Imagination: Four Essays*, M. Holquist (ed.), Austin: University of Texas Press.

Barthes, R. (1976) "The Death of the Author," in *Image/Music/Text*, London: Fontana Press, pp. 142–8.

Becker, H. (1982) *Art Worlds*, Berkeley: University of California Press.

Bourdieu, P. (1993) *The Field of Cultural Production*, Cambridge: Polity Press.

Bourdieu, P. (1996) *The Rules of Art: Genesis and Structure of the Literary Field*, Cambridge: Polity Press.

Burnett, R. (1996) *The Global Jukebox: The International Music Industry*, London: Routledge.

Carr, I., Fairweather, D. and Priestley, B. (1987) *Jazz – the Essential Companion*, London: Grafton Books.

Collier, J. (1989) *Benny Goodman and the Swing Era*, New York: Oxford University Press.

Driggs, F. (1959) "Kansas City and the Southwest," in *Jazz*, N. Hentoff and A. McCarthy (eds), New York: Rinehart, pp. 189–230.

Frith, S. (1983) *Sound Effects: Youth, Leisure and the Politics of Rock'n'Roll*, London: Constable.

Garnham, N. (1990) "Public Policy and the Cultural Industries," in *Capitalism and Communication: Global Culture and the Economics of Information*, London: Sage, pp. 154–68.

George, N. (1988) *The Death of Rhythm and Blues*, New York: Pantheon.

Gillett, C. (1983) *The Sound of the City: the Rise and Fall of Rock And Roll*, London: Souvenir Press.

Gracyk, T. (1996) *Rhythm and Noise: an Aesthetics of Rock*, London: I. B. Tauris.

Hesmondhalgh, D. (1996) "Flexibility, post-Fordism and the music industries," *Media, Culture and Society*, 18, 469–88.

Hesmondhalgh, D. (1998) "The British dance music industry: a case study of independent cultural production," *British Journal of Sociology*, 49, 234–51.

Jones, M. (1998) *Organising Pop: Why So Few Pop Acts Make Pop Music*, Liverpool: PhD thesis, Institute of Popular Music, Liverpool University.

Jones, M. (2002) "The Music Industry as Workplace: an Approach to Analysis," in *Cultural Work: Understanding the Cultural Industries*, A. Beck (ed.), London: Routledge Harwood.

Kealy, E. (1990) "From Craft to Art: the Case of Sound Mixers and Popular Music," in *On Record: Rock, Pop and the Written Word*, S. Frith and A. Goodwin (eds), London: Routledge, pp. 207–20.

Keil, C. (1994) "Motion and Feeling Through Music," in *Music Grooves: Essays and Dialogues*, C. Keil and S. Feld, Chicago: University of Chicago Press, pp. 53–76.

Lash, S. and Urry, J. (1994) *Economies of Signs and Space*, London: Sage Publications.

Lees, G. (1987) *Singers and the Song*, New York: Oxford University Press.

Lewisohn, M. (1994) *The Beatles' Recording Sessions: the Official Abbey Road Studio Session Notes 1962–1970*, London: Hamlyn/EMI.

McDonald, I. (1995) *Revolution in the Head: the Beatles' Records and the Sixties*, London: Pimlico.

Miège, B. (1989) *The Capitalization of Cultural Production*, New York: International General.

Moore, A. (1993) *Rock: the Primary Text, Developing a Musicology of Rock*, Buckingham: Open University Press.

Ogren, K. (1989) *The Jazz Revolution: Twenties America and the Meaning of Jazz*, New York: Oxford University Press.

Petrie, D. (1991) *Creativity and Constraint in the British Film Industry*, London: Macmillan.

Poe, E. (1976/1846) "Creation as Craft," in *The Creativity Question*, A. Rothenberg and C. Hausman (eds), Durham: Duke University Press, pp. 57–61.

Rietveld, H. (1998) *This Is Our House: House Music, Cultural Spaces and Technologies*, Aldershot: Ashgate.

Rollini, A. (1987) *Thirty Years with the Big Bands*, Oxford: Bayou Press.

Schuller, G. (1986) *Early Jazz: its Roots and Early Development*, New York: Oxford University Press.

Simon, G. (1981) *The Big Bands* (4th edn), New York: Schirmer.

Straw, W. (1990) "Characterizing Rock Music Culture: the Case of Heavy Metal," in *On Record: Rock, Pop and the Written Word*, S. Frith and A. Goodwin (eds), London: Routledge, pp. 97–110.

Straw, W. (1993) "Popular Music and Postmodernism in the 1980s," in *Sound and Vision: the Music Video Reader*, S. Frith, A. Goodwin and L. Grossberg (eds), London: Routledge, pp. 3–21.

Théberge, P. (1989) "The 'sound' of music: technological rationalization and the production of popular music," *New Formations*, 8, 99–111.

Théberge, P. (1997) *Any Sound You Can Imagine: Making Music/Consuming Technology*, Hanover, NH: Wesleyan University Press.

Toop, D. (1991) *Rap Attack 2: African Rap to Global Hip Hop*, London: Serpent's Tail.

Toynbee, J. (2000) *Making Popular Music: Musicians, Aesthetics and the Manufacture of Popular Music*, London: Arnold.

Tulloch, J. (1990) *Television Drama: Agency, Audience and Myth*, London: Routledge.

Wenner, J. (1973) *Lennon Remembers: the Rolling Stone Interviews*, Harmondsworth: Penguin.

Williams, R. (1981) *Culture*, London: Fontana.

3

BODIES ON THE BOUNDARIES

Subjectification and objectification in contemporary performance

Cathy MacGregor

Where was performance in the 1990s? In 1999 the theatre director Peter Hall spoke of the role of the arts in education as fundamental because of the revolutionary character of art. Hall went on to state "that [revolutionary art] is the only art, because artists are there to tell us about tomorrow not yesterday" (quoted in the *Guardian*, 2 November 1999). In a sense this statement could also be used to describe the general notion of art in the twentieth century, via the concept of the avant-garde as that which constantly pushes forward the boundaries of representation. In the late 1990s, some of the most exciting and vigorous pushing back of these boundaries took place in the realm of performance art and live art as opposed to traditional forms of theatre. However, in beginning to outline some of the main themes and pre-occupations of performance in the 1990s, I think it is also important to consider this work not merely in terms of pushing back boundaries (both its own and others) but also in how work of the time relates to performance work from the past thirty years. The notion of a canonical tradition and methodology is often missing from the consideration of performance as art – perhaps due to its significant lack of a finished product.

In this chapter I will outline some of the broad themes which have been evident in performance work over the past thirty years and how these same themes are being interpreted and reinterpreted in the work of artists who are producing performances at the current moment. This is not to say that the work is repetitive, rather I will show the way in which performance art is constantly interpreting and being affected by its broader cultural and political contexts. The major theme, which I have chosen to express, is that of the body in performance as it is both the most basic building block of performance but also the means for some highly complex explorations of, basically, what it means to be human. The body, the simple representations of the human body, the body of the performer, the body of the spectator and the interaction between the two is what it all really comes down to. As Robert Ayers puts it:

Live art allows the artist to enter the everyday lives of its audience and – quite literally – to touch them. And it is that moment free of preconceptions when flesh touches flesh, which as often as not is as unsettling for the artist as it is for the audience that, no matter what else they build upon it, is the essence of live art for many of the artists who make it.

(Ayers and Butler, 1991: 10)

The genesis of artists using performance is hard to define, but what we now term as "performance art" or in Britain "live art" is generally seen as having its beginnings in America in the 1950s and Allan Kaprow's "Happenings." (In this chapter where I will discuss work from both Europe and America I will use the term "performance art" to cover work that is also defined as live art as this term is specific to the British scene.) The activities of the influential Black Mountain School in North Carolina and also the work of John Cage and Merce Cunningham, particularly in terms of the notions of chance and "unintentional" events, affected Kaprow. The sense of something which "just happened" undercut the conventional methodologies of both theater and art. This concept of performance art as blurring and redefining the boundaries of artistic conventions returns again and again as perhaps its singularly most defining feature – defined by indefinition.

Other defining features of performance art introduced by the New York Happenings scene in the 1960s were fragmentation and lack of conventional narrative meaning: as Kaprow warned, "the actions will mean nothing clearly formulable so far as the artist is concerned" (quoted in Goldberg, 1988). The indefinability of performance art is precisely where its strength lies and, in many ways, making it a subject impossible to teach despite its growing presence in university curriculums in a variety of different formulas, both theoretical and practical. These two contradictory equations to modern performance – still indefinable and yet, increasingly becoming institutionalized – lead to an interesting point at the turn of the century. We now have a history and a recognizable catalogue of "classic works." This fact facilitates the teaching of performance art both within aegis of art and drama degrees yet, at the same time, the evolution of this tradition with the same impetus can only rely on the individual creativity and perseverance of a younger generation of artists coming from a wide variety of backgrounds. I wish to examine the work of some of these artists in relation to the past context from which this evolves, but to also recognize that the uniquely fragmented and individualistic nature of performance means that it can never really be adequately pigeonholed in a thematic survey as this leaves out the whole question of the spectators whose meanings are too multifarious for one critic to presume to prescribe. The themes which I will highlight in this chapter are the exploration of bodies and sexuality in contemporary performance, the medical body, the radicalized body and the role of other media in changing the nature of the body in performance in the late 1990s.

Bodies and sex

The body has always been a key subject in art, from the earliest cave painting through to Degas's odalisques. When artists began producing performances it was obvious that the body and its sexual presentation would be a major theme. Yves Klein's *Anthropometries* were an actualization of the preoccupation in art with the (female) body as object with female models as living paint brushes.

At the end of the twentieth century, as at the end of the nineteenth, there was an increasing artistic preoccupation with the boundaries of bodies and the boundaries of the sexualities that these bodies produce. Artistic production on these subjects is fraught with contradictions and displays the unease with which society views representations of the body and its desire, which do not conform to a stereotypical norm. Then, as now, the fears and anxieties of the cultural majority as much determine the cultural perceptions of otherness as it is by anything enacted by the "minority." The artist, obviously, can be seen to be situated in either camp but the notions of artistic value and suitability of subject matter constantly rear their head over and over again – the debate is never finished. Now, as then, the causes are deep rooted. In his study of *fin de siècle* art, Bram Dijkstra states that:

> Even many of the most comfortably situated men in late nineteenth-century culture felt a vague poorly defined sense of marginalization. If the robber barons and the already faceless trusts now seemed to have become the true movers and shakers – were the new executioners – the cloudy-browed middle aristocracy and middle bourgeoisie formed but an uneasy band of executioner's assistants. Aware that they were no longer executioners themselves, they looked around for someone to take the blame. And, as always, woman was conveniently available.
>
> (Dijkstra, 1986: 354)

In the 1990s, read woman, gays, blacks, disabled. The most striking example of the scapegoating of art was the NEA funding scandal of 1990 when three gay artists – John Fleck, Holly Hughes, and Tim Miller – and one feminist performer – Karen Finley – were defunded. Yet despite the risks of censorship and notoriety, the body and sexuality remains one of the most compelling themes in contemporary performances.

The performance of the body is linked fundamentally to the search for identity and adequate representation. I would disagree with critics who suggest the preoccupation with identity politics in the 1990s has depoliticized drama and performance; certainly in the arena of performance art this has not been the case. Performance, precisely because of its lack of boundaries and methodologies, can provide the ideal medium for the self-expression of the disenfranchised. Kaprow's earlier definition of this type of work as "something spontaneous, something that just happens to happen" (Goldberg, 1988: 130) does not, at least in theory, exclude anyone from the definition of "artist."

The concern with the artist's body in performance art can be seen as having a number of factors behind it. First, the ephemeral and subjective medium of the artist's own body in the *process* of performance replaces the object as the end *product* of the artistic experience. The rejection of the object as the supreme representation of artistic enterprise was also a rejection of the increasing capitalization of the art world. As early as the 1960s, Piero Manzoni was parodying the tension between process and product and between creativity and commodification. Manzoni's 1961 exhibition *Living Sculptures* turned people into works of art through the addition of the artist's signature onto their bodies; later, in 1961, Manzoni produced a number of cans of *Artist's Shit*, taking the notion of art as commodity to new self-parodic heights.

Much performance work using the body of the artist at its core has two objectives which are frequently linked or, in some cases, inseparable. These objectives can be defined as the desire to make the experiential subjectivity of the performing body central to the artistic experience or a desire to highlight the objectification and appropriation of imagery of the body running throughout society. The mass response to art, through media objectification/reproduction, eventually means that any creative or emotional value is lost. Baudrillard sums this up, referring to Benjamin's essay, "The Work of Art in the Age of Mechanical Reproduction": "in the age of mechanical reproduction the work of art loses its aura, the unique quality of its here and now, no longer destined for seduction but reproduction and in its new destiny takes on a political form" (Baudrillard, 1990: 162). The need for the control of the reproduction of images suggests the political dangers of uncontrolled bodies, sexuality or creativity. Boundaries are broken down between low and high culture, between art and life in many of these works.

Marina Abramovic is a figure who is key in understanding the presentation of the body and experience in performance art. She is a significant influence on many younger artists and is herself still producing work. Abramovic's work starts from the experiential presentation of the body but through this also questions notions of representation and identity. For artists of Abramovic's generation (a group which could be said to include Chris Burden, Gina Pane and Vito Acconci), the use of the body to replace the artistic artifact was pushed further from a critique of the commodification of artistic creation to a desire to push the physical limits of the body and thereby change the experience of art – both for the artist and the spectator.

In her performance work, Abramovic plays with the dualities of passivity and aggression. As with the work of the other artists discussed, this produces a contradiction at the heart of the work that is a positive rather than a negative aspect of the piece in performance terms. Abramovic's work is often highly ritualized in the repetitive and highly cathartic nature of the pieces. Abramovic's desire was to use her body literally as the material with which she works; as in the more recent work of an artist like Cindy Sherman, the boundaries of subject/object represented by the roles of artist and material are being transgressed. In Abramovic's most notorious performance, *Rhythm 0* (Naples, 1974) it was announced that the artist would remain completely passive for six hours. The visitors to the gallery were allowed to do whatever they wanted to her, ideas for such interventions were provided by a table of seventy-two objects, ranging from a rose and a bottle of perfume to razors and a loaded gun. The performance was stopped before its allotted time when a spectator placed the loaded gun in Abramovic's hand and pushed its nozzle against her head. In her adoption of complete passivity, Abramovic seemed to be questioning a variety of identity positions, the individual in relation to the collective, the artist in relation to society, women in relation to dominant male representation, the experience of an artist from a communist state working in Western capitalism. This exploration of the contradictions inherent in issues of representation and identity in late Western capitalism is an issue which a number of performers from a variety of sexual and racial identity groups are grappling with in their work. I will use Abramovic's work to introduce what I feel are two key themes which focus on the notion of the body and performance: these are sexuality and gender on the one hand and ethnicity and otherness on the other.

Sexy postmodern bodies: performing sexuality in the 1990s

To place a performer's body at the center of a performance makes a spectacle of it, and when this spectacle is both gendered and sexualized this raises a number of different levels of meaning. Putting performance together with a feminist sensibility deconstructs the dominant system of representation for women; to further couple this with a sexual sensibility deconstructs the sexual meanings attached to women's bodies. However, the attack on dominant sexual representation does not just exist as an out-and-out attack on conventional forms of sexual representation but can also work from within these discourses to try to reinvent them for the female performer and the female or male spectator.

To "make a spectacle" of oneself implies simultaneously to make oneself spectacular and transgressive. Culturally in the West, any woman who attempts to display a sexual subjectivity also makes herself into a spectacle. As we have moved into the later stages of capitalism, society has become one of spectacle where desire is projected onto a screen full of fetishized commodities (sexual or otherwise). The desire is both to have the commodity but also to become the commodity – like a fetish it will imbue us with its qualities if we possess it. For women this tension has always been greater and yet less problematic since it is so heavily internalized into our psyches, particularly in terms of our sexuality. Like the spectator at a performance, we are both affected by the objectification of the Other and aware of our own status as object/objectified. We are aware of the show but are often unaware of whether we are being called upon to perform. To make the performance of gender and sex obvious, as Rebecca Schneider terms it, to "show the show," can also throw into relief the terms of engagements between the genders and sexually desiring subjects when the performance is finished.

In 1975, Marina Abramovic performed *Role Exchange*. This was a dual performance, taking place in both a gallery and the red light district of Amsterdam where Abramovic swapped places with a sex worker.

This questioning of the boundaries between sexual representation and artistic representation was also questioned in the 1970s in Britain by the artist Cosey Fanni Tutti. Cosey worked in the sex industry and used these images in her performance work and exhibitions, most notably *Prostitution* at the ICA in 1976. The question of who owns the artist's body of work, and their ability to express themselves freely, also becomes a question of who owns women's bodies and their freedom to express themselves sexually. What does this mean when the woman is an artist also? The boundaries and overlaps but also the differences between the different ways of presenting the female body provided the impetus for Cosey's project of exploring the sex industry "as an artist (unknown to my associates) and as a woman within a man's fantasy world and also to see women through the eyes of men" (Fanni Tutti, 1993: 14). The female body presented in Western culture as the ultimate fetish of the logic of commodity was explored, subliminally, by an artist in terms of the varying levels of commodification and performance – a sliding scale of objectification and subjectification through and within the body. This process of investigation still goes on today in performance work on both sides of the Atlantic. Probably the most famous artist exploring the dichotomies of representing gender and sex at the moment is Annie Sprinkle. Sprinkle's definition of her self as a multi-media whore, like COUM's *Prostitution* exhibition, implicitly links the art industry with the sex industry. In fact, for the female performer, the experience of being a female body on display continually evokes connections with prostitution. This connection is still being played out in work being created by female artists now. As the transvestite performer Ru-Paul suggests in his comment, "You're born human and the rest is drag," we are all drag queens now. Perhaps the interest in the themes of sex work and prostitution in performance at the moment suggest that late capitalist Western society is now making whores of all women and even some men – particularly if they are also artists.

Annie Sprinkle's work has shifted from tongue-in-cheek takes on the relationship between bodies/commodities and art to a more spiritual experiential focus on the body. Sprinkle's sale of used underwear and her own piss (with which to produce golden showers) suggests a direct correlation with the avant-garde playfulness of Piero Manzoni over twenty years earlier. The more spiritual development of Sprinkle's work in recent years also shows a similarity in themes and preoccupations with both Abramovic's approach to her art and with the work of Cosey Fanni Tutti whose explorations of the sex industry were also informed by a sense of ritual and experiential exploration.

In common with many other female performance artists, Sprinkle's first major solo performance was autobiographical. The relationship between experience and performance in performance art is more often than not symbiotic: performances are signifiers that bear the traces of other experiences in much the same way that the body itself becomes traced with the marks of its lived experience. This referential element to much performance work (usually to specific events/experiences in the performer's life and by extension to a more general cultural experience of the issues) leads to what Elin Diamond refers to as the terminology of "re":

> as in *re*embody, *re*inscribe, *re*configure, *re-signify*. "Re" acknowledges the pre-existing discursive field, the repetition – and the desire to repeat – within the performative present.
>
> (Diamond, 1996: 2)

"Re" in terms of the depiction of the female body is the exploration of how its representation can be changed and modified through a re-contextualization and/or reinterpretation of the narrative frame. In her book, *Unmarked* (1993), Peggy Phelan refers to something she calls "re-posing." This refers to the re-positioning of a conventional human pose so that its one "simple" meaning is replaced by a multiplicity of meanings. Annie Sprinkle has created artwork that deals explicitly with re-posing the persona of the porn star or the whore. The title of *Post-Porn Modernist* suggests a number of different interpretations. It suggests an artist who is post or beyond porn and, if we take pornography in terms of the whole cultural conception of representing sex, Sprinkle's performance represents a way of moving beyond the simplistic popular understandings of porn. The title also suggests the artist as a post-modernist, someone who privileges micro-narratives (a myriad of interpretations) over macro-narrative (one universal interpretation or "truth").

The key notion in Sprinkle's ground-breaking *Post-Porn Modernist* is the live display which pre-empts the pro–anti censorship debate through the performer foregrounding the lived, corporeal experience of her own body. The performance works through simultaneously being too live to easily objectify the performer and also by parodying and playing along (in a highly

ironic way) with those very discourses of objectification and passive femininity. The set for the performance parodies the conventional expectations of a
porn star:

> a porn star's boudoir, with a glamorous bed, a large upholstered
> armchair and colorful sparkly lingerie hanging by a makeup table.
> There is a bathroom with a toilet. On the back wall is a large pro-
> jection screen on which slides will appear during the performance.
> There is soft, sexy lighting and the scent of cheap perfume in
> the air.
>
> (Sprinkle, 1998: 163)

Having set the stage, the performance which follows works to try to shatter
those preconceptions through the performer's own presence onstage as a
dialectical image which contradicts the easy stereotype. Through the testi-
mony of the piece, the audience is given the chance to see things from the
other side, an experience which is one of the key notions in performance.

Sprinkle's persona as a prostitute artist uses each role to contradict and
interrogate the other. The artistic representation of porn/prostitution uses
performance as a political act to bring a marginal activity into High
Culture; the mingling of high and low culture which this produces makes
the distinction itself a moot point. Sprinkle's persona as both sex worker and
now artist is so highly developed that, in some ways, the ultra performativ-
ity of her life and work do not unsettle or disrupt the expectations of the
spectator as much as the work of younger or less well known artists have the
potential to do.

Claire Shillito has produced works which rely for their power upon exploring the semiotics of the way in which we define sexuality and the way in
which the conventional "script" of the sexual contract can be manipulated.
This work relies less on the overt display of the female body as a sexual commodity and more on the exploitation of the performer/spectator interaction
with a sexualized twist. In *Fun, Loving, Female*, performed as part of the Expo
festival in Nottingham, Shillito took out a discreet newspaper advert for a
"friend" and interviewed the applicants in a hotel room. The purpose of the
interviews was to find a friend (a travelling companion) to accompany the
artist on her next working trip to Berlin, as opposed to a "friend" (a sexual
partner). Thus the piece used artistic intent to undercut and manipulate for
the artist's own ends the conventional tropes of sexual contract. In an even
more remarkable piece, *Hi I'm Claire* (1997–8), the audience is invited to
make individual appointments to see the artist perform. They are led to a
hotel room where Claire is waiting dressed like a high-class prostitute; she
invites them to take off their shoes and then unzips her own boots. They are
then asked to get into bed and Claire lies next to them and chats to them
casually, eventually getting them to reveal something personal and intimate.

Swiftly, the performer gets out of bed and asks her "visitor" to get their things. They are then led to the bathroom where the previous spectator has been listening and take this voyeuristic position. In this performance the close interaction between performer and spectator mirrors too closely the intimacy of the prostitute/client interaction, forcing the spectator to reflect on their own position. What is very interesting though is that this produces a great deal of discomfort through unsettling the expected boundaries of performative interaction, leaving the performer with a power to make the spectator and their own responses actually the focus of the performance. Shillito's interest is in "the way other people behave in potentially awkward situations, for instance when they meet someone for the first time" and her work is also heavily influenced "by risk, by sensations of shame and of getting 'caught'" (correspondence with the author, 1999).

In Sara Giddens's video piece *Not All the Time But Mostly* . . . the notion of performance art as a way to "speak" about the lived experiences of women is key to the work. Giddens (a choreographer) worked with a dancer to create moves inspired by the transcripts of interviews with prostitutes collected by sociologist Maggie O'Neill. The piece is performed in dim light; the main light comes from a strip of lamps that give the effect of suggesting a half-open doorway at night. Both the lighting and the camera focus are mainly on specific parts of the dancer's body. The camera angles, lighting and the quality of the movements all serve to deny the performer as merely objectified for the audience or the image of the prostitute as merely an object. The soundtrack of the transcripts, from one of which comes the title of the piece, further enhances the impression: "It's all set out in my head what I'm going to say and what he's going to say, so that I know what I'll say back. So when I know that I've got all my ammunition, then I'll go in. But I'm not going in beforehand because then I know that I'll come worse off. So I sort of work on that kind of basis . . . not all the time but mostly . . ."

The use of the transcripts highlights what I feel is one of the main reasons for this continuing interest in the boundary between sex and art. As in the earlier work of more established artists such as Abramovic, Cosey and Annie Sprinkle, the juxtaposition of subject (artist) and object (sexualized woman) are being continually explored in their relationship to each other and played off one another. The fascination with sex work in art is surely just a logical, but at times highly radical, continuation of society's own fascination with the bodies of women and signs and signifiers. By giving the most stigmatized of these signifiers a voice, either through the mediation of their own experiences or those of other women, these artists continue to use performance art in its most basic function as a direct communication which enters people's lives in a more immediate way than the more mediated art forms.

In the above section I dealt with the sexualized body; in the next section I shall deal with work that has explored what I will term "the medical body." I use this term incredibly loosely to describe work that is concerned with experience of the body in terms of bodily processes, pain and trauma and any work that explores or uses medical intervention.

The medical body

Probably the most famous exponent of art which focuses on the experience of the body, and that body's image through the intervention of medical procedures, is the French artist, Orlan. Orlan has for the past six years been engaged in an on-going work entitled *The Reincarnation of Saint Orlan.* This project involved surgical interventions to change her appearance. The surgery becomes the performance for Orlan, but this performance of the surgical modification of her body, and the recording and transmission of this is, at a basic level, a violation of the boundaries of inside/outside, of public/private. The surgical incisions and the interior of the body, which these reveal, are not usually spoken about, let alone shown to audiences. The rationale behind Orlan's work could be described as a desire to deconstruct the whole Western notion of femininity. Where an artist like Damien Hirst creates art about the body, Orlan is making art out of her body, becoming a spectacle – of beauty and ugliness – in order to provoke thought about surgery and the flesh. As in the work of those women engaged in representing the sexualized female body, Orlan's rationale is one of deconstructing the old binaries:

> Our whole culture is based on the notion of "or." For example, good or bad, private or public, new technology or painting etcetera. This forces us to condemn one element and to choose the other. All of my work is based on the notion of "and": the good and the bad, the beautiful and the ugly, the living and the artificial, the public and the private. It's always based on the notion of "and."
>
> (Quoted in Ayers, 1999: 4)

Orlan's work, rather like the explorations of so-called "modern primitives," challenges our notions of what is acceptable in terms of how our bodies are treated. Orlan's "enhancements" are not enhancements in the usual sense of the word, but serve rather to question why implanting silicone in breasts is more or less universally accepted, but that implanting it in the forehead to create small "horns" is seen as a form of body modification too far. Orlan's situating of the operation as performative breaks the modern Western taboo of censoring the body in extremis (either pain or death) but harks back rather to the early-modern conception of the body as something malleable, changeable and the ultimate performative artifact. The sixteenth and seventeenth centuries situated the spectacles of the operating theater and the dissection theater as *theater*, as a performative, site-specific spectacle. The recognition of the fluidity of gender and personal identity when the body is in extremis, particularly when it is being opened up in the operating theatre, is well documented in the work of early modern cultural historians such as Thomas Lacquer and Jonathan Sawday. The power of Orlan's work as both an artist and a female artist is interesting when seen in terms of Sawday's comments about the conception of the dissected, anatomized body in early-modern culture, the culture of dissection:

> The emblem of this culture was *Anatomia*, whose attributes were the mirror and the knife. These attributes were derived from the story of Perseus, the mythical hunter of the Medusa. In this book the image of the Medusa – or rather her petrifying glare – is a constant theme. The Medusa stands for the fear of interiority: more often than not a specific male fear of the female interior [. . .] But [. . .] once the body has been partitioned and its interior dimensions laid open to scrutiny, the very categories "male" and "female" become fluid, even interchangeable. This attempt at conquering the Medusa's realm with the devices of Anatomia involved a confrontation between an abstract idea of knowledge and the material reality of a corpse.
>
> (Sawday, 1995: 3)

Orlan's operations, in which she performs as an active and aware subject, confront the dichotomy of the body as meat versus the body as embodiment of subjectivity. Orlan's looking and being awake throughout the procedure mean that her gaze can provoke the same horror as that of the mythical Medusa but through a fear which is based on empathy and a horror for the frailty of our own corporeality. In a sense, much art which confronts the corporeality of the body is continually engaged in this same debate – bridging the gap between the abstract imagistic conception of the body and its experiential, material reality.

In a similar way, a younger Irish artist, Kira O'Reilly, produces work that focuses on the experiential reality of the body and its being, whether at the moment of performance that being is ecstatic or traumatic. The themes of the frailty of the corporeal and the edifices of identity and subjectivity that we construct around it are confronted head-on in Kira's work, particularly through imagery that confronts the cultural myths surrounding the female body. The mutability of the early-modern body, and its even more erratic medieval counterpart, are evoked in the title of her 1998 piece, *Bad Humors/Affected*. In this piece the live body of the artist, and very little else, is the focus of the experience. The performance normally takes place around an art gallery reception event. The audience is given a glass of red wine and invited into the room where the artist sits, wearing a long, wide, white skirt but naked from the waist up. An assistant wearing surgical gloves approaches Kira with a glass jar; from this she takes a leech and places it on

Kira's naked back this is followed by another. For an hour, the leeches suck the artist's blood until they fall off her back leaving bleeding wounds which seep blood down Kira's back and over her white skirt for the next twenty minutes until the audience is asked to leave the room. The use of the leeches is explained by the artist to be a means of producing "a direct intervention with the body: something actual, not represented, in front of an audience." Through this the audience is forced to confront the body as object. The passivity of the artist in this and the focus this brings to the body as a mutable object whose mutability is not always (or even rarely) under our control, bring to the fore notions of passivity and aggressivity which have been the focus of many female artists' work over the past few decades. The issues of control and testing the boundaries of subjectivity and objectivity also call to mind the work of the COUM group; particularly the implied analogy in Kira's work between the art reception audience and the real blood-sucking leeches and the blatant analogy in COUM's 1976 retrospective between art and prostitution. In a later piece, *13*, which is a collaboration with the photographer Irina Padva, Kira focuses on menstruation and the cultural myths and preconceptions around it. In the performance that I saw (in the Arena Theatre, Wolverhampton, October 1999), it again took place within a drinks reception. Kira emerges, dressed in a white slip with her hands and feet bound in red ribbon. She moves awkwardly around, at different levels, upsetting furniture and bumping into spectators. When she reaches the bar she takes off a pair of white knickers and places these in a glass of red wine. As Kira moves around the space, the red ribbons begin to unravel. The piece uses substances that are resonant with connotations of the Catholic mass: red wine and grapes, substances that are used to stand in for or actually become Christ's blood. The use of these in the performance performs a subversion of this substitution where the previously masculine symbols are transformed into metaphors for menstruation; an aspect of femininity traditionally represented as unclean and defiling. The performance culminates with Kira penetrating herself with the end of a three-foot-long plastic rose. The rose as a euphemism for menstruation and female genitalia is, through the performative action, made too real, too corporeal by the actual penetration, and the boundaries between the pristine, white clad exterior of the female body and the messy, bloody, incomprehensible interior are transgressed.

Racial bodies

Despite the shock that the spectacle of the body in extremis or the representation of the sexual body can still produce in the 1990s, perhaps one of the greatest taboos is also the least visible in discussion around performance, and that is race. Marina Abramovic's work has always been concerned with her ethnicity both in terms of what her specific background means in terms of her art and also how the artists can transcend the borders of race and ethnicity imposed by dominant culture. Abramovic has spoken of how "Artists work in the spaces in between – in waiting rooms, passport controls" (Abramovic, 1999), and Abramovic's own work dealing with race and ethnicity is always confronting the dichotomy of belonging and not belonging. *Capitalist Body/Communist Body* (1979) was a collaboration with Abramovic's then partner, the West German artist Ulay. In this piece, an audience was invited to the couple's loft in Amsterdam on their joint birthday. The artists lay together in a bed against a wall covered by a sheet. On two tables were food, drink and artifacts from their respective countries. On a nearby desk both artists' identification papers (birth certificate and student ID) were delicately joined together with tape. The performance played on both the similarity and separateness of the artists' identities: a contradictory mapping of duality and difference presided over by two performers who were both present and absent in the performative moment. As Kathy O'Dell writes of the assembled ID documentation, which was central to the piece, this constituted:

> A rich and multileveled emblem of sustained identificatory tension having to do with gender, nationality, politics and economics. Specifically the papers highlight the following differences: Ulay's gender is male and Abramovic's female; Ulay's birthright is German and Abramovic's is Yugoslavian; and West Germany was, in 1979, predominantly capitalist, whereas Yugoslavia was communist. There were shared traits too. After all, Ulay and Abramovic were a couple; a fact symbolized by the joining of their identification papers. Ulay was known for keeping his national origins vague, and Abramovic had been exiled from Yugoslavia. Together they had underscored their uprootedness by declaring that they had "no fixed living-place" . . .
>
> (O'Dell, 1998: 64)

One of Abramovic's most recent performances, *Balkan Baroque*, deals explicitly with the problem of Balkan identity in the light of the conflicts in the former Yugoslavia, a problem situated in the fact that, as Abramovic puts it, "the Balkan identity has too much of everything" (Abramovic, 1999).

The sense of a diaspora of bodies and identities has been fundamental to the work of a number of disparate artists. The act of performance itself is a trying out of personae. This can then function as a means of undermining the dominant forms of representation through a post-modern idea of the fluidity of what constitutes identity. By using performance, artists are questioning what it means to be both an artist and an individual. In terms of the discourse of ethnicity, a major theme has always been the racially marked body as "other" and therefore threatening to both the social body and the individual body identity of those supposedly unmarked by racial difference. Just as performance art serves to undo the boundaries between art and life, theater and non-theater, high and low, a thematic concern in much performance over the last twenty years has been to mark the "unmarked" and to undo the boundaries between those marked as "different" and those not so. The site of performance can, in an ideal world, function as the ultimate cultural melting pot, as the performance artist Guillermo Gómez-Pena writes:

> Cultural institutions can perform an important role: they can function as experimental laboratories to develop and test new models of collaboration between races, genders, and generations, and as "free zones" for intercultural dialogue, radical thinking, and community building.
>
> (Gómez-Pena, 1998: 16)

Gómez-Pena's own work is concerned with the "bastardization" of ethnic identity and its social and political ramifications. In Gómez-Pena's work, the borders of nationality are not so much being penetrated but becoming defunct in a post-modern age of identity bricolage or, as it is defined in the script to *The New World Border*:

> Imagine a new American continent without borders. It's a continent that has become a huge border zone. Think of it as the New World Border.
>
> We are living in the age of pus-modernity, a blistering, festering present. And in these times, all known political systems and economic structures are dysfunctional. They are being reformed, replaced or destroyed. Many see this as the era of *la desmodernidad*, a term that comes from the Mexican noun *desmadre*, which can mean either having no mother or living in chaos. The Great Fiction of a social order has evaporated and has left us in a state of meta-orphanhood. We are all, finally, untranslatable *hijos de la chingada*.
>
> (Gómez-Pena, 1998)

Gómez-Pena's work is rooted in the idea of transitional identity, of belonging nowhere and everywhere. Although he was born in Mexico City, he moved to America and has existed as a multicultural artist who explores the fluidity of national identity, as he says of his own identity:

> The Mexicans already consider me Chicano. My work has been Chicanized. My experience has been Chicanized. [. . .] Depending on the context I am Chicano, Mexican, Latin American, or American in the wider sense of the term. The Mexican Other and the Chicano Other are constantly fighting to appropriate me or reject me. But I think my work might be useful to both sides because I'm an interpreter. An intercultural interpreter.
>
> (Quoted in Carr, 1993: 196)

Part of Gómez-Pena's work is unsettling and interrogates the accepted notions of national stereotypes and racial interaction. Gómez-Pena's 1999 performance, *Borderscape 2000*, explored the problems of multiculturalism through a staging of Chicano identities and Western preconception via a Spanglish lounge operetta. Themes included kitsch, violence, cyborgs and millennium anxiety. Center stage is a large crucifix, stage right an exercise bike, stage left a toilet. At one point in the performance LaCultural Transvestite (Sara Shelton Mann) abandoned her Mexican costume for a flowered dress and floppy hat. She brings on a tea trolley and serves tea as a typical Southern belle. First a woman is cajoled from the audience and the audience is asked to help to persuade her up onto stage by clapping. After a few moments of embarrassment, the woman is allowed to return to her seat. A black man is then invited onto stage. The performer engages in some mild sexual banter and begins to comment about his skin color, "what a nice brown color you are." "I'm quite brown too [. . .] maybe we're related." This goes on for about five minutes. The audience of mainly white academics is not entirely comfortable. What seemed to be going on here is, as in the work of artists exploring sex, a deviation from the accepted cultural script. The character played by Shelton Mann was not merely a transvestite in the usual sense of gender but also a white person playing a Latin American. In the exchange with the audience member, the white performer plays a Latino performer playing a white woman. The different levels of performance going on interrogates the notion of roles which we consider given or unchanging, perhaps the one most fundamental role for the audience was that of white, middle-class, liberal which the theatricalized presentation onstage was chipping away at through its desire to offend those sensibilities.

Perhaps the real shock value in the work of performers like Gómez-Pena is not just in making "otherness" explicit, otherness and the experience of difference, but in the way in which this performance of the Other performs an estrangement of the "same." In the black British performer, SuAndi's performance *The Story of M*, SuAndi tells the story of her relationship with her mother and reminisces about the impact of her mother's racial identity on her own. SuAndi is recognizably black, her identity still marked as other in our culture; yet, only at the end of the performance is it revealed to the audience that her mother is white and that whiteness is being marked as a racial identity affecting the artist's personal history. Lacan's declaration that "There is no Other of the Other" (Lacan, 1990) sums up the problem of trying to adequately represent difference performatively, yet perhaps what the work of performers dealing with racial identity are often trying to do is to extend the debate of "who am I?", "where do I come from?" to those who are traditionally "unmarked" (white). The American performer Robbie Mac-Cauley's 1991 piece, *Sally's Rape*, about the experiences of her great-great grandmother, Sally, a slave, also features a white performer (Jeannie Hutchins). In descriptions of the performance, it is Hutchins's presence which is the most difficult for white audiences to take, for she functions as a constant reminder of the oppressive presence of the white race in slave narratives and a signifier who constantly prevents the white audience from identification with the performer's history. MacCauley herself comments on this phenomenon that: "White people have a problem because they don't want to be generalized as white. They don't understand that this is for all of us. We *all* participated" (quoted in Carr, 1993: 202).

The dialogue between radicalized bodies, particularly one that deconstructs the cultural expectations of otherness, and makes explicit the dialectic of racism, is possibly the last taboo in terms of the avant-garde. The fascination of avant-garde art movements with radicalized otherness, in terms of a desire to escape from culture and access the primitive, has obvious repercussions as more and more artists of color begin making works which they want to be viewed by the art world with as complex a view as possible, not just easy assimilation or fetishization. This desire to deconstruct the myth of the primitive was the inspiration behind Gómez-Pena's and Coco Fusco's itinerant performance, *Two Undiscovered Amerindians Visit* ... The artists dressed up as exotic savages and displayed themselves in a cage in a variety of public places. The spectators were invited to pay them to pose for photos or feed them, actions which firmly situated the artists as stereotypical others but which also refused the easy position of comfortable identification.

Conclusion

The theme which runs through all the work I have described, that focuses on the artist's bodily experience, is one of using the body, not as merely a metaphor, but as an actuality which can break through the merely metaphorical or conceptual and produce something real. The artists I have discussed are, in their different ways, all engaged in a project of blurring boundaries and questioning the imposition of boundaries or categories upon lives and experience in the first place. The artist's body still represents the defining feature of performance art through the way in which the artist's agency situates their body as both subject and object, turning it into something that therefore exceeds simple definition. The artists I have discussed in this chapter are all aware of this unsettling dichotomy between their agency and their representation, through and of their own flesh, in whatever sense, as sexualized, medicalized or radicalized.

The use of the body to blur the boundaries between subject and object also opens up dialogs between different discourses. The centrality of the artist's own body to their art often brings to the fore a dialog between high and low cultural representation, fundamentally questioning what is art. In work which focuses on sex, an unsettling dialogue is at the crux of the work: a dialogue between the conventional sex object representation of women through mass media and pornography, and the position of women as artists with the creative agency which that implies. The work of artists like Cosey Fanni Tutti or Claire Shillito has been concerned with blurring the boundaries between the high (the art world) and the low (the sexual) through the medium of the female body which – in both arenas – can be simultaneously idealized and despised through its representation. Introducing the artists' bodies there, with their experiences, pains and pleasures, complicates the judgements which society still wants to make about women and their sexual experiences. Work that focuses on the medicalized body is also operating on this same tightrope between the sure and the uncertain. The fixed, closed body is literally opened up in the work of Orlan and Kira O'Reilly. The opened body suggests a lack of agency and a vulnerability which can be used to question notions of identity in terms of what it means to be active or passive, male or female, or even what it means to be human. This questioning is also present in work that focuses on the body as racially marked. Performance becomes a means of unmarking otherness through its foregrounding of lived experience and making a question of the unquestionable. In the same way that chronic illness can fundamentally destabilize identity, the work of artists like those I have discussed in this chapter can be defined fundamentally as setting out a challenge to the boundaries of our bodies and what we think they make us, and not taking bodies or their representation for granted.

References

Abramovic, Marina (1999) *Artist Body* (lecture given at the critical forum "violent incident" at the Tate Gallery, Liverpool).

Ayers, Robert (1999) "The Special and the Unusual – Listening to Olan,' in *Live Letters*, No. 4, March.

Ayers, Robert and Butler, David (eds) (1991) *Live Art*, Newcastle-upon-Tyne: AN Publications.

Baudrillard, Jean (1990) *Seduction*, London: Macmillan.

Carr, Cynthia (1993) *On Edge: Performance at the End of the Twentieth Century*, Hanover, NH: Wesleyan University Press/University Press of New England.

Diamond, E. (ed.) (1996) *Performance and Cultural Politics*, London: Routledge.

Dijkstra, Bram (1986) *Idols of Perversity: Fantasies of Feminine Evil in Fin-de-Siècle Culture*, Oxford: Oxford University Press.

Fanni Tutti, Cosey (1993) *Time to Tell* (booklet and CD), Creative Technology Industries.

Goldberg, Rosalee (1988) *Performance Art: From Futurism to the Present*, London: Thames and Hudson.

Gómez-Pena, Guillermo (1998) *The New World Border*, San Francisco: City Lights Books.

Lacan, Jacques (1990) *Seduction*, London: Macmillan.

O'Dell, Kathy (1998) *Contract with the Skin: Masochism, Performance Art of the 1970s*, Minneapolis: University of Minnesota Press.

Phelan, P. (1993) *Unmarked: The Politics of Performance*, London: Routledge.

Sawday, Jonathan (1995) *The Body Emblazoned: Dissection and the Human Body in Renaissance Culture*, London: Routledge.

Schneider, Rebecca (1997) *The Explicit Body in Performance*, London: Routledge.

Sprinkle, Annie (1998) *Post-Porn Modernist: My Twenty-five Years as a Multi-media Whore*, San Francisco: Cleis Press.

4

"I AM WHAT I PLAY"

The radio DJ as cultural arbiter and negotiator

Steve Taylor

Note

This chapter uses as its source material Steve Taylor's experiences as one of the launch DJs at Xfm. His chapter reflects on the early days of the radio station in the late 1990s. While changes have been made to programming policy, his chapter still has much to say about what it is like to work for a music radio station committed to innovative practice in unstable and insecure times.

Introduction

British commercial music radio is ubiquitous; it is part of the aural fabric of everyday life. It has been steadily expanding, attracting ever more listeners and, as a result, more advertisers, since 1990 when the Broadcasting Act altered the corporate structure of the industry. The Act (which softened the rules concerning the limitations of ownership, allowing the most powerful radio groups to increase their portfolios, and which created three new major players, namely Virgin, Classic FM and Talk Radio) was a response to continued criticism of the monopoly in place at the BBC. It provoked Radio 1, hitherto the primary broadcaster of music that falls within the descriptive paradigm of "popular music," to radically alter its music and presenter policy. More tightly focused under Matthew Bannister, it embraced dance and indie music and promptly shed its audience of over-thirties. In keeping with the prevailing political mood for laissez-faire economics, a new audience, rich in disposable income, became available to the newly oligopolistic commercial sector.

Radio 1 retained and strengthened its delivery of new music, developing a brand identity that incorporated the cutting edge approach synonymous with John Peel's understanding of public service music radio, a philosophy which had previously been at odds with much of the station's output. No longer was it the case that, to paraphrase Peel, an interest in music was a considerable disadvantage at the station. The new commercial oligopoly, content that Radio 1 was, at last, playing the public service role it always should have done, set about putting its own house in order. Local stations, many now under the new ownership of one of the major radio groups, focused on developing strong brand identities where the key factor was, ironically, music. Having witnessed the success of the offshore AM hit music station, Atlantic 252, which played long sweeps of music with minimal input from DJs, they now used this as a model. Playlists became the key programming tool and output was carefully controlled to ensure that the brand identity of the product was not undermined.

More people are listening to commercial radio, a fact borne out in the quarterly listening figures prepared by the industry research body, Radio Joint Audience Research (RAJAR), indicating that commercial radio stations must be getting something right. This chapter will attempt to explain the strategies which have produced such impressive results. However, it will also suggest that, from a cultural perspective, these achievements are at best irrelevant and, at worst, deprive the listening community of a part of its potential cultural and aesthetic experience. Put another way, commercial radio is accused of neglecting its audience and, in the process, reducing itself to a secondary medium which suits advertisers looking for the biggest reach but, as is posited here, is characterized by an ambivalent listener who expects little of much significance from the radio station they are listening to. There are many others who choose not to listen at all who, it is argued, have been failed by the industry and its governing body.

I intend to substantiate this argument by reflecting on my own experience as a cultural worker within the industry. The focus is on my employment as a presenter at London station Xfm, which from its inception consciously adopted certain alternative working and programming practices to those existing in mainstream commercial radio in the UK. Retained as a presenter following the takeover by the station's philosophical antithesis, the radio giant Capital, I have been able to continue as a participant observer of Xfm's transition into a radio station which now more closely resembles the industry standard, albeit based on the relatively innovative American model of alternative format radio.

What follows is not a philosophical attack on the British commercial music radio industry. There are many people, amongst whom I would number myself, who enjoy listening to formatted stations especially when all of the factors – music, presenter, production and, significantly, listening context – come together to produce twenty minutes of audio which perfectly compliments a certain mood or scenario. At times, format radio is an aesthetic which can trigger emotions, and it is not always simply coincidental. Radio professionals, particularly those programmers with responsibility for the overall sound of a station, are motivated to achieve these twenty-minute "highs"; indeed, it is a widespread aim of many of those whose vocation is music radio. The disputes concerning which music is played and how it is presented or scheduled are related issues (indeed, they are central to this chapter) but the desire to reach an audience and to elicit some kind of emotional response is paramount. The issue is the philosophical distinction made over the quality or efficacy of that emotional response, and the extent to which the strategy in place to elicit such a response is motivated by economic imperatives.

There are different types of response, ranging from the purely emotional – where a particular track is liked or disliked, a factor which may change depending on the time of day or listening context, or because it is unfamiliar or too familiar – to the response which has a more cognitive and reflective aspect; in this instance there is a need to understand the aesthetic, its intellectual or cultural significance, to know where it fits within a musical hierarchy and to question the criteria on which that hierarchy is based. This is the response of a listener who is interested in music per se, or its associated cultural role, as opposed to the listener who craves something more superficial. Uses and gratifications theory might describe the former mode of consumption in relation to the categories of entertainment and social interaction and integration; and describe the other cognitively driven mode of consumption as informational and identity forming. These responses are not mutually exclusive for the individual listener but, unfortunately, there are fewer attempts to elicit the latter response from listeners due to the "safety in numbers" approach adopted by large parts of the British commercial music radio industry. There will always be a place for "wallpaper radio" which is as valid as an aesthetic form as more provocative music radio, but the economic and structural rules associated with the format should not inform the criteria by which the success of smaller, independently-minded radio stations are judged.

The focus of this chapter is the role that music plays in the contemporary radio industry. There is a degree of creative freedom afforded certain presenters at some commercial stations but this does not include any substantial authority to determine the choice of music. At the point of writing, this is certainly the case at Xfm where there has been a move toward employing presenters with a background in television and comedy who, like their counterparts at Radio 1, are able to develop their own show features through interaction with guests, assistants and listeners. New music is still central to the brand identity of the station, but there has been a significant shift in policy that allows certain presenters more scope to use their time on air as a platform to enhance their own media profile. This differs from the philosophy inculcated in presenters at the original Xfm which dictated music first, station second and presenter third. Indeed, that was apparent in the station immediately after its acquisition by Capital Radio where the station took priority over the music, and presenters, with the exception of Bob Geldof who presented the drivetime show, were reduced to continuity announcing. (Bob Geldof presented the weekday drivetime show (4 pm to 7 pm) for 104 days. His producer was Des Shaw, a colleague from the Planet 24 media production company, who also assumed the role of overall program controller of Xfm.) The creative freedom currently given to presenters does represent some progress toward the acknowledgment of aesthetic imperatives within the contemporary radio industry but the key factor, music, is still utilized as a corporate branding tool with little attempt to explore its aesthetic potential.

A neglected cultural industry?

Theodor Adorno's use of the term "culture industry," adopted by cultural and media theorists as a shorthand description for those industries which deal primarily in ideas and aesthetics, notably the media industries, is a term which continues to point to the fundamentally ideological process by which culture becomes standardized. However, the philosophical arguments concerning the character of culture, particularly the significance of postmodern culture, have blunted the phrase, so that it has become a more descriptive term. Whilst not exactly defending postmodernism against such charges as the decline of cultural standards and disappearance of rules and hierarchies of quality and talent, Frederic Jameson has suggested that a cultural aesthetic which interacts with capital at least offers the opportunity for us to understand, and cognitively map, the world of international money and information flows in which we find ourselves (Jameson, 1992). As facilitators of the production of culture, the cultural industries are central in this respect, and it is the degree to which the aesthetic dimension of contemporary culture is allowed to exist alongside the economic which determines the progressive or regressive significance of a particular cultural industry.

Jameson draws on the film industry, particularly the conspiracy theory films of Alan Pakula, to support his argument. Films like *All The President's Men* and *The Parallax View* are good examples of the interrogation of economic and political power paid for by a major film studio. The mainstream film industry, like the music industry, is aware of the significant role played by the independent production sector, which has led to a sophistication of its mainstream counterpart. Audiences are still keen to be "entertained" but also demand a degree of self-reflexivity and sometimes, parody, within cultural products. From *Die Hard With A Vengeance* through to *Scream 3*, blockbuster movies no longer take themselves too seriously, and certainly do not patronize their audiences by producing cultural products which are simply a collection of economically viable generic constituent parts.

By comparison, the contemporary British commercial music radio industry lags behind. The centrality of economic imperatives, and related suppression of aesthetic innovation, is evident almost universally in the range of music broadcast and, to a lesser extent, in the creative freedom afforded the presenters in terms of speech. The increasing aestheticization of life in contemporary society requires some form of communication between the agents of capital and the culture which forms its consumer base. As radio pays its bills through attracting advertising which, in turn, is achieved by the nurturing of a mass audience, there is no incentive to stand out amongst the media clutter; it is already achieving its aim in its secondary capacity as a kind of subliminal message board. Unlike the advertising industry which must connect with potential consumers and prove itself through increased sales, radio does not need to tap into the cultural capital held by those employees who are more aesthetically motivated. Music radio occupies a different position within contemporary culture. It is part of the wider cultural industry but, rather than being a conduit for the transfer of cultural ideas, it merely provides a framework for the delivery of those cultural artifacts produced by other cultural intermediaries. (The character of these other cultural intermediaries could form the basis of a further study but it is significant that much of the music played on mainstream commercial radio is funded by the major record companies and their offshoots. It's also significant that the radio industry struggles to attract such first-time radio clients as Doctor Martens, Durex and Smirnoff, who have since decided not to renegotiate deals with Capital. It could be suggested that radio is out of step with an important sector of the market that needs to be addressed as it represents today's new customers and tomorrow's core consumers.)

The assumption of this secondary role requires the suppression of aesthetic imperatives and can be explained from two perspectives. The first of these concerns the economic reality of an industry which tends toward oligopoly and whose major players are in a daily contest to attract mass audiences. Such high stakes make it difficult for the independent sector of radio broadcasting to attract an audience and, as a corollary, advertisers, unless they adopt similar programming techniques. RAJAR is the industry research body jointly funded by both commercial and BBC sectors which provides information concerning radio listening figures and habits. It exacerbates this situation due to its limited definition of what constitutes a listening audience. Additionally, management philosophies and strategies inspired by the circulation of institutional discourses are also important, specifically the concept of format and its associated programming techniques.

The second perspective requires an examination of cultural workers within the music radio industry. Drawing on Bourdieu's explanation of cultural industries staffed by cultural intellectuals, or cultural arbiters, it is possible to identify conflicting working philosophies which attach more or less weight to economic or aesthetic imperatives. Many cultural industries achieve a balance of the two, notably in advertising, where contemporary working practice affords "creatives" a significant amount of philosophical and practical input into advertising campaigns, sometimes leaving capital open to subversion and undermining. Whilst the music radio industry might employ specialists in symbolic production, it is generally the case that these cultural specialists, especially DJs, are not fulfilling their vocational potential, particularly with regard to the aesthetic potential of popular music. In fact, because of the reliance on the concept of format as the key unit of organization within the industry, a new job description has been developed which calls for different skills to be emphasized or imported into the role. Indeed, it is more accurate to think of the DJ and the radio presenter as two very different vocations, each emphasized to a greater or lesser degree depending on the policy of the individual station. British commercial music radio tends to utilize the skills of the latter, namely consistency and structure, which once more confirms its preferred role as a message board for existent cultural products rather than a framework for the construction or transference of culture.

The reach and how to get it

Xfm's reach for the first quarter of 1998 was 219,000 listeners (source: RAJAR/RSL). This figure is the weekly total of listeners calculated by adding up the amount of people who regularly tuned in to the station for more than seven and a half minutes per week. This number is arrived at through a process of weighting. In fact, during this period, just under 5,000 people representing a potential listening audience of around ten million people were asked to keep a record of their listening habits in a diary over a period of three months and from the results of this sample an overall figure was arrived at. In the diary, each hour of the day is divided into four quarters. If the member of the sample listened for a period in excess of seven and a half minutes a tick was placed in the box. Xfm's listening hours were 5.5, the average amount of time a listener tunes in for in a week.

These figures compared unfavorably against Xfm's competition in London. It was hoped that the station could achieve a reach of 5 percent or 500,000 listeners early on and then start working toward the 10 percent attained by dance station, KISS 100. A reach of 219,000 was less than that of JazzFM and more in line with RTL Country, which was automated for a significant amount of its output. It was certainly a long way short of Capital, Heart, Virgin and easy-listening station, Magic, which was regularly attracting 1,100,000 listeners with a policy that focused on long sweeps of continuous music and presenters who did not announce their own names. These stations know how to play the figures game. Funded by major media groups, they have access to the latest programming tools, and apply the fundamental industry knowledge accrued by its antecedents in American radio. Within a year Xfm's shareholders had decided to sell to Capital Radio, their economic investment of the previous year cashed in before the financial risk became too high. It was possible that Xfm's listening figures would rise after this initial showing in the competitive London market, and, in fact, they did in the second quarter of 1998, to 329,000 with listening hours of 5.1, whilst the sale was being investigated by the Radio Authority. (In the third quarter of 1998, the figures fell to 283,000 with hours of 6.1 (source: RAJAR/RSL).) But there may have been another reason for the shareholders' cold feet – the lack of format and consistency in the on-air sound of Xfm which was evident in its more successful competitors.

The techniques employed by RAJAR to calculate listening figures changed for the third quarter of 1998 but the principle remained the same: a listener is someone who is within the vicinity of the output of a particular radio station for at least seven-and-a-half minutes in a given week. As the sample is so small, stations know it is vital that as many potential sample subjects are listening and are aware of their product as possible. The reality of the situation is that a mass audience is required to ensure a high proportion of sample subjects, so a mass audience is sought. The quality of the listening experience is not at issue. The search for mass listenership necessarily means adopting an inclusive policy that focuses on the lowest common denominator, a policy which means broadcasting the most popular music to encourage the largest number of listeners. The fact that competitors also adopt this policy and because listeners tend to remain detached from the sounds playing in the background means that clarity of brand identity becomes the key factor. The individual listener must be made aware of the station's existence and recognize it when they hear it.

Brand marketing is clearly important. For Capital FM marketing budgets allow for television advertising and perpetual billboard and flyposting campaigns, as well as the link with "Capital cabs" and annual events such as "Party in the Park" and the "Help a London Child" charity campaign. The media profile of presenters like Chris Tarrant, Steve Penk and Neil Fox is also a key factor. Heart FM and Virgin can mount similarly large-scale marketing initiatives. Xfm, on the other hand, was criticized for its lack of marketing savvy, despite being handled by Saatchi and Saatchi. A flyposting campaign which included straplines such as the ultimately ironic "Nine out of ten Londoners prefer Capital" was deemed too subtle and confusing. Fraser Lewry, former head of music at the station, complained: "We needed to let people know that we were a radio station called Xfm before beginning an advertising campaign as pretentious as that."

In 2000, Capital had only embarked on a low-key marketing campaign for the relaunched Xfm consisting of posters which simply displayed a list of featured artists and the revised Xfm logo, with the emphasis on developing a satisfactory programming policy first. This is perhaps a recognition that brand marketing to make people aware of a product can be undertaken relatively successfully providing there is access to a large budget, but that the most important aspect of brand marketing is inherent within the sound of the station itself.

In the contemporary music radio industry, a strong and successful brand image is built on two factors – the perceived *quality* and *consistency* of the product available to the listener at all times. To suggest that the definition of quality is problematic is hardly a new idea, and although it is an issue that cuts to the heart of this chapter, it is unhelpful to claim that one type of radio is better than another. Rather, the point is made that there is a predominance of a particular type based on certain objectives and principles at the expense of other potential forms with different sets of objectives and principles. For Des Shaw, an international radio consultant employed by the Planet 24 media group who became Xfm's program controller immediately after the Capital takeover, the two guiding principles of good radio are "consistency and entertainment, in that order." Capital FM, with the largest reach in the London market, is exemplary. It is marketed by drawing on its brand identity as a hit music station that will make the listener "feel good"; hence the "smiling sun" logo. The output of the station needs to confirm this image at all times; in fact, a regularly reproduced industry truism is that when the listener turns on the hot tap s/he expects to get hot water and, conversely, when the listener is getting hot water then s/he knows that they have turned on the hot tap. If, as is the case, the listener is hearing tightly segued hit music and a professional and approachable presenter who appears to be enjoying her/himself then, so the logic goes, they are listening to Capital FM.

The privileging of consistency is significant and goes some way toward explaining the centrality of the format in contemporary commercial music radio, and the consequent necessity for entertainment to be a corporate determinant. Des Shaw is in agreement with Fraser Lewry that the original independent Xfm was "consistently inconsistent" and qualifies the comment by acknowledging that this anti-brand image is a powerful one for a smaller, culturally specific audience, but is certainly not in keeping with the attraction of the large-scale listenership demanded by the Capital Radio Group. For Shaw, Xfm needed to adopt the principles of alternative radio that had proven successful in the United States and Australia, which entails placing the all-important factor of music firmly within a formatted structure. Xfm, he claims, failed to build a strong brand image because it was too unpredictable both in terms of the music played and the manner in which it was presented: "Presenters had too much freedom, one show bore no resemblance to the one before or after it. The wrong songs were played at the wrong time of day and there was no attempt at 'separation.'"

In this context, "separation" refers to the process whereby similar tracks are scheduled apart. Shaw is particularly keen to alternate songs featuring male or female vocals, or those by British or American artists. He is also critical of Xfm's tendency for playing hip-hop and dance music which, he felt, further undermined the creation of a consistent brand image. The choice and placement of music within an individual program was, to a large extent, left to the presenter. Daytime programs included approximately 75 percent playlisted tracks but these could be placed in any order within the program and, in reality, many tracks were dropped completely if the presenter felt that they did not reflect the overall mood of their show. Program controller Sammy Jacob occasionally raised the issue of omitted playlist tracks but presenters were never penalized. This approach to scheduling marked a fundamental break with the policy in place at most mainstream commercial radio stations where the presenter is given a scheduled list of the tracks and running order for their program, together with specific instructions concerning the interval, duration and basic content of each speech break.

A key programming tool is a software system called *Selecter* which is able to schedule playlist tracks based on a variety of criteria. This might simply mean scheduling the rotation of tracks to ensure they receive the stipulated number of plays but, depending on the information entered for each individual track on the playlist, can become a more sophisticated tool. For example, the proximity of tracks to one another can be determined due to their style, pace, instrumentation or vocal timbre. Des Shaw believes that Selecter is an essential tool but, if not used properly, can be detrimental to the music policy of a station: "Like any software package, it is only as good as its raw material. The person responsible for inputting information about tracks should know music and station policy, and be able to humanize some of the results that it throws out."

Unsurprisingly, Xfm under Shaw utilized Selecter, and did not allow the presenters any freedom to choose the music they played. Speech breaks were kept to a minimum in the initial stages, with the focus on the music, an approach designed to emphasize the new identity of the station on which a brand image could be built. Shaw insists that presenters need to learn the format first before being given more freedom (a point we will return to later).

Allied to scheduling is the process by which tracks are chosen for inclusion on a playlist. The process of selection under the new regime seems to draw on a number of factors. In a sense, the final decisions as to whether a track should be added to the playlist owes a good deal to "gut feeling," but is based on certain objective criteria which can be observed in other parts of the music industry. A central factor is the current media profile of the artist, although tracks by artists with a low profile in the UK that appear on the playlists of alternative stations in the United States are often added as they are perceived to be integral to the brand genre. In addition, there is a reliance on record companies and pluggers who can advise the playlist committee on their own expectations for a particular track or artist, expectations which hinge on substantial media support; in short, a symbiotic process. The aesthetic form of the track is also important. Does it have a "hook"? How long is it? Is it too "hard"? Tracks may be tested before they are added, a standard process that the bigger commercial radio stations apply to songs already on the playlist, whereby members of the potential target audience are contacted by telephone and asked to give their opinions of certain tracks. Each respondent will hear a short section representing the "hook" of a track. From their answers, the suitability of the track for playlisting is judged. Des Shaw points out that, once again, the results of such a tool should be considered in context. The respondent is only hearing the most accessible part of the song, is required to focus on their reaction to the song, and is hearing it over the telephone, none of which reflects the reality of radio listening.

Inside/outside thinking

The concept of "burn" is interesting. This is the term used to refer to a track that has declined in popularity over a period of tests, suggesting that it should now be removed from the playlist. The Gomez track "Whippin' Piccadilly" was released and added to the playlist in September 1998 and reached "burn" in February 1999; this was read as an indication that the station's listenership had risen as Xfm was the only radio station in London to have regularly played the track. At the original Xfm, tracks remained on the playlist until the date of their release, or were taken off before this if the committee felt that they were sounding stale. The Gomez track remained on the Xfm playlist for nearly six months, receiving approximately six plays per day. This would not have happened at its predecessor where a decision would have been made to remove the track much earlier, because to leave it on the playlist any longer would have been considered detrimental to listening enjoyment. Testing clearly informs music policy and, regardless of whether or not it is the correct decision to leave a song on the playlist for this length of time, it is instructive that, in this case, it functioned as an indicator of audience research and evidence of listening, rather than as a positive scheduling choice made with the enjoyment of the listener in mind. There is clearly a cynical aspect to such a decision but, it could be argued, based on the results of the testing, the audience's listening enjoyment had not actually been compromised to any significant degree. The issue is whether or not testing can be relied upon to satisfactorily explain the reality of radio listening.

Commercial radio discourse would claim that much of the original Xfm's approach to programming policy suffered from "inside thinking," claiming that the audience does not focus on a particular radio station's output as closely as those who work within it. At Xfm the audience was not perceived, as in mainstream commercial radio, as an "other," albeit the ultimate focus of programming policy, but rather as part of the same cultural field – a specific type, reflected and represented by those who worked there. The perceived audience did not have to be repeatedly told "this is what we do" but, it was felt, could be relied upon to know the policy of the station because they were part of the culture that defined the philosophy and associated policy of the station.

However, it could be argued that the refusal to view the core audience as "other" was both inclusive and exclusionary. Listeners within the same cultural milieu could enjoy having their cultural capital confirmed whilst also being informed of the shifting boundaries of the cultural field. For this sector of the audience, Xfm was a primary medium; it spoke to them, it connected with them. Alternatively, there are also those potential listeners who might enjoy the content of the station's output but sense, at times, that they are excluded because they lack the required cultural capital and are merely eavesdropping on a communicative process that they are not part of. This becomes particularly apparent if an artist, hitherto considered to be part of the "scene," is criticized and seemingly cast outside the boundaries of the cultural field. Artists with large fanbases, that would have included a large proportion of potential Xfm listeners, were often underrepresented in the output and on occasion might have been openly criticized on-air. This behavior can be read as a necessary aspect of a cultural field, where its members consider it crucial to constantly distance themselves from the mainstream, and from what might be viewed as its insidious colonization of alternative culture.

Des Shaw uses the industry term "aspirational" to describe alternative radio. It targets those who have an interest in contemporary popular music and is more exclusive than what he refers to as "wallpaper radio." He points out that the original Xfm was too exclusive. Presenters retained by Capital were instructed not to refer to the station or its output as alternative at any time and to drop phrases such as "of course" when delivering links as this can alienate listeners who were not aware of any fact prefaced in this manner. This attention to detail is indicative of "outside" thinking, the privileging of the objective over the subjective. Indeed, a favorite mantra used by Shaw at presenter meetings concerned the requirement for presenters to "leave their own tastes and opinions outside the studio door." He is less inclined, however, to treat the audience as an homogeneous "other" and criticizes British commercial radio stations for their focus on demographics rather than the more sophisticated science of psychographics, which takes account of different taste publics and addresses the more intricate aspects of lifestyle and the way in which this impacts on radio listening. Psychographics attempts to personify the consumer beyond simply physical characteristics and takes a step closer to making a connection with her/him, but the communication is still corporate in character. Based on his experience of aspirational radio, he suggests, for example, that the traditional importance of a celebrity-driven breakfast show does not apply, and that there are more opportunities for building an audience in the evening. The introduction of an on-air "feedback line," giving listeners the chance to opine about the music being played or provide a soundbite concerning a topical issue, also recognizes the listener's desire for interaction – not as a listener who phones in and becomes part of the output itself but rather as a contributor, responding to the output of the station.

Fraser Lewry states that Xfm was set up to provide a service for those who were hitherto "musically disenfranchised"; and when asked for a definition of the target listener, he simply comments that it was someone who was "into music." Capital refer to their target listener for Xfm as male, in his twenties to early thirties. The music played on the station (album artists defined by the music industry as rock or indie) is clearly associated with this target audience. In both cases, subjectively and objectively, the audience is defined or thought of in relation to a musical type. Within mainstream commercial music radio the audience is not defined by a specific musical taste, other than a general recognition that the individual listener will enjoy that which is familiar and generally considered to represent good aesthetic and musical practice; that is, songs which are well crafted and carefully produced. This goes some way toward explaining why many mainstream radio stations select the same tracks for their playlists, because they are the songs that are most likely to entertain.

Other aspects of broadcast output at these stations are also standardized in line with industry belief as to what makes good radio, based on the guiding principles of consistency and entertainment. On the surface this situation surely seems to undermine the development of definitive brand identities. For example, rather than signifying an individual station, a certain track can become a "radio record" or, taken a stage further, a certain *type* of track can become a radio record. In fact, the mainstream commercial music radio industry as a whole benefits from an overall consistency where certain tracks, and other aspects of programming output, become essential elements of radio output as a whole. To remain consistent, these rules have to be obeyed. The individual station's brand identity becomes secondary to the wider understanding of what makes "good radio." For smaller stations, and those competing in a particularly volatile market, this means having to playlist a track which is more widely associated with the brand image of a competitor, whilst attempting to differentiate themselves through a subtle reshuffling of the mandatory elements.

This scenario of a music radio industry consisting of sub-genres differentiated by the most conservative variations is likely to continue whilst a vast amount of the potential listening audience is being ignored. It is interesting to note that in the RAJAR results dealing with the second quarter of 1999, it was calculated that 8 percent of the potential London audience did not listen to the radio at all. However, this is not just about those who do not listen to the radio, but also about those who are listening and only being addressed at the most basic and superficial level. There is room for this type of music radio, just as there is room for its equivalent in television, film, popular music and paperback book publishing, but the independent or alternative sector which exists to varying degrees in other media is not being given a legitimate chance in music radio. There should be room for other forms of radio that attempt to entertain or provoke potential listeners in ways which include developing other strategies for delivering music into people's lives that go beyond the superficial. This means rethinking the relationship between station and listener. The adoption of psychographic techniques, whilst useful, still only addresses shadows. To really connect with the listener using music radio as a primary medium, the skills of the music expert, or DJ, are key.

The DJ as cultural arbiter, the radio presenter as cultural worker

Before discussing the specific skills of the DJ and the way in which these skills could be utilized by the radio industry, it is useful to briefly outline an approach to contemporary cultural practice described by theorists keen to develop a "sociology of culture." This can certainly help to explain the individual working philosophies within cultural industries generally, and might go some way toward understanding the original Xfm as a specific example of the possibilities and potential problems associated with this type of music radio, if it exists, in the future.

In order to explain the individual's role in the dialectical and continually developing process of hegemony, Gramsci refers to "common sense" as an organizational structure for understanding everyday experience. The individual has a dual consciousness characterized by a form of conflict between an often buried innate sense of right and wrong (equated with anti-capitalism) and a consciousness informed by the prevailing ideology which operates through and in social practice (equated with capitalism). Gramsci has argued that the former consciousness tends to give way to the latter and the chances of revolutionary action are diminished. It follows that an expedient contemporary "common sense" leads employees to contextualize their opinions concerning management practice within the framework of the prevailing societal structure, itself informed by economic factors. This is not to say that non-economic factors are completely sidelined; use-value for the customer, employee or society at large will often be considered but only if this is not to the detriment of the economic health of the companies or industries that support the employee.

Gramsci is more optimistic when he refers to the cultural figure of the traditional intellectual. This individual is a different entity to the organic intellectual. The traditional intellectual has the potential for opposition to prevailing ideologies, unlike the organic intellectual who tends to be directly tied to the system. Pierre Bourdieu's description of a contemporary society driven by both economic and cultural capital, and populated by individuals who attach more or less importance to the economic or aesthetic, resonates with Gramsci's earlier division of type.

Bourdieu's work is inflected with a certain structural Marxism that points to the economy as the ultimate determinant of the social order. Like the Althusserian concept of the ideological state apparatus it is inspired by the idea of a relationship between base and superstructure. It offers a description of the cultural process by which society becomes stratified in the form of a definite hierarchy where economic capital is the defining factor of power in the last instance, but where cultural capital is the everyday currency of distinction. Bourdieu explains that "there is, diffused within a social space a cultural capital, transmitted by inheritance and invested in order to be cultivated" (Bourdieu, 1971: 201) and that cultural intellectuals are constantly engaged in attempts to raise the significance of cultural capital above that of economic capital. The result is a culture where "a work of art has meaning and interest for someone who possesses the cultural competence, that is, the code, into which it is encoded" (Bourdieu, 1994: 2).

Central to Bourdieu's explanation is his appropriation of Kantian aesthetics theory. The circumstances surrounding an individual's nurture and associated social expectations, encapsulated in Bourdieu's term "habitus," will determine the way in which that individual interprets art. They will be informed either by a Kantian aesthetic which prioritizes form over content and judges art on its own terms within its own discourse (and only then extrapolated to, and compared with, other discourses) or by an anti-Kantian aesthetic which reduces the significance of art to the merely functional. The former is detached and cognitive in character; the second is tied to the manifest significance of the aesthetic and is characterized by a purely functional response. Importantly, this ability to appreciate art is not innate, but is the result of the structured knowledge learned in childhood and dependent upon the centrality of economic imperatives at this time. The analogy is drawn between the ability to appreciate art with critical distance, detachment and objectivity, and the "distance" from economic necessity apparent in an individual's upbringing. This provides a good starting point for understanding contemporary social structure and cultural practice once the increased significance of popular culture in daily life is acknowledged.

John Frow argues that the link between economic wealth and the accumulation of cultural capital that Bourdieu makes is too rigid and as a result the categories of "high" and "low" culture become mutually exclusive. For Frow the root of the problem is that Bourdieu does not properly address a more traditionally defined popular culture focusing only on certain discourses, or fields, of little or no interest to large sections of society. Bourdieu refers to classical music, theater and literature as legitimized cultural fields; jazz, photography and cinema are said to be in the process of becoming legitimized, whilst popular music falls into a category which he describes early in his academic career as "other daily aesthetic choices" (Bourdieu, 1971: 174). Frow notes Bourdieu's apparent support of the "warmer" and more "natural" culture of the dominated or working classes compared to the "cold" and "mediated" culture of the dominators or new cultural intermediaries and their superiors, but argues that too much is made of the disadvantageous position which the former find themselves in. They are not necessarily excluded from particular cultural or intellectual fields. Furthermore, the character of fields in general is always changing:

> The category of cultural disadvantage is, of course applicable only *on the ground of high culture*. Bourdieu assumes that the legitimacy of this ground is still imposed on the dominated classes; but it may well be the case, particularly since the massive growth of a television culture in which working-class people tend to be fully competent, that high culture, or rather the *prestige* of high culture, has become largely irrelevant to them.
>
> (Frow, 1995: 37)

Popular culture has become a backdrop for a heterogeneity of cultural fields, or territories of knowledge, each with its own particular group of intellectuals. Drawing on the work of Jamous and Peloille who have noted "a charismatic mode of ascribed knowledge which forms any profession's 'mystery'" (Jamous and Peloille, 1970: 112), Frow explains that such intellectuals distinguish themselves, and ensure the stability of the intellectual field, through a process which diminishes the significance of accepted knowledge about cultural products or ideas so that "as disciplines of knowledge become institutionalized, it is *particular* territories of knowledge, and the disciplinary mysteries appropriate to each, rather than the knowledge in general, that come to be invested with value" (Frow, 1995: 126).

The cultural industries can and do benefit from the specific cultural knowledge of such intellectuals, often allowing them a good deal of freedom. The advertising industry is a notable example which will sanction outright attacks on capital, in certain campaigns, to maintain integrity with potential customers. The advertising industry has a definite vocational split between "creatives" and "account managers" who, it might be suggested, fall neatly into the categories of Kantian and anti-Kantian described above. The creatives are allowed freedom to parade their cultural capital, simultaneously raising its significance by apparently undermining its rival economic capital. But, all the time, the creatives are kept in check by the account managers who are responsible for ensuring the continued domination of social and cultural life by economic capital through the efficient functioning, by whatever means, of consumer society. This characterization is simplistic, not least because individuals cannot be placed wholly within one or other of the categories, Kantian or anti-Kantian. In fact, the very purpose of advertising, tied so closely to capital, surely requires some recognition of the importance of economic capital by the "Kantian" creatives. The primary importance attached to the reinforcement of a product's brand identity in even the most surreal and aesthetically driven campaigns is evidence of this. There is a functional aspect to all advertising which is, at its core, economic; just as there is a detached aspect, recognized by the "anti-Kantian" account managers who allow aesthetic imperatives to thrive. A continuum running from Kantian at one extreme to anti-Kantian at the other is a more useful tool for interpreting the character and philosophy of individual cultural workers who might move along the continuum in differing scenarios, circumstances or discourses.

As I have suggested, the music radio industry tends to prioritize economic imperatives. This is reflected in the anti-Kantian activities of many of its employees who are encouraged to treat music as a means to an end and their own input in the form of speech breaks as an opportunity to reinforce the brand identity of the station. There is scope within a "link" to inject a degree of "personality," indeed this is expected of the best "format jocks," but it is essential that the process of entertaining does not undermine the consistency of the brand identity.

The rule "one thought per link" is imbued in the rookie radio presenter in order to ensure that s/he does not become confused and flustered, and this "thought" is generally based on a station promotion, written down for the presenter in the form of a "liner." The presenter is encouraged to use the liner as a basis for their own interpretation of the message to be conveyed and to alter the delivery of the message each time it is spoken, usually once an hour. Along with the announcement of the station's name and strap-line (e.g. "today's best music"), this is the basic requirement of a standard link. During the day most stations will operate a policy of four or five standard links per hour, leaving aside key moments such as a weather or travel announcement, a competition requiring the presenter to take a caller to air, or a "what's on" guide. No matter how simple or complex the link, it should adhere to the rule of the "three Cs," i.e. clear, concise and conversational, which means rehearsing and editing the link before opening the microphone fader, but without losing a sense of spontaneity. The experienced, confident format jock will be able to "do the sell" from the liner without sounding cynical or rehearsed and, in addition, cross-promote another show or feature or, with the target listener in mind, include a local reference, news story, joke or information relating to an artist or track just played from the playlist. Every phrase counts. My own comment, having just played the Red Hot Chili Peppers' original version of "Under the Bridge" that "it's good to reclaim that one from All Saints," whose version was, at the time, ubiquitous on British radio, was met with a reprimand. I was told to be careful with statements like that because "All Saints do not exist in our world," that is, the new Xfm.

There is some room for creativity within the formatted structure of a link, but it is a very subtle creativity. This is due to the pressure felt from above to keep within the format rules but also due to another kind of pressure described by radio trainer Dan O'Day at a speech made at the 1999 Radio Festival:

> There is one secret known to every presenter: every time he opens the microphone to speak a small voice inside says, "I hope I don't make too big a fool of myself this time." This feeling never leaves a presenter and the easiest way to suppress it is to go through the motions, count down the time to when the slot would end, which does not make for good presentation.

According to O'Day, this fear exists because program controllers are disinclined to accept mistakes from their presenters as this can quickly undermine professionalism, a key aspect of the brand identity of the station; hence the tendency to be "safe," resulting in the construction of links that are consistent and functional, an anti-Kantian trait, and a form of self-censorship when viewed in terms of aesthetic innovation. Of course, there are those presenters who are allowed more freedom to develop an idiosyncratic radio personality, and this is increasingly the case, as more and more television personalities are recruited to present radio shows. It is also true that Chris Evans, Mark Radcliffe and Chris Moyles are examples of radio professionals who have developed their own personalities within the medium but, with the possible exception of Radcliffe, these presenters are not defined by their relationship to the music that they play. Before being sacked, Evans turned his Virgin Radio breakfast show into a virtually music-free zone, focusing instead on the interaction between himself and his presenter assistants. The remainder of the Virgin schedule and commercial music radio schedules in general are dominated by music. Although radio presenters, whose job is to play music, may have some scope to devise links and, in this respect, indulge in an element of aesthetic creativity, when it comes to the music itself, either by choice or not, the role is, in keeping with the economic imperatives of the industry, characteristically anti-Kantian.

The role contrasts with that of its former nomenclature, DJ, to the point that the two vocations are now perceived to meet different demands and serve separate publics. Furthermore, institutional rules and pressures have coincided with the development of cultural boundaries to make it less viable for the roles to overlap. The consequence for commercial music radio is the failure to reach a large section of its potential audience, culturally defined by their enthusiasm for new and alternative music for whom the DJ, as a technician of beats or an informed selector of music, is a central cultural signifier. Further, those people who do listen to music radio are denied access to most new music produced, and older styles and genres considered unsuitable for the mainstream target audience in which they have been included. The DJ, a vocation which requires an historical, cultural and aesthetic knowledge of music, who is qualified to make selections and determine the context of those selections, is denied access to the industry unless they are willing to leave their taste outside the studio. This requirement for the DJ, essentially a music fan, to adopt a cynically anti-Kantian position, has contributed to a situation of entrenchment, characterized by the tendency for DJs to shun the mainstream and radio presenters reluctant to talk about the music on air lest they should sound like an "anorak." To reiterate the incisive observation made by John Peel: "an interest in music is a distinct disadvantage in radio."

It is the significance attached to music which ultimately differentiates the two roles. The DJ defines her/himself through music; it is a vital part of her/his life. This enthusiasm for the form is the basis of an ongoing campaign to make others aware of music's potential. The DJ is constantly discovering new music and contextualizing older music within an ever developing canon. Indeed, the most unlikely examples of the form have been appropriated by DJs primarily associated with hip-hop culture. An archive has been created that includes music from many different genres, and additionally, specific sections of music that have been used to create new musical forms. The aesthetic potential of all music is taken for granted amongst DJs.

Cultural value and the importance of context

The aesthetic imperatives of music radio are stifled by the constant necessity for music to serve the maintenance of a consistent brand image. Andrew Bowie has noted the potential for the economic appropriation of music in his book *Aesthetics and Subjectivity*: "Music engages the individual subject in both emotional and intellectual ways. Music's non-representational character does, of course, make it liable to indiscriminate use in conjunction with non-aesthetic practices like advertising. On the other hand, this non-representational character can enable music to resist commercial or other appropriation" (Bowie, 1990: 178).

He is referring, primarily, to classical music, and it could be countered that the paradigm of contemporary popular music is infected, at the point of creation or production, with a distinctly capitalist logic. Certainly, the music industry is dominated by five major companies who have made significant inroads into the independent sector, establishing deals that have effectively turned such companies into research and development departments for artists and styles which have marketable potential whilst others are neglected. Nevertheless, the range and amount of musicians making popular music is such that there are many sources of new, "uninfected" music, and the degree of "infection" is always dependent upon the artistic intention that resonates within each individual piece of recorded music. The music industry as a cultural industry which facilitates the creation of cultural and artistic artifacts from scratch necessarily requires the talents of more aesthetically motivated cultural intermediaries, those who display Kantian tendencies in Bourdieu's conception. The value inherent within individual tracks will always be subjective, and the aesthetic or economic decisions involved in the process of production can become irrelevant when consumed by an individual listener. However, the DJ, as a cultural specialist, will make judgements as to the suitability of certain tracks for consumption by her/his audience. These judgements might or might not take account of the perceived aesthetic or economic motives behind the production of the track and will depend upon the extent and rigidity of the cultural field that the audience represents.

Richard Meltzer, in his book *The Aesthetics of Rock*, described as earnest investigation and crypto put-on, explains the underlying principle that makes the ultimate cultural value of a single track irrelevant. He writes that "Rock 'n' roll is now in the midst of a cataclysmic acceleration, both in this mode of repetition and in the cognition of its nature. And it always has been" (Meltzer, 1970: 72).

He goes on to list examples from a whole range of industrialized popular music, most notably Motown's "germplasm" approach that has the guiding principle of "if anything can unfailingly accomplish an end, why not repeat it again and again" (Meltzer, 1970: 73). This is an updated version of Theodor Adorno's standardization argument – except that where Adorno attached an ideological significance to the process, Meltzer does not. His conception of "rock 'n' roll" is of a world hermetically sealed off from political or economic interests, where questions of quality or aesthetic value are irrelevant. He claims that "the unit of rock significance is the whole of rock 'n' roll." In his example, the emotional and musical poverty of "I Think We're Alone Now" implies the luxuria of "I Am The Walrus" and vice versa. According to music journalist Dave Marsh, the music fan will always be aware of the communicative relationship between tracks, across musical boundaries and time periods:

> As much as anything else pop music fascinates me because it continues to spawn so many public and private discussions. I don't just mean the conversations that you and I have with our friends. One of the things I hope this book demonstrates is how often and how clearly singles speak to one another, in a continual cross-talk of style and content, shape and substance. In the grinding rhythms of "U got the look" you can hear Prince practically telephoning Sly Stone and James Brown, getting on the cosmic horn to Elvis and Jimi [. . .] We listen to the music and it speaks to us.
>
> (Marsh, 1989: xvi)

John Frow is concerned that Pierre Bourdieu's insistence on classifying cultural products in terms of taste leaves the product no integral or inherent value of its own. Frow agrees that value is a relative concept which is continually being fought over, but disagrees with the implicit assumption within Bourdieu's work, that, in his words, the "sole or primary" function of aesthetic texts is status-distinction. Frow does not offer an alternative "primary" or any specific purpose for aesthetic texts other than the suggestion that pleasure might be significant. This is apparent in the positioning of individuals within particular cultural fields; if distinction can be achieved through a knowledge of film or popular music, is it a purely arbitrary choice to learn about one rather than the other, or does personal interest and enjoyment influence such a decision? Frow's point is that the terminally indefinite meaning of aesthetic or cultural products means that they could have any number of purposes, or none at all.

For Frow, knowledge and the meaning of cultural products are transitory, ultimately dependent upon the particular discourse in operation within the cultural field in question. It follows that cultural products from outside a cultural field can be appropriated by members of the field and invested with a new meaning and associated cultural capital. This process can be allied to the concept of "regimes of value" which operate independently of intellectuals and cultural fields "permit[ing] the construction and regulation of value-equivalence, and [. . .] cross-cultural mediation" (Frow, 1995: 144). As texts and objects have no intrinsic or inherent meaning outside of social relations and mechanisms of signification, the process of passing from one cultural field to another is theoretically possible.

The point is made that the cultural value of products is determined by the cultural field that appropriates them. It is also the case, according to Frow, that those doing the appropriation are not always motivated by the cultural capital they can accrue. Furthermore, in the specific case of popular music, if Meltzer's explanation of the form is accepted, the affinity between certain musics and the market is not a disincentive to appropriation. I would suggest that the DJ as a member of a cultural field who has direct influence concerning the soundtrack of that field and with knowledge and respect for its bounds is able – and keen – to introduce to it new sounds and styles normally associated with different genres.

Xfm, in keeping with its guiding philosophy, made the concept of the DJ the fundamental basis of the station, and offers a test case to explore the above assertion.

DJs on the radio: the case of Xfm

Xfm began in 1991 when Sammy Jacob provided a round-the-clock radio service for the Reading Festival, and followed it with an initial restricted service license running for a month in London in 1992. Between 1992 and 1997, with the backing of Chris Parry from Fiction Records and Robert Smith of The Cure, and later Pinnacle Distribution and Allied Entertainments Group plc, the largest concert promoter in Europe, Xfm staged a concert in Finsbury Park which attracted 27,000 people and was later shown on Carlton TV, released two albums featuring exclusive tracks by major artists such as Oasis and U2, and operated regular Restricted Service Licenses (RSLs). It also applied to the Radio Authority for a full license on three separate occasions, eventually winning the last full London license to begin broadcasting in September 1997.

Fraser Lewry claims that Sammy Jacob's primary motivation for creating Xfm was economic – "he spotted a gap in the market." This is an interesting inference, particularly as my own experience of working with Jacob was that he was driven by a guiding philosophy best described as the antithesis of the mainstream music and radio industries. This took the form of a policy best summarized as, "if they do it like that everywhere else, then we don't do it like that here." For example, after my first show Jacob told me not to brand (i.e. mention) the station in every speech break, but just to do it "every third link or so." Further, whilst it was certainly the case that Jacob believed that his presenters should have significant freedom of music choice, on many occasions he would criticize selections, particularly within the weekly playlist meetings.

According to Fraser Lewry, the music policy of Xfm was to focus on songs which were made with "a spirit of adventure." Xfm operated a playlist to ensure that each week new releases which reflected this sense of adventure were given the greatest exposure because "record companies and the (music) industry generally like to gauge the success of their promotional activity." The playlist was not designed to reflect the tracks most popular with the target audience, or even an estimation of such, and it was certainly not informed by an intent to brand the station drawing on notions of consistency. A playlist committee made up of Jacob, Lewry, and several presenters, including me, decided on additions by listening to new releases and debating the merits of each individual track. This could often be a long, drawn-out process as the criteria for inclusion on the playlist were particularly vague, and did not contribute to objectivity. Indeed, when an objective viewpoint in support of a certain track was offered, perhaps in terms of the artist's current profile or popularity within the cultural field that represented the target audience, this often served to undermine the validity of the proposed track. It might also have drawn attention to a track's perceived aesthetic cynicism. The track *Mulder and Scully* by Catatonia was considered to be a blatant attempt to achieve mainstream success, with its reference to the popular television show and Cerys Matthews adoption of a distinctly broader Welsh accent when singing certain words or phrases. A process of "group-think" accounted for many playlist choices although, on occasion, Jacob would veto certain tracks regardless of the opinions of other voters. At one meeting the normally placid Gary Crowley was moved to exclaim, "but it's the fucking Bluetones, how can the new Bluetones single not get on the Xfm playlist?"

A common accusation leveled at the original Xfm, notably made by those pluggers representing the bigger radio promotions companies, was that the station, specifically program controller Sammy Jacob, purposely omitted releases by major artists from the playlist in an attempt to undermine the work of individual pluggers. Certainly, Jacob was keen to prevent pluggers from cultivating relationships with presenters, and would often contact pluggers to gleefully inform them that the track they were working had not made it onto the playlist. On 13 July 1998, prompted by an article entitled, "BBC Radio 1 at U.K. music's leading edge – the pluggers' view," which appeared in the July 1998 edition of *Music and Media*, Dylan White of Anglo Plugging sent a memo to all Xfm staff and certain industry figures (including Alan McGee at Creation Records) which accused Jacob of self-grandeur. This was a response to Jacob's claim that White had neglected to mention Xfm alongside Radio 1 as a champion of new music in a recent music industry magazine article. Central to this disagreement are the criteria by which new music is judged, and how and where it is generated and nurtured. Jacob was deeply suspicious of the industry structure and was keen to uphold "alternative" values, an approach which did not sit well with certain shareholders, and which was fundamentally cultural, given his own alleged economic interests. This kind of positive discrimination was certainly practiced to a degree by most of the workforce at Xfm but the character and extent of this skepticism differed for each individual.

The branding statement, or strap-line, employed by Xfm at its launch – "London's only alternative" – was perhaps problematic. Although this is not as vague as "today's best music" or "the better music mix," it was still referring to a particularly large and unstable descriptive paradigm. At its most expansive it incorporates all music not considered part of the mainstream and at its most modest it refers to a particular genre, acknowledged by the mainstream music industry which, it could be argued, represents the mainstream albums market in the UK, including bands such as Oasis, Blur, The Verve, and Radiohead. For many involved with Xfm, their own personal definition of "alternative" fell somewhere in between these two extremes and this was reflected in the individual programs and the content of the Xfm playlist each week. It was also the subject of the most discussion and argument within the station.

Simon Williams, a writer for the *New Musical Express*, began his first radio show on Xfm, "London's only alternative," with a song by Glen Campbell, *Wichita Lineman*. He left a few weeks into the station's license because he claimed that he did not have enough musical freedom. Keith Cameron, another *NME* writer, noted for his championing of cutting-edge new music in his show, The Carve-Up, would regularly play Bob Dylan, Bert Jansch, Terry Callier and Boston; and was deeply concerned when a memo suggested that Spiritualised and the Jesus & Mary Chain were a fair indication of his show's content. David Keenan, producer, occasional presenter, and guitarist with the Scottish avant-garde band Telstarr Ponies, commenced one of his programs with a quotation from Lester Bangs and a thirty-six-minute track by Japanese hard-core band Acid Mothers Temple. He rated *Crazy, Crazy*

Nights by Kiss as one of his favorite songs, which could move him to tears due to the power of the message and its performance.

The station represented a microcosm of the contemporary music industry. It was staffed by journalists (Cameron, Williams and Steve Sutherland, editor of the *NME*), musicians (Keenan, Tim McVey, once guitarist with Family Cat, Caspar Kedros of the Headrillaz), national radio and television professionals (Gary Crowley, Claire Sturgess), label managers, A&R men, pluggers, concert promoters, successful club DJs and ex-regional specialist radio presenters such as me. Inevitably, there were disagreements concerning the music policy of the station, particularly the playlist. Many staff were opposed to some of the guests who appeared on the station, notably Robbie Williams and Kylie Minogue because they were not perceived to be "right" for the station's image, and the credibility of some of the presenters was also called into question.

Individual presenters had free choice, more or less depending on their position in the schedule. Occasionally, a presenter might be told not to play a particular track by the program controller, but other than this there were no restrictions on music played. This does not mean to say that presenters did not feel the weight of "getting it right," as to get it wrong could result in criticism from within the organization or sometimes from a listener. As the presenter of the show before Cameron's Carve-Up, I can draw on first-hand experience of this. The track used to finish the show was always a difficult and fraught decision. He did not appreciate Stiff Little Fingers' "Alternative Ulster" on one occasion and said so on-air. In his role as letters editor of the *NME*, the reply given to a letter received from another ex-presenter, Marc Sheldon, admonishing the Radio Authority for depriving a specific culture of its music, read: "Alas Mark, when it came to your singing along to crap Real People records on Saturday mornings, I'm afraid you were the minority" (Cameron, 1998: 62).

The correspondence that was in evidence after the take-over suggests that Keith Cameron's program was most popular amongst those who are most critical of radio in general and who are distinguishable by their desire for unfamiliar and difficult music. These listeners had an affinity with Cameron's show. In such instances these presenter/audience relationships can be considered distinct cultural fields, but this relies on the nature of the cultural field being manifest at all times. Mainstream commercial radio deals with this through a policy of broadcasting consistent and narrowly defined output, but this approach would defeat the objective of a station like Xfm.

The key issue is the way in which the audience is addressed. In mainstream radio the focus is on the target audience, knowing the listener through demographic or psychographic research. This necessarily translates the audience into a mass from which the concept of an individual member can be created. At the new Xfm this was initially described as a "jeans and t-shirt guy who likes guitar-based music" and, of course, a string of signifiers can be developed from this to make him seem more real. The alternative is to work within the paradigm of a cultural field. The DJ places her/himself within the bounds of the cultural field they are most comfortable with and simply talks to the other members of that field.

The scenario is analogous to that of the club DJ, except that the radio DJ is separated in space and, often, time from her/his audience or cultural field. Furthermore, there is no direct peer group pressure to reinforce or undermine music selections so that the individual listener, it seems, is free to interpret a particular track selection for themselves, based on its quality and relevance to their own perceived cultural field. The concern for the radio DJ is that, without the direct backing of their peers, the individual listener will turn off if a less obvious selection is made. It is vital therefore that the listener is aware of a distinctive context surrounding such a selection. At Xfm, the station's independent credentials and history provided this necessary context at a macro level, but it was also the case that individual shows were aimed at quite specific cultural fields, each with their own boundaries and rules, particularly governing the acceptable level of affinity with the market displayed by a certain track or artist.

Keith Cameron's show, although clearly part of a commercial institution, appeared to be the show most driven by notions of art and the avant-garde. The form and content of the show were not informed by the traditional rules of radio. He would often play a track before firing his introductory identity sweeper (a piece of audio with sound effects but no music which serves as an identifier of the station or show on which it is played) announcing the beginning of his program; a song may be played twice, in slightly different versions, in order to contrast them and, as already mentioned, the selection of music was often from genres which seemed to have no relation to a standardized notion of "alternative." The disregard for conventional radio practice is indicative of a distancing from the market, and the appreciation of such anti-radio bestows cultural capital upon the listener whilst strengthening the legitimacy of the presenter. The idiosyncratic choices of music, whilst also showing a disregard for conventional practice, emphasize the power of the cultural intellectual to bestow cultural value on a hitherto insignificant object within the cultural field in question. Taken out of the context of Cameron's show, unlike those tracks which will retain cultural value within the cultural field and neighboring cultural fields, a track, for example *Wichita Lineman* by Glen Campbell, may become problematic as an indicator of cultural distinction. This would tend to suggest that it is not appropriation or knowledge of the individual object per se that is indicative of cultural distinction but rather it is knowledge of the process by which such objects can be imbued with cultural value. This process should not be confused with the postmodern strategies that center around pastiche and kitsch. In a sense it could be conceived of as an intellectual game, in the tradition of "the emperor's new clothes," but to indulge in such a game could undermine other elements of the show, particularly other music. This suggests that such idiosyncratic musical choices are informed by certain rules.

Simon Frith has attempted to make sense of the operation of cultural fields by updating Bourdieu's monolithic division of Kantian and anti-Kantian sensibilities. Perhaps influenced by the comments of those fans of aesthetic and cultural production like Meltzer and Marsh, who are unwilling to let economic imperatives taint that which they love, he refers to three discourses which dominate cultural judgements of value:

> an art discourse – the ideal of cultural experience is transcendence; art provides a means of rising above the everyday, leaving the body, denying the significance of historical time and geographical place; a folk discourse – the ideal of cultural experience is integration; folk forms provide a means of placement – in a space, a season, a community; a pop discourse – the ideal of cultural experience is fun; pop provides routinized pleasures, more intense than the everyday but bound into its rhythms, and legitimized emotional gratification, a play of desire and discipline.
>
> (Frith, 1997: 575)

These discourses can be applied to the music played on Xfm. The first could be summarized specifically as those pieces of music which represent the ideals of the avant-garde, e.g. the mostly instrumental post-rock of Tortoise, Mogwai or Quickspace but, more generally, any music that evokes the timelessness and placelessness described by Frith. *Wichita Lineman* may fit into this category, as might Radiohead. The second are those songs which have a particular organic subcultural resonance, for example dance music and more traditionally folk or rock-based songs that have some degree of political or social content, from Bob Dylan to the Manic Street Preachers. The third discourse might incorporate a large proportion of the current Xfm playlist, indie music which falls into the rock/pop category such as Catatonia, Space, even the Fall.

Transcending these categories is, I would suggest, a master discourse, inflected culturally rather than aesthetically, which is reinforced by both the need for intellectuals to distance themselves from economic capital and the guiding "alternative" philosophy at Xfm. This master discourse is defined in terms of Xfm's Other, the mainstream, which is itself defined as those objects which are obviously in league with the market and, as such, can be written off as in any way "real." It is clearly the case that virtually all of the cultural products that circulate within Xfm are implicated in such a way, but it is those that seem to have been so infected with the demands and strategies of the market that are to be avoided; tracks which have let the market use them rather than the other way around; those which are created demographically rather than personally, generically rather than idiosyncratically, economically rather than culturally; tracks which are fake rather than real. This charge was leveled at several artists added to the new Capital XFM playlist. This was evidenced by correspondence from disgruntled former listeners who criticized Semisonic, Eve 6, and Goo Goo Dolls, acts who were mainstays of American alternative radio stations. To reiterate the Head of Music, Fraser Lewry's, guiding philosophy for the station, tracks played on-air should display a spirit of adventure.

This guiding principle, reinforced by the day-to-day working and social practice of the station, sets aside the original Xfm as a distinctly cultural phenomenon, driven by a desire to offer an alternative selection of music to that available elsewhere; in short, an ideological project. The cultural capital of the specialist presenter and the positioning within the context of other cutting-edge, new music bestowed enough relevant criteria upon the song for it to fit with the attitude of the station. In a similar relationship to that of the club DJ who provides the "crowd" with their music, certain bold choices can be made which are given validity by the transference of cultural capital within a peer group. In a sense, cultural workers at mainstream radio stations are setting the cultural agenda but it is always contributing to a confirmation of listeners' identities rather than provoking a reflection upon such identities by throwing in something unexpected from time to time. Xfm could do this because it refused to regard itself as anything other than a primary information and entertainment source, and was not afraid to risk losing listeners. Of course it was always less likely to lose listeners because its audience was willing to persevere and expected innovative selections. Any other radio station would undermine their role as a safe haven for occasional listening by such behavior. The industry rule that when listening hours are down the rotation of core tracks should be increased is born out of the reality that the listener feels let down if they do not hear what they have tuned in to hear. At Xfm, the repetition of tracks did occur but it was always felt that this undermined the message of the station. Presenters often dropped songs with little or no comment from management.

Ironically, to an extent, the didactic and democratic possibilities just outlined created a feeling within Xfm that it was a cultural project, and this in turn had some influence on policy at the station. This was as evident in the failure to play some mainstream alternative artists as it was in the positive discrimination of hitherto under-represented artists and musics. Of course this undermines the potential of the DJ who should transcend the notion that the cultural value of an artist or track is based on its proximity to the market. Indeed, it confirms the centrality of cultural capital. As Bourdieu would suggest, this is an essential task of the intellectual who emphasizes her/his autonomy from the market by enhancing the prestige and relevance of cultural goods. However, if the DJ described above is thought of as a purely normative concept, so that its position becomes analogous to that of the traditional artist when describing the role of advertising creatives, film directors, authors or musicians, all of whom rely on cultural markers and boundaries to define and position their work, then Xfm is immediately recast as influential patron of a developing cultural aesthetic.

Radio now – a better music mix – please!

The DJ, in contrast to the radio professional discussed above, and the traditional artist or cultural intellectual who gathers cultural capital through a policy of distancing themselves from any functional aspects that a cultural artifact might have, is keen to include rather than exclude through her/his original choice and scheduling of music. As I hope I have demonstrated, the radio DJ is not free from cultural capital concerns, just as the radio presenter is closely tied to the needs of economic capital. Mainstream commercial music radio needs to take on the role of training future presenters so that they understand the relative importance of both cultural and economic concerns, allowing them to apply such training to their own scheduling decisions. If this is not done properly, music radio will continue to lose credibility amongst that large section of the population which consumes popular music.

In early 1999, the Radio Authority reacted to complaints concerning the output of the new Xfm and imposed a paltry £4,000 fine on Capital. In terms of broadcast output it cited the failure to play live sessions and made a vague reference to the changed on-air attitude of the station. This has resulted in two new DJ-choice specialist programmes, John Kennedy's *Xposure* and Ian Camfield's *Rock Show*, and the introduction of the aforementioned personality presenters but, unfortunately for the music fan, the station continues, through its corporately-driven music policy, to undermine itself, through the wrong music choices and contextualization of those choices. For example, having drawn attention to three songs featuring Richard Ashcroft's vocals scheduled within twenty-five minutes of each other, I was told: "So? We'd play The Verve every twenty minutes if I had my way." A memorandum circulated in late October 1999 reinforced the rule that all the scheduled tracks should be played and in the order in which they appear on the playlist sheet, confirming the station's attitude toward any notion of DJ freedom. Fraser Lewry, whilst not inclined to be particularly objective, nevertheless neatly sums up the output of the current station: "the ultimate prick-tease, you get two good tracks and then the third one ruins it. In fact, no-one I know has a record collection made up of the stuff that Xfm now plays – it doesn't make sense."

Veteran broadcaster Paul Gambaccini, speaking at the 1999 Radio Festival in Cardiff, prominently referred to the station's format and music policy, listing it alongside other less cutting edge stations, noting, "There's a Bermuda Triangle where formats go to die – Xfm, Capital, Heart, Virgin – you have to ask yourself, 'Which station am I listening to?'"

Clearly, for some listeners, there is insufficient choice, and the moves toward a more adventurous music radio industry, represented by the new Xfm, are still too conservative. The role of the DJ is central to the process of bringing music alive through selection and contextualization, transforming radio from a message board for other cultural products into a cultural product in its own right. If the original Xfm still existed, there would be a different choice for the listener. The fact that it, and other culturally significant stations like the dance-oriented forerunner Kiss 100, no longer exist in their original form is partly due to the pressures of the marketplace which seem to demand mass audiences. This is largely due to the failure of the industry's governing bodies to protect such stations when they do not achieve these audiences. This is a matter of great concern. It is also profoundly undemocratic.

References

Bourdieu, Pierre (1971) "Intellectual Field and Creative Project," in *Knowledge and Control – New Directions for the Sociology of Education*, M. F. D. Young (ed.), London: Macmillan.

Bourdieu, Pierre (1994) "Distinction and the Aristocracy of Culture," in *Cultural Theory and Popular Culture*, John Storey (ed.), Essex: Prentice Hall.

Bowie, Andrew (1990) *Aesthetics and Subjectivity (from Kant to Nietzsche)*, Manchester University Press.

Cameron, K. (1998) Letter to the editor, *New Musical Express* xx, 62.

Frith, Simon (1997) "Defending Popular Culture from the Populists," in *Cultural Theory and Popular Culture*, John Storey (ed.), Essex: Prentice Hall.

Frow, John (1995) *Cultural Studies and Cultural Value*, Clarendon Press.

Jameson, Frederic (1992) *The Geo-political Aesthetic: Cinema and Space in the World System*, London: British Film Institute.

Jamous, H. and Peloille, B. (1970) "Changes in the French University Hospital System," in *Professions and Professionalization*, J. A. Jackson (ed.), Cambridge: Cambridge University Press.

Marsh, Dave (1989) *The Heart of Rock and Soul: the 1001 Greatest Singles Ever Made*, Cambridge, MA: Da Capo Books.

Meltzer, Richard (1970) *The Aesthetics of Rock*, Cambridge, MA: Da Capo Books.

Part III

ORGANIZATION

Dina Berkeley's chapter discusses the constraints which determine television drama production during the current turbulent conditions facing the industry. It argues that the climate of fear that proliferates in the industry, and which leads to conservatism in what is being chosen to be commissioned and transmitted, is counter-productive for the health of the industry. It presents a five-level framework for mapping influences on a production and discusses the degree to which the media industry itself has the power to direct them to its benefit. It concludes with an argument that creativity is also essential in the managerial side of the production process in order to cope with all external and internal influences. It argues that the typical assumption that creativity is only to be found in the artistic side of the work is a fallacy which needs to be dispensed with if the British drama production industry is to sustain its reputation. Her chapter draws on some of the results of a three-year project, Study of Industrial Modes of Production of Television Drama (funded by the Media, Culture and Economics Program of the Economic and Social Sciences Council 1995–8) which was carried out through in-depth interviews of key executives in the British television industry and case studies of a variety of television drama productions.

Skillset and BFI studies have shown that more women are coming into the television industry and more younger women are securing producer/director jobs. Skillset findings also show that 70 percent of women working in television production are under forty compared with less than half of the men. So will the young female entrants be able to sustain a career in television or will they have to make social adjustments and sacrifices to stay in? Statistics imply that many women, both in the past and currently, leave after the age of forty. Janet Willis and Shirley Dex's chapter looks at the implications of casualized employment practice and the demands of production work for women working in this sector, and uses data from interviews to examine the effect of family formation on the career orientations of a group of mothers with experience of a range of production jobs and environments. Their chapter draws on recent research analyzing the effect of

101

interruptions on women's careers and on cross-national studies which look at the conditions which discourage women from continuing employment as well as those which enable women to make career progression and to close the gender pay gap.

Film and television producer Sally Hibbin was the founder member of Parallax Pictures. She is also a founder and board member of The Film Consortium and one of the major architects of the successful franchise bid for Arts Council of Great Britain funding. She began her career as a journalist but became a documentary film-maker with *Live A Life*, which was shown at the 1982 London Film Festival. She followed this with *The Road to Gdansk*, and *Great Britain United*, which looked at black footballers in Britain. She went on to produce a number of award-winning films and drama. Among her film and television credits are: *A Very British Coup*, which won the 1988 BAFTA Award for Best Drama Serial, together with an International Emmy; *Riff-Raff*, which won both the 1991 Cannes Critics' Award and the Felix European Film of the Year Award; *Raining Stones*, which earned the 1992 Cannes Jury Prize, as well as the 1993 *Evening Standard* Award for Best Film; *Ladybird, Ladybird*, which was premiered at the 1994 Berlin Film Festival where it carried away the Critics' Award for Best Film, as well as the Berlin Silver Bear Award for Best Actress; *i.d.*, the feature debut of writer–director team Vincent O'Connell and Phil Davis; and Ken Loach's *Carla's Song*, which was in competition at the 1996 Venice Film Festival. Sally has also acted as Executive Producer on other feature films: *Bad Behaviour* (winner of the 1993 *Evening Standard* Peter Sellers Comedy Award), *Land And Freedom*, *The Englishman Who Went Up A Hill And Came Down A Mountain* and *The Governess*. She is uniquely placed to reflect upon the organization of the production of films in a British context.

Mike Jones spent ten years as a member of the British pop group Latin Quarter. In that time the act had only one hit single in Britain, *Radio Africa* (1986); yet in Northern Europe a considerable market existed for Latin Quarter from 1985 into the 1990s. Latin Quarter released six albums, four (*Modern Times*, *Mick And Caroline*, *Swimming Against The Stream* and *Nothing Like Velvet*) for major labels (Arista and RCA) and two (*Long Pig* and *Bringing Rosa Home*) for German independents (Verabra and SPV). Although Jones's lyrics are still used by Latin Quarter co-founder Steve Skaith, Jones himself has retired from work in the popular music industry. Jones's chapter draws on his own experience of making pop records. He reflects on the character and type of access to other pop acts and to industry figures his role as a song-writer and band member gave him. Essentially, his chapter functions more as a search for theory rather than as an application of an existing body of theory.

5

CREATIVITY AND ECONOMIC TRANSACTIONS IN TELEVISION DRAMA PRODUCTION

Dina Berkeley

Introduction

Television drama has always been, and still is, the most expensive type of programming in Britain (ITC, 1994). Since the beginning of the 1990s, the drive to decrease the costs in drama production has resulted in pressure to create low-cost, high-volume drama which will leave enough of the overall production budget of a company remaining to fund more expensive drama projects (Brown, 1998). Economies are usually being achieved by trading-off location work with purpose-built sets (producing what is known in the trade as "precinct drama"), or moving production to out-of-London locations, where resources are cheaper (although lack of local facilities may create problems of their own).

The general drive is to find ways of saving on production costs without making it noticeable on the screen. Guaranteed short-term profits from programs that bring in mass audiences are preferred investments to developing high-quality programs in the long run. The current tendency is to move from "prestige" to "popular quality" drama. Reliance on majority audiences means building programs with the widest popular appeal (Sutherland, 1989) or programs which will attract the target audiences the advertisers want (Stoessl, 1998). This tendency has the adverse effect that established formulas, which have proved to have worked in the past (i.e. attracted large audiences), tend to get preference over experimental formulas. ITV, for example, has been accused of becoming like Hollywood: looking for a simple concept, backed by a well-known cast, the "talent" (Brooks, 1994). This challenges the once traditional strength of British television drama of being author-led. (Key figures in the British television industry – Andrew Davies, Tony Garnett, Ken Loach, John McGrath, Alan Plater – speaking at a conference organized by the University of Reading in 1997, all voiced the same concern.)

In such an environment, risk aversion and conservatism tend to proliferate. As Richard Williams (1997) comments:

> The trouble with television [...] is that even at the fringes it is staffed by people who think of themselves as radical, yet whose idea of progress is to clone the last thing their peers raved about. [...] This is perhaps not surprising, in view of television's wholesale capitulation over the past decade to the imperatives of market forces, a phenomenon much remarked upon in its manifestation at the bureaucratic levels of the medium, but at least as evident in the matter of what actually appears on the screen. A destructive form of synergy is at work here, one suspects.

Mulgan's (1990) prophecy that "in the future 'quality programs' will depend less on a nod and a nudge from a regulator and more on funds and organizational structures that grow up alongside and within a more conventional, internationalized, industry structure" (1990: 30) seems to have come true. An increasing proportion of drama consists of material produced to suit the demands of the marketer, exporter and co-production sponsoring institutions, while a shrinking proportion results from the determination of individual authors to achieve self-expression (Dunkley, 1988a, 1988b; Nelson, 1996). The 1997 Edinburgh Festival, for example, witnessed the condemnation of such practices by established and respected authors and scriptwriters like Troy Kennedy Martin. It could be, perhaps, for this reason that "drama is drooping" (Phillips, 1998: 20).

Creativity, in such an environment, tends to get reified. The assessment of the potential value of a drama production under consideration is thus determined by the "talent" that it includes in its bid which, it is assumed, will attract the audience and, hence, deliver audiences to its producers and financiers.

In this chapter I look at the constraints under which decisions are made in the industry concerning the "value" of a particular prospective television drama production. Each particular product, I argue, is assessed for its audience-attractability prospectively, on the basis of the value that each of its attributes (or a selective combination of some of its attributes) had achieved in the past. The product, looked upon as an object, is the focus of evaluation and of negotiation between different stakeholders. But, by being seen throughout the negotiations as a fixed entity, valued in fragments, the possibility is negated for it to develop into something better, given a new, emergent, combination of elements. Conservatism, as the decision rule in operation, results in its own propagation as the appropriate rule.

Television drama as a commodity

A drama program is the final product of the results of a series of negotiations between a variety of stakeholders with different levels of responsibility toward its production and eventual delivery to its intended consumers, the viewers. Its development process typically starts with just an idea or concept, communicated through its originator (an author, a producer) to the first decision-maker in the "chain" (an executive producer, a commissioner). As it moves through the "chain" of decision-makers it gets, progressively, more tightly specified (as specific resources and budget items are included in its definition), enabling the concept to be envisaged as *the* final product.

At each stage the concept remains, more or less, the same; it is the attributes of the final product that are being negotiated so that its attractiveness to the next decision-maker approached will increase. At the end of the "chain," if the negotiation process has been successful, a commissioning agreement or contract fixes all the central attributes of the final product (budget, timescale, major resources, etc.). These define the brief for the project which will make the final product. The process continues from then on within the frame of reference of the project until the original concept, often changed and developed on the way, emerges as the final product.

However, a drama program is not just like any other product. As a cultural commodity, it circulates in two contiguous economies, the financial and the cultural (Fiske, 1987). The financial economy is primarily concerned with exchange (monetary) value while the cultural economy exchanges and circulates "meanings, pleasures, and social identities" (ibid.: 311). Within each economy the product changes role as soon as it starts circulating: in the financial economy, the commodity which has been sold to distributors becomes, itself, a producer of audiences to be sold to advertisers; in the cultural economy the commodity that is being "sold" turns into a producer of meanings and pleasures (ibid.: 312). The typical perspective of the media industry focuses on the role of this cultural commodity as producer of audiences (hence, homogeneity and consensus tend to become the guiding principles) while the audience itself focuses on the role of the commodity as a producer of meanings and pleasure (individually defined and, hence, drawing attention to the principle of heterogeneity and difference from the consensus).

Fiske suggests that the failure to predict what type of product will do well in the market is a manifestation of the fact that, in the cultural economy, commodities do not move in a linear fashion from production to consumption (as is the case with the financial economy), mainly due to the power of the audience. He claims that this is

> one reason why the cultural industries produce what Garnham
> (1987) calls "repertoires" of products; they cannot predict which of
> their commodities will be chosen by which sectors of the market to

be the provoker of meanings/pleasure that serve *their* interests as well as those of the producers. Because the production of meaning/pleasure occurs in the consumption as well as the production of the cultural commodity the notion of production takes on a new dimension that delegates it away from the owners of capital.

(ibid.: 313, original emphasis)

Accurate prediction of the direction that this production of meaning/pleasures will take at the point of consumption is vital for success in the industry. Utilizing popular formats and genres is one way of binding this direction within relatively predictable bounds, whereby the risk of failure is minimized, often alongside the possibility of innovation.

Each different format of television drama carries its own assumptions about its target audience and what would appeal to it, within the frame of that format. Television drama formats, essentially, consist of one-off productions (anthology) or continuous productions (series or serials) of varying lengths, with a stable cast, that either follow an ongoing storyline or present a new storyline in each segment (Cantor and Cantor, 1992). The mini-series, a very popular format in the UK, is viewed as a particular type of the serial format. Tunstall (1993) suggests that this popularity is due to the fact that it fits well with how ITV allocates its broadcasters' drama productions to the network. Its very popularity also sits well with the BBC's "deference" toward writers of television drama and satisfies producers' perceptions that quantity often leads to reduced quality.

Each format is typically assigned to a position in a "moral hierarchy" of values, defining a piece of drama as a "high" or "low" cultural artifact. The prevailing assumption of an association between "high quantity" and "low quality" results in an elitist attitude within the media industry toward people involved in the production of certain drama products (e.g. soap operas). Involvement in the production of soap operas is often the starting place for many people in the industry. Soap operas provide a good training ground as well as a source of income for people in the industry in between other productions.

In terms of format the cultural high ground resides with the single play. Single plays are viewed as upholding the quality standard. Here the writer is seen as the spearhead of innovation and is usually expected to break away from "mirroring everyday reality," the driving style for series and serials, and to focus instead on naturalism, authenticity and realistic surface texture. This difference may largely stem from difference in ancestry with the single play, as anthology, developing primarily from theatre, and the series or serial developing primarily from the medium of radio.

In terms of costs "high prestige" drama costs significantly more than "low prestige" drama. The determining cost factor is the volume of episodes made per year; the higher the prestige, the lower the number of episodes made per year. Tunstall (1993) suggests that the mini-series is the format that provides some economies of scale while still offering a "high" level of prestige. Hence, we encounter a proliferation of mini-series at the expense of single dramas. Moreover, single dramas are increasingly being produced for the film market as their primary target. Thus, television companies produce or co-produce films (Fuller, 1998) or co-finance them (as was the case with Channel 4). Conversely, a panel discussion on *What's the Story* at the 1998 London Film Festival raised the issue that only 40 percent of the films made for the cinema get distributed and many of those which do not get distributed search for a place in the television market.

In terms of content, "innovation" is often accorded the highest prestige. The ambition of people involved in drama production is often declared as being able to deliver "innovative" drama to their customers. For example, Peter Salmon, on taking his appointment as controller of BBC1, stated that he was "looking for the next big series, a bit of derring-do, a bit of ambition" (Longrigg, 1997). However, what type of prospective product will be characterized as "ambitious" depends greatly on whose perspective will be employed in the characterization, and on the relative power this person has within the hierarchy of decision-makers involved in deciding on the fate of the prospective product.

The perpetual tension between "being the same" and "being different" which proliferates in the industry under conditions of fierce competition for audiences (Abercrombie, 1996; Elliott, 1972), is evident at all levels. This constitutes the terrain where differences between the perspectives of different stakeholders (producers, executive producers, commissioners) materialize. The audience, as an image in each stakeholder's mind, plays a major role as the tension moves to the conflict between images of audiences' desires for a new TV drama product. In essence, the tension is between "playing safe" and "taking a risk."

To be or not to be?

Failure or success of a television drama program is determined retrospectively, i.e. after it has been produced and transmitted, by the audience ratings it has achieved. Nevertheless, decisions about what will be produced and transmitted are taken prospectively. Responsibility for the failure or success of a piece of drama (using the ratings as its measure) is often ascribed to some externally observable elements which describe the product itself (e.g. quality of script, content, lighting, director, actors' performance) and, less often, if ever, to issues related to scheduling, pre-transmission publicity, competitive scheduling, or budget and time allocated for its production. However, producers are all too aware of the importance of such elements to the success of their product and they try to ensure the best possible deal with broadcasters so that their production is given a good chance.

While positive decisions to produce a drama program can be "assessed" for their wisdom in the above terms, negative decisions which have prevented a particular piece of drama materializing are rarely demonstrated to have been either wise or mistaken; projects which have not been financed, in general, tend not to be ever produced. A rare exception was the example of a mistake in terms of a negative decision by the Independent Television Network Centre not to commission a comedy series featuring redundant Yorkshiremen turned male strippers. This concept eventually materialized as a film (*The Full Monty*) which became the UK's most successful film, in terms of box office takings, since *Four Weddings and A Funeral*. A Granada-produced one-hour pilot (*Bare Necessities*), watched by eight million viewers, failed to interest the network (Wainwright, 1997).

Moreover, competition between different broadcasters generates a situation whereby, if a particular type of drama, in terms of content, has recently appeared to be "successful," everybody starts trying to finance the production of something of the same type. A current example of this kind of successful theme is costume drama, one of the most expensive types of drama. Costume drama has the added advantage of also being a marketable commodity abroad, as "it is increasingly seen worldwide to be the area of British Television expertise" (Nelson, 1997: 149) and, hence, it has a potential market which is wider than the UK. However, costume drama is not always successful in delivering audiences; there have been many classic costly flops (characterized as such on the basis of the ratings achieved; 45 percent or more audience share of all broadcasting at the time on all terrestrial TV channels is the benchmark for a hit (Phillips, 1998)). For example, the first episode of Andrew Davies's adaptation of Thackeray's *Vanity Fair*, a BBC1 costume drama transmitted in November 1998, won a mere 28 percent share of the audience while a feature-length episode of *Taggart*, a fifteen-year-old television series shown on ITV at the same time, won 46 percent share of the audience (Gibson, 1998a), despite intense advertising orchestrated by the BBC (Parker, 1998). While the BBC was explaining the low audience as a typical occurrence with first episodes, ITV was celebrating the success of its own "classic," albeit of another type.

Another example of a currently popular theme is science fiction. Jed Mercurio, who wrote *Cardiac Arrest* and recently *Invasion Earth*, a science fiction drama, was reported as saying that getting his series commissioned was easy, since:

> If I tried to pitch the idea five years ago, I would have got nowhere. They would have said, "Is it for kids? It'll have to be very low budget. The mainstream audience won't watch science fiction." But due to the success of the *X Files* and movies like *Independence Day*, there was a feeling that science fiction was now a mainstream, commercial product.
>
> (Griffiths, 1997: 21)

This feeling that Mercurio talks about is part of what is employed as a stable referent in the drama production/commissioning enterprise. A project which fits in with a prevailing trend (in terms of content) is more likely to encounter a number of "open doors" in seeking to get commissioned. Moreover, the negotiations that take place between the various stakeholders involved typically tend to focus on how the project's profile can be improved (e.g. by incorporating more highly valued talent than the one proposed, irrespective of the higher cost, often compensating for the difference by cutting costs in some other function which could threaten the eventual success of the project). This attitude, although an instance of "playing safe" behavior, is counter-productive for the well-being of the industry. Nevertheless, it forms part of the unspoken "rules of engagement" in negotiations between different stakeholders (commissioners, producers, authors). Innovative drama production concepts (e.g. *Our Friends in the North* or *Boys from the Blackstuff*) which gain wide acclaim when they are finally given the chance to be made into a product, are often treated as exceptions to the basic operating principle of "playing safe," not as a proof that the operating principle functions only well on average (i.e. taking into account all that has been produced) and must change.

The dominant rule concerning television drama (that is, that the past should inform the future) effectively reconstructs the past, as all negative decisions do not form part of it and all positive decisions which have ended up in flops are treated as exceptions to the rule. It also propagates the idea that those who made the decisions are always right when the product has been successful, while it is always the fault of the implementer (e.g. producer) if the product has failed in attaining the desired audience ratings. In all instances, the audience is considered the final arbiter in the ratings battle and most decisions are taken in its name. However, the audience is treated en masse while nobody seems to consider that, even using the ratings discourse as a measure, the audience votes amongst the alternatives decision-makers have made available for it. The cloud of "fear" of failure in the ratings arena (often voiced by our interviewees) that has overshadowed the industry throughout the last decade or so has actually removed the possibility of delivering to audiences new alternatives which will be producing new notions, challenges and ideas, rather than merely reproducing the status quo.

A system in flux

In the 1990s we witnessed tremendous changes in the media industry, not only in terms of regulations that are imposed by legislation but also by general structural transformations and, even more specifically, by the movement of individuals, at executive level, from one broadcaster to another or to/from the independent sector. During the three-year period of data collection for the purposes of our project (1996–8), we came across many instances whereby a person we had interviewed in his/her particular function within a particular organization had moved on to another post and/or another organization within the next month, or that a person we would approach at some point had moved on by the time we would finally interview him/her, a month or so afterwards.

One can characterize this movement of individual players in significant posts in the industry either as a result of the usual tradition of upward (vertical) mobility that exists in the industry or as a result of a response of individuals to the particular structural transformations in the industry that are taking place. The fact that, on a number of occasions, the mobility is, in reality, horizontal (even if the newly acquired title is slightly different to the previous one) indicates that it is more likely that, in the majority of moves, the latter case holds true. This point was made in 1986 by the dramatist John McGrath: "I would say that about 80% of the independent drama producers producing for Channel 4 are refugees from the BBC, who have set up their own companies to escape its oppressive structure" (quoted in Tulloch, 1990: 177).

The fact that a number of significant figures in drama production, not only from the BBC, frequently leave their employers to set up their own companies or move on somewhere else would indicate that oppressive structures are becoming more ubiquitous across the entire industry. It is less certain whether the recent development of an apparent "climate of fear" is due to changes within the UK industry itself or due to the expansion of the market, foreign competition, lack of funds, technology advancement, or a mere reflection of eighteen years of Conservative rule in the country, and the philosophy it propagated and implemented (Curran and Seaton, 1997).

In the last decade of the twentieth century, a number of changes which have taken place in the industry, mainly due to legislation under the Conservative government, have had tremendous repercussions for the functioning of the industry. For example, the 25 percent quota obligation of BBC and ITV companies to commission programs from independent producers, which is often exceeded (Westcott, 1998), has led to an excessive increase in the number of independent producers (Robins and Cornford, 1992). It has also led to the loss of stable resources in the production side of broadcaster/producer organizations. The "producer choice" initiative at the BBC, which started in 1991, allowed producers to opt out of using "in-house" facilities. Although a number of independent producers seem to see it as a positive development, this had certain ill effects for the BBC itself. One of our interviewees stated:

> Producers were given the chance to use people whom they already knew and worked with before and did not want to use in-house people. The creative producers chose to recruit their staff from the

outside because they knew people from outside were cheaper. Meanwhile, you had departments that had to be paid for, so the overhead had to be put somewhere. This made in-house programs more and more expensive. This could lead the BBC to become only a broadcaster which would be a shame because historically the BBC had staff, arguably some of the best in the country and, as a production house, it is a fine one. Now, most of the people have gone. Whole departments have gone; there is no more Design, no more Make-up and it becomes hard to defend an in-house production.

The developments in the television broadcasting industry of the move, during the mid-1950s, from monopoly (BBC) to duopoly (BBC and ITV), to the current quasi-open market system, created a shift toward a fragmented and disaggregated situation. The business functions necessary for making programs available to viewers have come to be seen as separable rather than integrated entities. In the current climate, we often encounter three separate business functions: (a) production, (b) channel management/scheduling and (c) delivery/transmission. Often, different organizations fulfill these functions, bringing along different interests, different cultures and operating principles. This necessarily gives rise to incompatible perspectives being employed in valuing a production and often leading to conflicts in the context of the production process.

On the commercial side, the establishment of the Independent Television Network Centre (through the 1990 Broadcasting Act) centralized decision-making concerning commissioning and led to a substantial struggle amongst the ITV broadcasting companies which collectively own the ITV Centre and wish to supply the bulk of ITV programs themselves. Since the last Channel 3 franchise round (1993), independent producers have the possibility of either obtaining commissions through a Channel 3 franchise holder (i.e. an ITV broadcaster) or through access to the ITV Network Centre. Nowadays, because of the increase in supply of production companies, in order to stand a reasonable chance of obtaining a commission, it is becoming increasingly important for independent producers to carry out a considerable amount of development work on projects prior to submitting them to broadcasters. This requires a considerable investment of capital which is often borrowed from banks and results in the financial handicap of having to pay thousands of pounds in interest charges (Westcott, 1998).

The emergence of new channels and subscription-funded television, during the 1990s, increased the competition for sharing the advertising "pie." Cable and satellite television, for example, in 1997, accounted for around 36 percent of the £4.7 billion revenues of commercial television and 11 percent of the £2.6 billion total advertising revenue (ITC, 1997). Curran and Seaton point out:

Commercial broadcasting is based, not on the sale of programs to audiences, but on the sale of audiences to advertisers. Thus the introduction of more competitors will reduce advertising revenues both by spreading them between a greater number of channels and by splitting potential audiences into even smaller groups. As the main incentive will remain the attraction of the largest possible audience, the competing channels, less constrained by regulation to produce a variety of programs, will tend to show more of the same or similar programs.

(1997: 313)

Moreover, in 1996 changes in media ownership rules, allowing an increase of the number of broadcasting licenses which can be held by any one company, has led to significant changes in Channel 3 with concentration of ownership in major corporate owners. This, again, leads to repercussions for what is being made available on the screen:

The small number of corporate owners are not competitive in a sense that could conceivably be expected to produce an improved product; but their financial rivalry will undoubtedly impose pressure to produce a cheaper one. That means an almost inevitable lowering of standards since it is cheaper to buy in international soap opera than to make your own drama, and so on. Thus, the victims of media concentration are variety, creativity, and quality, while the proliferation of broadcasting channels in the hands of a small band of operators, "liberated" by government policy from the obligations of public service variety, is likely to make matters worse. "Choice," without positive direction, is a myth, for all too often the market will deliver more – but more of the same.

(ibid.: 313–14)

Changes effected in November 1998 in the way payments to the Treasury by the regional television companies are calculated implicitly acknowledge the fact that the government's policy, in the 1980s and 1990s, of forcing companies to bid high for a franchise was not wise. Many bidders have run into financial trouble by overbidding. Moreover, more changes in ownership may be forthcoming. As Gibson (1998c) states:

A further bout of mergers and acquisitions seems likely. Granada, Carlton and United News and Media, the big three owning three or more franchises each, are expected to consolidate. A further Broadcasting Act is not likely until after the next election but it will almost certainly contain another overhaul of media ownership laws, possibly even the creation of a single commercial television network owned by one company.

Pressures on costs have led companies to look for cheaper ways of obtaining quality programming. This has led to a trend from producing in-house to out-sourcing, an increase in the search for co-finance and secondary markets, and striving to achieve economies of scale with high-volume/low-cost productions and greater use of repeats. Co-financing, in particular, especially when one has foreign partners, increases the probability of things going wrong during the production process as each partner has an over-riding concern with gaining a high share of audience in a different cultural market. In one of our case studies, the quality of the final product suffered greatly because of internal strife and the demand of the major co-financier to make it appeal to the American market (i.e. changing the script to make it have a happy ending).

Outsourcing has also had the effect of creating a huge expansion of the freelance labor market, employment insecurity due to temporary contracts and unemployment, lack of providing training opportunities (traditionally associated with institutions such as the BBC), deskilling and loss of opportunities of transferring expertise through hands-on experience and apprenticeships. As Paterson notes:

> In the UK television industry the previous certainties of employ-ment in the BBC or one of the ITV companies have been replaced in the 1990s by increasing casualization of employment (estimated by 1996 to be about 60 per cent of the workforce) with potentially disastrous consequences for creative endeavor.
>
> (Paterson, 1998: 136)

All our interviewees, from both broadcasting and production companies, have commented negatively on the repercussions of this trend for the "health" of the industry as a whole. Valuable skills which can only be learned through hands-on experience are getting progressively lost while those who do have the skills are becoming progressively more expensive to employ as they have come to represent a rare breed. Hence, although the casualization of the labor market has given producers more opportunities for getting a cheaper labor force for certain unskilled tasks, expert skilled labor is becoming an expensive resource to employ.

Moreover, advances in technology have changed considerably the organ-ization and resourcing of the production itself. The possibilities offered by the general adoption of digital technology for post-production work, for example, have cut down considerably the amount of people needed during the production process, further limiting the possibilities of newcomers getting exposure to the work involved. Preparations for the introduction of digital broadcasting technology is creating even more far-reaching changes in the industry (Puttnam, 1998).

These operating conditions facing the industry that I have briefly mentioned here generally affect what television drama is being produced, by whom, as well as its quality (for more detailed accounts see Saundry and Nolan, 1998; Swales, 1997). They represent constraints which apply to all persons involved in this business but listing them in such a general manner (typical of reviews of the conditions prevailing in the industry) has the effect of implying that they affect the work of everybody involved in the industry equally, which is not the case. Successful organizations, even working under these general constraints, are successful because they focus on the possibilities these constraints leave open for their activities and develop practices which capitalize on them.

In order to be able to predict how any one prospective production will be valued by significant decision-makers or how it will finally fare once it is commissioned, one needs to think about constraints in a different way, so that the possibilities available also come into focus. A generative scheme of influences on production will also enable positioning any new change in the conditions prevailing in the industry at the right level, estimating its effects for one's own practice, and responding accordingly. This could influence the "health" of the industry and remove the "climate of fear" that currently informs its functioning, to its detriment.

In the next section I outline a scheme which we have used in our study to map the in-depth case studies we carried out within the remit of our project. It enabled us to identify instances of "best practice" in the industry and some of its characteristics.

Constraints and possibilities in television drama production: a systems view

A particular television drama program, as produced and transmitted, is the end result of a series of interactions between a number of different systems, each with its own personal/institutional goals as well as responsibilities (broadcasters, producers, actors, directors), and concentrating on a specific goal common to all: to realize a particular drama production. However, each system has its own notion of what creativity entails and its own notion of value of a prospective product. The end result, the particular television drama production, through its transmission, becomes subject to public scrutiny and, thus, an object for evaluation through which the work of all the systems involved in the production itself gets assessed. Such assessments, usually predicated on the "ratings discourse," feed back into the entire system which was used to transform a concept into a final product.

Constraints within which a television drama production takes place are imposed at different levels, each level making its unique contribution to the success or failure of a concept to materialize into a final product and, eventually, to the final product being successful or not. Understanding influences in this way enables one to predict the effects of some change materializing at some level on all the other levels below it (and the consequences for drama production itself). Each level has infinite possibilities of defining how the one below it can be affected (i.e. define the constraints under which it can operate). And each definition of a level by the one above it confines what is possible for any level below it. It is very important to understand this propagation of constraints, through the levels, in all its magnitude because only then will the industry be able to effect change at the appropriate level. Conversely, the character of constraints set at a particular level also define the degrees of freedom one has to cope with them and produce a successful product.

At the highest level, one encounters the constraints set by:

A: the social world at large, especially as it pertains to the entire media industry (e.g. economic pressures, regulation, legal issues, politics, relevant technology);

which affects and determines

B: the general *climate/structure* of the drama producing/commissioning industry (e.g. character of competition, market forces, seller/buyer relations, regulations specific to drama production/commissioning).

Although, in the discourse of producers and broadcasters, one always encounters a link being made between governmental policies (at level A), for example, and the state of the existing climate in the industry (at level B), it is not the usual case that these two domains of influence are seen as operating at different levels. Instead, the two are seen as one, acting as the background against which organizations involved in drama production or commissioning believe they have to operate. However, by doing so, they negate for themselves the possibility of acting at level B (while they have no agency to affect level A). They focus on the constraint-setting character of these two levels, constraints that they take for granted and as unchangeable. This, however, is not necessarily so. What takes place at level B is the result of the industry's agency and this can take different directions, either opting for competition for the share of the audience attention or collaboration toward improving on what the audience is being offered. (A rare exception to this competition was the cooperation initiated by the playwright Dennis Potter whose request that his final two plays, *Cold Lazarus* and *Karaoke*, be conjointly produced by BBC and Channel 4 was realized after his death.)

Both levels A and B are culture- and country-specific. However, with the globalization of the market, producers need to have a purview on how both these levels are defined in other countries and cultures if they wish their product to have access to foreign markets (and, hence, enlarge its potential revenue). Under prevailing conditions (e.g. Westcott, 1998), producers do not have the time or skills to pursue such ventures, effectively leaving them dependent on the success or failure of distributors to understand how levels A and B are set in other countries.

Moving down the levels of influence on drama production, we encounter three other levels of influence on what the final product will look like (or if it will materialize at all). While levels A and B influence in common all types of media organizations involved in drama production within a particular country, levels C, D and E enable us to differentiate various organizations and drama productions, thereby gaining a clearer understanding of the different perspectives employed in assessing the value of a prospective drama product.

At level C, we encounter the constraints and possibilities an organization encounters by virtue of

C: the position the organization holds within the drama-producing and commissioning industrial structure (e.g. motivations, management structures, role in the industry, power, responsibility).

At this level, different organizations are positioned according to the role they play within the industry. An independent drama-producing organization, for example, has a completely different position and locus of power in the industry to the one a broadcasting/producing organization has. Even the various UK broadcasting organizations encounter different expectations by viewers, as a survey conducted in 1998 by the Independent Television Commission has found.

There are, of course, cases where an organization occupies more than one position at level C. The BBC, for example, is still both a broadcaster and an in-house drama-producing organization. Such a position enables it to have a strong say on what is being shown on the screen. The two functions, while embedded into one at level C, hence identifying the overall mission of the organization, split at level D (see below) into two separate functions, each guided by different objectives and interests. However, the organizational culture that exists by virtue of a common understanding between broadcasting and producing functions at level C entails that the organizational forms of each function remain the same even if they relate to different functions. For example, the production structure of *Eastenders*, a BBC in-house product, mirrors the complexity of the organizational structure of the BBC and is a completely different structure to the production structures of soap operas originating in the independent sector (e.g. *Brookside*, *Coronation Street*) which are of more or less similar quality and which have the same frequency of transmission schedule. This structure, however, does not make it more efficient.

The position of an organization at level C determines the power it will have in any negotiation it may wish to carry out concerning a particular TV drama production. As we move "down" the levels, functions become more specific to a particular production. Thus, level D relates to

D: the management of drama productions/commissioning within the particular organization (e.g. rules, portfolios of drama productions sought after, principles of working, policies).

Media organizations vary widely in how they operate at level D, but knowledge about specific instances (e.g. concerning BBC, Channel 4 or ITV commissioning practices) exists within the media community. This is how decisions can be made, for example, by a producer to identify which commissioning organization he/she should approach for a particular project. Conversely, commissioning organizations may have some knowledge about the capabilities of a production company on the basis of the success of what it has produced so far. Of course this creates a bias in commissioning decisions toward a preference for established production organizations, leaving little space for newcomers to become established. While in the broadcasting and commissioning arena the "players" are more or less stable and predictable in their preferences (if one keeps up with the changes in the climate of the industry which affect them), the drama production arena is volatile to changes as more and more new people wish to enter it.

Finally, at level E, we have

E: the particular drama production process itself and its management (e.g. content, format, resources, production management practices) which will produce the commissioned product.

Success or failure of particular projects is typically associated with what took place at level E, usually neglecting to identify that constraints set at higher levels narrowed down the options available. The production management of a particular television drama is the terrain where all constraints set at levels A through to D are brought together. The role of the producer is to perform a balancing act between the different interests and concerns voiced by the different stakeholders involved in the production as well as coping with all emergencies that come his/her way (Abercrombie, 1996).

The tendency to resort to ratings discourse in determining referents, at all the above five levels, instigates a process where the image of what the audience wants or what the audience should have available proliferates in the negotiations which take place at each level. Decisions are made on the basis of such images which are often not the same for different organizations. But an implicit agreement seems to be made in perpetuating a common image. This leads to the tendency of following the current "fad" which results in producers "knowing" what would appeal to financiers/broadcasters while financiers/broadcasters are either given the option to choose out of similar prospective products, or to define any new prospective product which is not similar to what else is on offer as a question of deciding between "taking a risk" and "playing safe" on their part. A vicious circle is thus set in operation which, if not broken, could lead to further recession in the industry.

The role of the audience as the final assessor of a product is undoubtedly important. But what is missed in the current practices is that the audience "votes" by selecting to watch a particular program in comparison to what other programs are available on the screen at the same time. The closer each program resembles others (due to current "fads" and competitive scheduling), the more uncertain the audience's watching choice becomes. Scheduling practices encourage anchoring on genre as the lever which draws audiences. Such practices effectively draw attention away from the quality of a television drama production as what appeals to audiences and into the "pull" that the nature of its content would generate. If a product does not succeed in attracting a satisfactory level of audience, its failure is blamed on intrinsic deficiencies of the product. In some instances, this may be justified but, in others, inappropriate choice of transmission time or falling prey to competitive scheduling should carry at least part of the blame, but this is rarely acknowledged by the commissioning organizations. However, producers often cited this to us in cases where low ratings were registered for their own productions.

Conversely, stress is placed on aspects of a product's "quality" that would make it "different" (and, therefore, more attractive to an audience) from whatever else is in circulation. While the audience is seen as active in choosing out of what is available, and while the industry decides on what is being made available, on the basis of an agreed-upon version of what would appeal to the audience, this vicious circle will continue. As Nelson writes:

> Whereas flexible specialization's adaptable small-scale production units may potentially serve different market segments in television by narrowcasting, British TV drama as yet strives to maximize audience for popular drama. In recognition of the heterogeneity of audience members, however, attempts are made to establish what is attractive to a number of audience segments and aggregate them by including in the drama elements that will appeal to each.
>
> (1997: 74)

Breaking this circle entails taking risks. But how many producer or broadcaster organizations are prepared to do so? There is a lot of creativity in the industry but, unfortunately, it is habitually located in the artistic and "craft" aspect of the drama production process (following the creative versus managerial split that exists within it). Managerial creativity is often not given due credit for part of the success of a production although it is, often, given full credit for a failure!

The character of creativity in television drama productions: prevailing assumptions and the difference they make

The fact that television drama productions circulate, simultaneously, in two different economies (Fiske, 1987) makes the value of their currency uncertain. This leads decision-makers to opt for "playing safe," effectively perpetuating the myth that audiences are simply receivers and assessors of what is being provided to them rather than active decision-makers on what they would want to watch.

Quantitative or qualitative audience research focuses on assessing audience responses to what has already been decided to broadcast, given the industry's prevailing view of its target audience. It informs only a range of variations on the same theme and does not challenge the prevailing tendency within the industry to assume what the audience wants and act accordingly. The dominance of the ratings discourse at all levels perpetuates the myth that there is one audience out there, and each producer/broadcaster should attempt to grab the largest proportion of its attention, thus delimiting the possibility of the products of the media industry fulfilling their cultural role.

There is a great deal of creativity in the industry. This does not only materialize in the artistic spectrum of television drama productions. In fact, unless creativity is utilized in the non-artistic part of the enterprise, productions have a very small possibility of succeeding, given the current climate. Tulloch criticizes academic accounts of what is going on in the industry as follows: "Recent ethnographic accounts have been slow to extend analysis to the creative ways in which people resist the deleterious effects of their social situations *within the media industry itself*" (1990: 20, original emphasis).

This chapter has attempted to identify, at a number of different levels, the conditions which can enable organizations involved in drama production to break through the "deleterious effects" which Tulloch references and which amount to a "climate of fear," and to identify creativity in both artistic and managerial ventures which can, in their joint effort, guarantee television drama production of a quality fit to sustain the reputation of the UK drama production industry.

Acknowledgments

I am thankful to Patrick Humphreys for his very useful comments on earlier versions of this chapter. I would also like to thank all the people from the industry who shared their experience with us, and the Economic and Social Research Council for its funding.

References

Abercrombie, N. (1996) *Television and Society*, Cambridge: Polity Press.
Brooks, R. (1994) "ITV takes vow of populism," the *Observer*, 16 January.
Brown, M. (1998) "Thinking big for the BBC," the *Guardian*, 27 July.
Cantor, M. G. and Cantor, J. M. (1992) *Prime-Time Television Content and Control* (2nd edition), London: Sage Publications.
Curran, J. and Seaton, J. (1997) *Power Without Responsibility: the Press and Broadcasting in Britain* (5th edition), London: Routledge.

Dunkley, C. (1988a) "The dangers of formula drama," *Financial Times*, 27 April.

Dunkley, C. (1988b) "Formula drama bodes ill for the future," *Financial Times*, 7 September.

Elliott, P. (1972) *The Making of a Television Series: a Case Study in the Sociology of Culture*, London: Constable and Co.

Fiske, J. (1987) *Television Culture*, London: Routledge.

Fuller, C. (1998) "Auntie's film role," *Broadcast*, 20 November.

Garnham, N. (1987) "Concepts of culture: public policy and the cultural industries," *Cultural Studies*, 1, 1, 23–37.

Gibson, J. (1998a) "Sharp shock for BBC as Taggart beats Thackeray," the *Guardian*, 3 November.

Gibson, J. (1998b) "ITV networks get £90 m 'rebate' in fees reappraisal," the *Guardian*, 26 November.

Gibson, J. (1998c) "ITV franchises: double or quits," the *Guardian*, 26 November.

Griffiths, N. (1997) "Where next for fantasy TV?," *Radio Times*, 2–8 August.

ITC (1994) *Annual Report & Accounts*, London: Independent Television Commission.

ITC (1997) *Annual Report & Accounts*, London: Independent Television Commission.

Longrigg, C. (1997) "BBC1 'people's channel,'" the *Guardian*, 3 September.

Mulgan, G. (1990) *The Question of Quality*, London: British Film Institute.

Nelson, R. (1996) "From *Twin Peaks*, USA, to lesser peaks, UK: building the postmodern TV audience," *Media, Culture & Society*, 18, 677–82.

Nelson, R. (1997) *TV Drama in Transition: Forms, Values and Cultural Change*, Basingstoke: Macmillan Press.

Parker, I. (1998) "Look under the bonnet," the *Observer*, 8 November.

Paterson, R. (1998) "Television," in *The Media: An Introduction*, A. Briggs and P. Cobley (eds), New York: Addison Wesley Longman, pp. 127–139.

Phillips, W. (1998) "Drama in a crisis," *Broadcast*, 30 October.

Puttnam, D. (1998) "Digital vision," *Stage, Screen & Radio*, October.

Robins, K. and Cornford, J. (1992) "What is 'flexible' about independent producers?," *Screen* 33, 2, 190–200.

Saundry, R. and Nolan, P. (1998) "Regulatory change and performance in TV production," *Media, Culture & Society*, 20, 3, 409–26.

Stoessl, S. (1998) "Audience Feedback," in *The Media: An Introduction*, A. Briggs and P. Cobley (eds), New York: Addison Wesley Longman, pp. 250–61.

Sutherland, A. (1989) "Why Jewel won't be crowned," *Sunday Times (Screen Section)*, 5 March.

Swales, V. (1997) "Television in the United Kingdom," in *Television in Europe*, J. A. Coleman and B. Rollet (eds), Exeter: Intellect Books, pp. 21–34.

Tulloch, J. (1990) *Television Drama: Agency, Audience and Myth*, London: Routledge.

Tunstall, J. (1993) *Television Producers*, London: Routledge.

Wainwright, M. (1997) "Monty type film strip failed to excite ITV," the *Guardian*, 30 August.

Westcott, T. (1998) "Selling indies short abroad," *Broadcast*, 6 November.

Williams, R. (1997) "Telly without the vision," the *Guardian*, 25 August.

6

MOTHERS RETURNING TO TELEVISION PRODUCTION WORK IN A CHANGING ENVIRONMENT

Janet Willis and Shirley Dex

Introduction

The process of women returning to the labor market after having children has been studied extensively (Brannen and Moss, 1988, 1991; McRae, 1989,1991; Dex *et al.*, 1998). Decisions about labor market participation and hours of work at this point in women's employment careers have been shown to have important consequences. Returns to part-time work or having lengthy breaks carry a penalty in terms of foregone earnings, occupational status and career advancement (Dex, 1987; Joshi and Newell, 1987). In this sense some of the increase in so-called "flexible jobs" in Britain's restructured labor markets, especially increases in part-time jobs, have hindered rather than helped women to gain equal opportunities with men, largely because part-time jobs have predominantly been low wage and low status. We know from other studies of flexible work that there are some benefits and some disadvantages for women who take part-time jobs (Dex and McCulloch, 1997). However, it is not clear whether all types of flexible jobs will have this effect on women's status and career prospects. Fixed-term contracts and different types of self-employment have not been investigated to the same extent (Dex and McCulloch, 1997). This chapter sets out to examine women who became mothers when working in television production in the early 1990s as a particularly interesting group as far as new flexible jobs are concerned.

The British television industry changed over the 1980s and 1990s from employing largely salaried staff on unlimited contracts to employing around 60 percent freelance workers (Skillset estimate, 1996). In this sense, the television industry experienced in an extreme way what other British industries have experienced to a lesser degree. This group of women television workers who became mothers has had to face a fast-changing environment, major organizational changes and changes in the contracts of employment and conditions of work. The research described in this chapter examined mothers' experiences and decision-making under such conditions, and how this is likely to influence equal opportunities now and in the future. We are interested in knowing how the changing conditions affected these mothers' ability to sustain or progress their career in television. Mothers who returned to work after childbirth found it very difficult to sustain a career in the current working conditions. In addition to factors noted in other studies, like childcare problems and low levels of partner support in some cases, working in television introduced added difficulties because of the nature of freelance work, the vulnerability to the bosses' discretion and favor, and the demands and expectations of organizational cultures.

This chapter first reviews the relevant literature about mothers returning to work and women in professional careers. The data analyzed in this chapter are then described, after which the organizational and industry setting of working in television are summarized. The results of analyses are presented under a number of subheadings: career histories, career goals, timing of family formation, culture and conditions of the workplace, attitudes and commitment to work, flexibility at work, childcare and balance, and the return to work. A discussion of the more general conclusions follows.

Professional careers after childbirth

Brannen and Moss (1988, 1991) studied dual earner households in the mid-1980s, a time when relatively few mothers were returning to work full time after childbirth. They found that a number of factors shaped the experience of returning to work: labor market opportunities, current ideologies of motherhood and of the workplace, and support from partner and social networks. The decision to return was a personal one, though financial needs of the household were cited as significant and women were largely responsible for the demands, problems and tensions that dual earner households imposed. These findings are echoed in larger-scale surveys from the early 1980s (Martin and Roberts, 1984). McRae's (1989, 1991) studies of maternity leave found a marked increase in those taking maternity leave and returning after short gaps (eight to nine months) to the same employer and the same job. The return to work was aided where family-friendly working opportunities were available and this was more often the case in jobs with higher status and in the public sector. Other studies have supported this point (McRae, 1990).

Fogarty et al.'s (1981) early study of professional women included television in an era when most employees had unlimited contracts. Women tended to start lower down the hierarchy and took a long time to reach the point where they were competing with men. Few women held senior posts and women were found to have better prospects in gendered niches like education and children's television. There was inflexibility about the return to work after childbirth, the majority failing to return and many women stating they would value the opportunity to work part time. Other studies of professional women in different organizational settings have shown many recurring patterns: gendered niches for women in management structures (Spencer and Podmore, 1987; Crompton and Sanderson, 1994); a strong shared institutional ethos generated by men and for the benefit of men (Smith, 1976; Walters, 1987; Cockburn, 1991; Crompton, 1997; Mc-Dowell, 1997); mothers sidelined for not fulfilling notions of ideal employees (Lewis and Taylor, 1996); and the demands of the job preventing genuine flexibility in work options for new mothers (Hantrais, 1990; Hantrais and Walters, 1994; McDowell, 1997). Studies of organizations and women in management have also identified ways in which women have been disadvantaged by organizational cultures: the pressure to work long hours (Bailyn, 1993), men's formal and informal networks (Smith, 1976; Kanter, 1993; McDowell, 1997), the performance measurement culture (Halford *et al.*, 1997) and recruitment methods (McDowell, 1997).

The data

A group of thirteen women who had either taken maternity leave from working in television or were taking a career break to have children was drawn from a larger survey of television production workers and interviewed at the beginning of 1995. Interviews were conducted, mostly in the women's homes, using a semi-structured schedule. The topics covered in the interview included their career history, their last employment before childbirth, the career break and its implications, future career plans, attitudes to work before and after childbirth, arrangements for childcare, and broader questions about family and social life. One woman had just begun a maternity leave before the birth of her second child and two others had already returned to work by the time of the interview. The other ten had already given birth and were contracted to return to work or were considering their work opportunities. In total, for five of the women it was their first child, for seven it was their second child, and for one it was a third child. All were married or in established partnerships.

Since these women were part of a larger survey, it was possible to supplement the interview material with information they had given in their survey questionnaire responses. This material both preceded the interviews and continued for several years afterwards. In effect, therefore, longitudinal data were collected about these women and their experience, covering a period of five years.

The larger survey of which these women were a part was the Television Industry Tracking Study (ITS) conducted by the British Film Institute between 1994 and 1998, and it aimed to study the effects of TV industry changes on a panel of 450 creative production workers. Respondents were sent diary/questionnaires twice a year from May 1994 until May 1998 (nine waves in total). More details of this survey are available in Pettigrew *et al.* (1995, 1997) and Sheppard and Dex (1998). All of the women in this survey who were taking maternity leave in late 1994 were interviewed. These interviews, plus their completed diaries and questionnaires, form the data which are analyzed in this chapter.

The women, aged between thirty-one and forty-three in 1995, came from the BBC, regional ITV companies, the independent and satellite sectors. They were all part of the delayed childbirth cohort, all having their first birth in their thirties after a fairly substantial period of establishing a career. Most lived in or near London and three lived within reach of regional television centers. Nine were graduates and eight of these were producer/directors or assistant producers at the time of their first child. Four of the graduates had started as secretaries, two going on to producer grades from this starting point. The four women who did not have any higher education had also started as secretaries and only one of them had reached a director grade. One became a production manager, one a researcher, and the last a PA before the birth of the first child.

Working in television in the 1990s

Before 1980 the British television industry was characterized by a few vertically integrated hierarchically organized broadcasting institutions. By the 1990s, after regulatory changes, the industry has changed to be one in which the private sector broadcasters compete first to get the license, then to attain maximum ratings and revenue (with the exception of Channel Four). The BBC also reorganized, with internal markets and a split between broadcasting and production. Part of the programming is now supplied by many small and a few large independent production companies competing with each other, as well as with the internal production of broadcasters. There is now uncertain demand, technological developments, pressure on costs and increasingly fierce competition from an increasing number of channels. The organizational structure and ethos may differ by company, by department, or by program genre. Most companies employ a core of staff, although this core is extremely small in most independent companies. Most employees in all organizational settings are on short-term contracts of less than a year and are freelance workers.

Program proposals are put forward and commissioned in different ways. Most jobs are obtained through personal contacts or recommendations rather than by advertisements or interviews. The workplace is largely unregulated and workers, especially young workers, are largely unrepresented. Contracts are in smaller work units. Job roles and job descriptions have been forced to change alongside the change to flatter organizational structures. There is an additional swelling labor supply with pressure from young media studies graduates willing to work for free or for very low wages to get a foothold in an industry based on who you know. However, more young women are reaching producer/director status (Pettigrew *et al.*, 1995; Woolf and Holly, 1994). It is against this background and these organizational settings that our small sample of mothers were studied.

Career histories

With the development of small independent companies since the early 1980s, the access points for a career in television have multiplied, and this may account in part for the increased numbers of younger women in the television workforce. For some of these women the culture and informality of the independent sector enabled them to make quite rapid progress but for others it was very random. Serena, a graduate, had progressed fairly quickly to production manager grade in the independent sector and although she preferred the independent culture she nonetheless felt that her career might have been better planned at the BBC: "I think it's very difficult to plan a career in television [. . .] particularly in the independent sector. If you are not working for somebody like the BBC or an ITV company so much depends on the company you are working for, and their particular structure."

A series of short-term contracts in the North, the West Country, the BBC in London and corporate sectors for Jane, a graduate, illustrates the unpredictable character of career progress in a casualized job market: "It's just sheer opportunism. If an opportunity arises I have just grabbed it – no plan at all."

For a short period she became a producer, although this was not sustained: "I started working with them just doing a bit of research then I PM'd [worked as production manager] on a couple of jobs and then the executive producer turned me into a producer because he wanted to go off on another contract."

For those who worked in the independent sector there was apprehension of the formality of the BBC, even though it was understood that the BBC might have offered better training and prospects. However, for Carole, a graduate working inside the BBC, it was hard to make the switch from a secretarial role to a creative production job in current affairs.

Many comments relating to career progression were underscored by feelings of gender difference both in the BBC and in the independent sectors. It was perceived by most of the women that there were certain accepted ways of making progress and achieving promotion, and it was generally felt that men adapted easily to this. At the BBC it was mostly to do with the politics of who they were associated with and how these networks were maintained. Beverly, Karen and Jean, working in the independent sector and at the BBC, found they had made less progress than male colleagues who had started at the same time and on the same grades, perhaps partly as a result of male networking but ultimately because of the constraints a family had imposed (Smith, 1976; McDowell, 1997).

Some felt that the casualization of the industry, and the changes at the

BBC in particular, where short-term contracts were now the norm, had effectively removed the ladders of career progression: "There isn't going to be the same sort of job structure and continuity of work" (Sally). ITS evidence shows that networking and personal work contacts are the most important ways of finding out about work and obtaining work. For these women there was a risk in taking a maternity break of losing touch with contacts.

Another feature of this environment with less structured career routes was to find workers being paid and graded at a lower rate than the job they were doing. Amanda and Laura both did director and producer work over long periods, but were paid as assistant or associate producers. It was felt that it was probably easier for women to gain entry to the TV industry but that it required determination and often just luck to sustain a career progression and achieve the security of a staff job before having a family.

Career goals

The women's career ambitions at the time of their maternity breaks were marked by caution: a consideration of the constraints imposed by family responsibilities and partner's work, by a reckoning of the realities of the work options available, and by reflections on their own skills, experience and marketability. Those who were not fully confident of their skills learned "on the job," and who had not been on formal training schemes, tended to feel easily undermined in an aggressive male environment.

Six respondents mentioned a lack of confidence as a problem for career advancement. Training or education was a factor. Anita and Carla would have liked to have become producers, but as they didn't have a degree or any formal training they felt unable to push themselves forward. Jane had felt her confidence undermined when she had been a victim of sexual harassment on an all-male shoot: "It was there and it happened and because you are so desperate for work [. . .] I had to go through a lot of abuse on location [. . .] nobody said a word because he was the director."

Amanda had found directing a male crew difficult in the early days and suffered from low esteem: "I can remember weeks of weeping in the toilets [. . .] I had an awful feeling that people out there were probably doing it much better."

Laura, Karen, and Amanda, who were well established as full-time producers, were more confident of sustaining their pre-family position and two of them declared an interest in becoming series producers. Serena, who returned to freelance production management, said she would eventually like to become a head of production with a large independent, but no one interviewed thought that being a company executive or a broadcast executive was an achievable goal with a family. Those mothers whose attitudes to work and a future career were much more positive were generally those who had felt confident and valued at work. Amanda, the ITV producer, said that she knew that she did a good job under stressful conditions.

Others were content to continue in their current grades because they enjoyed the work, or they found it easier to manage home and work, or they were no longer prepared (or able) to work excessive hours or to compete with young people with no responsibilities. Some anxiety was registered that taking a slower route might cut off future career options. Others found that former ambitions to be a director or a producer had simply evaporated. Sally, a graduate, was very cautious about returning as a producer after her second child because she had been put under severe pressures when she had returned after her first. She said that she wasn't sure whether her views about her future career were more affected by her children and her changed priorities or by the way the television business had changed. From all interviewees it was clear that decisions about career goals were inextricably bound up with family responsibilities and with the security and demands of the partner's career.

Timing of family formation

All the women interviewed were over thirty for the birth of the first child and four were forty. Some talked of delaying a family because they were enjoying their jobs or wanted to be well established. The book *Social Focus on Women* (Whitmarsh, 1995) shows that women are marrying and having children later. Brannen (1987) found that women in high status jobs gave birth on average at thirty, and so spent an average of nine years in the labor market, making it easier for them to return. Karen, a successful producer who had a long apprenticeship and training in an ITV company, but who had been working in the independent sector as a producer for some time before the birth of her children, was able to continue at the same grade afterwards:

> I think I certainly delayed having the first one until I was reasonably established as a producer because I had seen lots of other friends have babies when they were assistant producers and they just could never seem to crack being a producer or director afterwards.

But for some, the strains of trying to recover a career after one child deterred them from contemplating a second. Anita had worked as a PA and a production coordinator and had her first child at forty. After being made redundant and then returning on short-term contracts she was worried that the progress she was making in a more family-friendly niche in the Education department at the BBC would be lost: "It would put me back another three years. With the job market as it is, it would take me right back to the beginning [. . .] I have noticed that I am working with a lot of people who just have one [baby] in the BBC."

Women in their late twenties and early thirties in the main ITS panel have also registered anxiety about the idea of having children in such an uncertain and demanding job market. Petra was working as an associate producer for a major ITV company: "On the lookout for more stable jobs particularly as I want to start a family within the next few years and don't think I can do the job I am doing with a baby."

Studies have shown the importance of women spending longer on the labor market before family formation, and of having protected job maternity leave to minimize the effect of a family on pay and grades (Bird and West, 1987; Dex, 1985; Joshi and Paci, 1995). Contract workers were more likely to suffer, in this respect, than permanent workers with no employment protection or contracted maternity pay. Of the five short-term contract workers who did not have contract enhanced maternity leave we found that three did not return to television work: one returned part-time for an independent company run by a woman, one worked on short contracts for non-broadcast production, and the third worked on short contracts.

Culture and conditions of the workplace

Organizational studies have indicated how women are bound up with the workplace organizational structures and processes (Kanter, 1993). Lewis and Taylor (1996), in their case study of the impact of family-friendly policies in a firm of chartered accountants, found that organizational cultures were grounded in deep-seated beliefs about gender, the nature of work and the ideal employee. The interviews with the ITS mothers demonstrated the significance of experience of the workplace culture and how the leadership of the department or company largely determined the work environment (Fogarty et al., 1981). Those workplace experiences before the birth of their children had considerable impact on the idea of returning to work. And those who did return were also keenly aware of the current conditions and ideologies of the workplace.

Those women who had faced impossible work schedules, with long hours and with little or no administrative support, before the birth of their children, were the most cautious about returning. Sandra, a graduate with PA experience at a former ITV company who was then elevated to producer when she joined a satellite company, found what started as an exciting challenge quickly became a nightmare, and did not return to television production work:

> They didn't understand anything about copyright [. . .] you were being asked to do things you just couldn't do with the money that was there [. . .] I was working ridiculous hours [. . .] I seemed to be getting in earlier and earlier and coming home later and later.

The long hours "visibility" and "macho" culture of some broadcaster departments and independents put huge pressure on some who returned (McDowell, 1997; Smith, 1976; Lewis and Lewis, 1996; Jones, 1997). Beverly, who worked full time after the birth of her first child with an independent company doing current affairs programs, had difficulty with her boss over controlling her working hours: "It was kind of manic [. . .] you were expected to sit at the desk from 9 in the morning until 7.30 at night and if you went home he would always say, 'Oh, having a half day Beverly?' and I would say, 'No, I've got my briefcase.'"

Jean also worked full time and found the ways in which men organized their working hours affected women working on lower grades in the office:

> A lot of them [the men] haven't got families, are single and they have got no need to rush home. So they have a long lunch and they come back, rush into the office and don't actually start getting going until about 4 o'clock and the poor secretary is panicking that she won't be able to go by 5.30 pm.

The "long hours" male culture was also sometimes adopted by some women (Jones, 1997; Lewis and Taylor, 1996). Three women, in interviews, talked of the difficulties they encountered from other more senior working mothers who had committed to the long hours working culture. Mothers returning part-time were made to feel that part-time work was the "soft" option. An experienced woman executive producer with three children had organized a late and last-minute meeting and insisted on producer Beverly's attendance, though she had to collect her child from childcare: "She was adamant that I had to stay [. . .] in the end I was in tears and I explained I had to go. She just went on and on."

Carole, producer, who had worked in BBC Current Affairs said: "It's weird, it's as if they [working mothers] have to appear to be just as macho as the men."

Two women talked of recent interviews, where, despite equal opportunities legislation, they had been asked whether they would be able to cope with long hours, working away from home, and their childcare.

Another found the competitive male environment of the Current Affairs department at the BBC alienating. Carole, a graduate who had made the grade from secretary to researcher and then producer, talked of huge egos and said that you always had to seem very confident and totally assured, "If you showed any worry or anxiety, that would be seen as weakness and a problem" (Jones, 1997; Spencer and Podmore, 1987). As a fledgling producer she had not been given the editorial support she needed and was a casualty of staff cuts, three days after the transmission of her first program. She has not returned to television production.

Employment research has shown that women are more affected than men in their attitudes to work by favorable and unfavorable elements in the workplace (Dex, 1988; Agassi, 1982). Women who returned to the BBC were very appreciative of those departments which showed flexibility about working hours and encouragement in career progression. But experience varied with departments. Anita, whose work after her return varied between a production assistant and production coordinator, said that she had been afraid to say that she had a child in one department, but was delighted to find a more sympathetic environment in another. In this department she had even begun to think that she might in time achieve a producer grade. Fogarty *et al.* (1981) and Crompton and Sanderson (1994) talked of gendered niches in the BBC, such as Education and the Children's department, where women were able to secure more senior posts. Sally, who worked at the BBC, praised her male head of department in the early 1980s, a time before the widespread casualization of the industry: "It was one of the best departments to be in for training, they were supportive of all grades [. . .] secretaries, PAs, researchers. It was a policy in the department to give people opportunities."

The independent sector also provided good examples of stimulating but nurturing environments, but for this group of women these tended to be companies led by women. Carla, who worked four days a week, talked of a strong team spirit, led ably by a woman, where it was possible to share ideas and criticize and not feel threatened. She described her boss as supportive and understanding, who boosted her confidence and pushed her to make the most of her career: "It's a nice environment to work in and it makes a difference to how you work [. . .] the way we think [. . .] just getting things done [. . .] the understanding, co-operation."

Attitudes and commitment to work

All the women interviewed demonstrated a high degree of commitment to their work before the birth of their first child. They talked of long hours and of complete dedication to work at the expense of other parts of their lives, in many ways describing the features of the ideal employee described by Lewis and Taylor (1996) in their case study of chartered accountants. There was, however, a marked change in attitude toward work before and after childbirth. Amanda, an associate producer who worked for an ITV company, had decided to sacrifice family life to reach her career goals. But a late partnership and the birth of a child had changed her:

> I used to think, "if you don't like doing such a demanding job, you shouldn't be doing it" [. . .] Now I am on the other side. There should be a way of meeting your commitments in television and having a family. And that's for men as well, because their careers are out on the road, now that their hours are flexible [. . .] They don't see their families from one week to the next.

Nearly all interviewees referred to a dramatic change of priorities and described very strong feelings about the responsibilities and constraints of motherhood, and how, even with a supportive partner or husband, management of time was complex. Work in the workplace, work in the home, childcare, the demands of the partner's job were all interwoven (Dex, 1988; Allat *et al.*, 1987).

The discourse of time was a potent one for these women as they talked about the workplace and home. Commentators have noted that time and commitment are socially constructed, and those who don't work beyond office hours are seen as less productive and committed and therefore don't conform to the notion of the ideal employee (Cooper and Lewis, 1995; Lewis 1997). The mothers said they felt that, with full-time work, they were either guilty for not being home or guilty for not being able to meet the exacting demands of the job. BBC producer, Laura, who returned to full-time work, described it as a juggling act: "It is never easy and I don't think you feel 100 percent that you have done the right thing once you have had children."

Producer Beverly, who worked full time but on short contracts, talked of the anxiety and strain she felt as the afternoon progressed when she had to pick up her daughter by 5.30 p.m.:

> From lunch time onwards you've got this sack of potatoes on your shoulders thinking, "Well if I had that meeting at 4 pm is it going to be finished by a quarter to five so that I can rush out of the door?" [. . .] It's a big [. . .] suddenly a big strain on you, a big pull to get home.

She also talked of falling for a 1980s philosophy which made women feel that they could easily manage both lives. Her view in 1995 with three children was that that was unrealistic.

The women had difficulty in resolving their former total commitment to their occupational work with their new commitments to the demands of household and family, and then with the increasingly competitive and casualized work environment to which they were returning. All the women who returned to work either full- or part-time felt that there was really no room for any kind of social life. Dual-earner studies have described a high degree of tension in these households (Brannen and Moss, 1988, 1991; McRae, 1989).

For these reasons several women talked of the need to find a balance between work and home, of the need to preserve some notion of the quality of life (Wilkinson and Mulgan, 1995; Lewis and Lewis, 1996). Carla, the production manager working in the independent sector, talked of the importance of her family's interests: "I want to be a rounded, happy person so if it was in my family's interests to move and live in the country then I think I would do that."

Carole, who was a producer who left the BBC just before childbirth, said that although she had worked long hours right up until the birth of her baby: "I think I realized about life outside work being much more important."

Flexibility at work

Carla, a production manager/researcher, and Karen, a producer, for example, were both able to return to work for independent companies run by women on four-day weeks, but their work was mostly office based and this made it easier for them to manage work and family responsibilities. All the women interviewed were interested in the idea of having some kind of "control" over their job, principally in relation to working hours. However, most of the women expected that their employers would not be receptive to the idea of returning to work part-time hours. Serena, the production manager who returned to short-term contracts in the independent sector, said of her employers: "They want people in the office and they want them there full time [. . .] they have a sort of loyalty. But in the end there isn't a lot of sympathy or flexibility."

However, Beverly, the producer with three children, found that her short-term contracts, producing non-broadcast programs, enabled her to avoid working during the school holidays. Amanda, one of the three women who returned to full-time work after maternity leave, and who worked for an ITV company, found no flexibility from her employers. Indeed a restructuring and rationalization of the company and cutbacks in support staff had increased the pressures on her working week. Amanda recorded working 65 hours in the week she completed the diary, six months after her interview.

Measures of flexibility were found at the BBC, although part-time work was not considered possible for most women at that time. Laura thought that her head of department would assign her programs which did not require much travelling and would understand if she wished to do some work at home. Jean was to be assigned studio-based programs so that she did not have to stay away from home. Pat, however, was offered part-time work in a trial job-share, because this BBC department was concerned about excessive turnover of trained staff in this specialist area. She found the arrangement worked very well and because she had time off with her child she was very motivated to work hard when she was there.

Short-term work contracts gave a measure of flexibility to Beverly for a while, producing non-broadcast videos, but she noted after two years that she might find it hard to return to television work. Pat had been able to job-share her director's post at the BBC without loss of status, but she had been told that she would not be able to job-share in any grade above her current one. There was also a view that most TV production did not in general suit part-time or job-share contracts.

However, as Jones (1997) found, employers on the whole pay little attention to the needs of employees' care responsibilities. Amanda, for instance, found herself falling asleep at the wheel of her car when she returned to full-time work and her baby was not sleeping at night. When she told her personnel department they sounded sympathetic, and gave her the number of a crisis line, but didn't offer practical help by offering her shorter working hours on a temporary basis.

For the women who were returning to casual contracts, there were great anxieties arising from the uncertainties of this environment. Some mothers interviewed experienced the stress and fear of not having regular work and therefore not being able to make firm childcare arrangements or indeed afford them. Serena, for example, had obtained a short-term contract after the birth of her second child and yet the start date and length of the contract were unclear: "I don't know how I am going to organize my childcare from here on in [. . .] I mean it is going to be very difficult for someone to just work for six weeks."

Uncertainty was an even greater problem where a partner was also facing uncertainty in an insecure job. Anita, having been made redundant soon after her return, and needing the income as her partner's work was insecure, had to seek a series of short-term contracts. Karen, who was working part-time on short-term contracts, said: "At least once a week I worry, am I ever going to have a pension, and am I ever going to retire?" Serena, who returned to short-term contracts said: "I don't like the uncertainty and I feel quite envious of other people who are in permanent work [. . .] it seems a very unforgiving environment that you are going back to."

Childcare and balance

All the women interviewed who were intending to return to work, experienced a great deal of anxiety in getting the childcare provision right, especially when there were unforeseen long working hours. All showed a strong ideological commitment to the idea that childcare was their responsibility (Brannen and Moss, 1991), but it was also clear that in nine cases the partners' participation was vital to complement other arrangements and, in two cases, partners shouldered the responsibility entirely for periods of time – one to enable the mother to continue her demanding full-time job (Amanda), and the other (Karen) to enable her to produce a program abroad for six months. The producer, Sally, said that her husband would consider giving up his job (teaching) if they found that her career had more prospects. These findings show how the ideology of the male breadwinner has been somewhat modified amongst this professional group, as Brannen and Moss (1991) also found. Furthermore, these examples also demonstrate some flexibility and dynamism about the notion of which partner's career should have priority in a dual earner household (Hardhill *et al.*, 1997), but also shows how hard it is for both partners to pursue a career to the same degree. The three who were most cautious about returning to work were those mothers who said that their partners were unable to provide support because of the demands of their own careers.

Each respondent expressed very strongly a commitment to the ideology of good parenting and expressed anxieties about getting this right. Ten of the respondents particularly noted that they were anxious to get the balance of work and home right in their lives. Their attitudes perhaps reflected a more general change in attitude to the "having it all" philosophy of the 1980s, but may also have been a reflection of the very "unforgiving" nature of the industrial world they inhabit.

The long, unpredictable and often unsociable hours made childcare arrangements difficult and those who had sporadic work patterns and uncertain contracts could not afford to make expensive childcare arrangements for short periods and at short notice. The practical aspects of covering childcare, which did not necessarily fit office hours therefore required intricate planning and negotiation and most of the women relied on a combination of childcare types. No one used facilities provided by an employer – respondents complained of waiting lists at the BBC and shortages of nursery places near their homes – but also questioned the desirability of taking a small baby into central London every day for childcare.

The intricate childcare arrangements made by these women also confirm that they felt that domestic pressures or emergencies should not be seen to interfere with work performance. Even Carla, who talked of a "mother friendly" work environment, said that she was unlikely to take time off when she was ill as she sometimes had to take time off when her daughter was unwell.

The return to work

Full-time work with the same employer over time has been shown to encourage women to return and to enable career progression even after childbirth. Evidence from national and cross-national studies shows how relatively little UK mothers are supported in their need to return to work. Ferri and Smith (1996) show that most couples now feel that two earners in the family are necessary for the maintenance of the household and yet parents have to find their own private solutions to childcare. Almqvist and Boje (1998) in their pan-European survey have demonstrated the salience of national childcare and maternity provision for mothers' participation in the labor market and found that British mothers have comparatively low rates of employment and precarious employment conditions. Other cross-national studies, comparing women's employment in the US and in Britain (Dex and Shaw, 1986) and French and British mothers' employment (Dex et al., 1993; Hantrais, 1990) have shown how enforcement of equal opportunities legislation, generous maternity leave and pay, credits and childcare provision, have encouraged women to return to work. However, evidence from the ITS interviews with mothers shows how problematic a return to full-time continuous work can be in a demanding and pressurized job, even with the same employer. Nine of the thirteen mothers interviewed mentioned financial need as a significant reason for wishing to return to work after a maternity break, though nearly all also talked of the strong interest factors of the job. Those who had been able to establish themselves well in a producer job grade before the birth of the baby or who had staff jobs which entitled them to full maternity pay and leave found it easier to return to work without loss of status or pay.

Two years after the interviews, only two of the respondents were in full-time continuous work: Amanda, who worked for a regional ITV company, whose partner was able to take on most of the childcare; and Serena, who had returned to work on unsatisfactory short-term contracts in the independent sector, but then secured a full-time, office-based job with regular hours, a more secure contract and with better chances of promotion, at a regional ITV company. Four women had found part-time jobs in television, of which one was a job-share at the BBC. One had done short periods of non-broadcast work and three had worked part-time for short periods in other industries. Jane, whose production experience had been scattered around the country and did not have sufficient confidence to return to television production, found work in the university media studies sector, after retraining. Although she was earning half the salary she would have earned in television work, she was glad to have more secure employment and more clearly defined hours and holidays, which matched those of her children.

Laura and Jean, however, who had worked full-time continuously for many years for the BBC and had returned to full-time work after staff paid maternity leave, eventually left their posts. Both had partners working in television and had talked in their interviews of the intricate juggling acts necessary to keep both worlds of work going. Both also noted that their partners' work roles had increased in the two years following the births of their second children. Laura recorded in her diary that the new budgetary regimes had increased pressures to cut production times and made her work even more demanding. And even though the BBC offered part-time work after a career break she decided to leave work for full-time childcare. Jean also noted the strain of returning to an environment which was changing, where there were new production finance systems and procedures. She was also unhappy, when she left the office at 5.30 p.m. to pick up her children, that freelance staff working alongside her were working longer hours. She found lack of control of her working hours hard to manage and, as she was making the painful decision to seek redundancy after fifteen years at the BBC, she was expressing anxiety that she would be unable to recover her position.

It is evident from this small sample that, in the two years following childbirth, some had managed to sustain but not improve their job grades but most of the women were not in jobs of comparable status to their pre-childbirth work. Amanda had maintained her associate producer position but had not secured her producer grade, although she had been continuously in full-time producer/director work. Serena was working in a less creative area but felt that she had more chance of career progression working for a large company. Karen had remained in part-time work for an independent, but felt that she had remained in the same job at the cost of her career development. She would have preferred to be working part-time for a broadcaster.

The long-term career prospects for women who opt for flexible work have been well documented. Dex (1987, 1988) found, from her analysis of the Women in Employment Survey, that women who worked part-time suffered most downward mobility, though women in high-status jobs were less affected. Evidence from this small group does suggest that those in part-time work were more content with their jobs but were concerned about career progress. The example of the two mothers who were working full-time at the BBC shows how difficult it is for women in a pressurized and changing work environment to stay.

Conclusions

Evidence from these interviews and diaries demonstrates that women face a complexity of factors which affect or constrain their choices about the return to work; these impact upon their ability to stay in work over time. It is also clear that there is a complex interaction between their occupational careers and their family careers. From the moment of family formation, these mothers had to incorporate their existing ideologies of unstinting commitment to a demanding occupational career into a new ideology of care and commitment to the needs of a family. This involved an uncomfortable resolution of competing demands, particularly if demands at home or at work changed or were unforeseen. In practice, demands and pressures at work – especially to work longer hours – were perceived as increasing substantially.

We set out to examine a number of questions and issues. Our analysis has helped us formulate testable theoretical propositions around these topics. One of these questions was: what helps women to sustain a career in television post childbirth? Women were helped to return to work and sustain their participation by a number of factors: these included maternity leave arrangements, supportive partners, some types of flexibility, autonomy and control in their hours and job tasks on return, sympathetic female bosses, confidence, self-worth and reputation, smooth-running childcare arrangements, restricting births to one, and working in a larger, more bureaucratic (broadcasting) organization. These factors are in addition to women having a strong financial incentive to return. Clearly, maternity leave provided the necessary but not the sufficient conditions for many of these women to carry on working in television post childbirth; its availability was also linked to working in the larger broadcasting organization. Many of these factors – maternity leave, childcare and supportive partners – have been identified as important to women's return and continuation in employment in other large- and small-scale studies. It was the effect of changes occurring simultaneously which proved disastrous for these women's continued participation. Our study has served to emphasize the importance of these variables and the weight of their acting in combination. This is because the working conditions and hours in television production are rather extreme in the spectrum of hours distribution for women workers in Britain – extreme, but increasingly common

The factors which our study has added to the established understanding of women's labor force participation concern the problems created by being freelance, the importance of the attitudes of key individuals and the role of organizational structures. Freelance workers faced a level of uncertainty which was sometimes impossible to combine with parenting and childcare responsibilities. Childcare is not easy to arrange at short notice, or to drop if insufficient work and money are available to make it unnecessary. Strategies of trading off uncertainty for lower pay helped some to find an equilibrium for this problem, possibly at the expense of their career. These choices and decisions are not unlike those women in other circumstances have made – to take part-time jobs for convenience, accepting downward occupational mobility as a trade off (Dex, 1987). Freelance workers also share common problems with those with on-call or zero hours contracts. Freelance workers differ from many other workers in the way that reputation is a vital part of staying in work, as well as keeping up with contacts and networks. These vital qualities and activities were put at risk from periods of maternity leave and having other responsibilities to fulfill. Of course, having built up a rep-utation before becoming a mother could be an advantage subsequently, and facilitate organizing flexibility around her needs. Some women felt that they were having to compromise their career aspirations because they wanted to care for their children, attributing their lower status, position and some-times a sense of failure to their own attitudes and priorities. However, it is difficult for individuals to have a correct assessment of how much is their own responsibility and how much is caused by the extreme working con-ditions they faced, and an environment over which these individuals had little control. These are factors women were well aware of.

The role played by organizational structures and cultures in all this was also complex. The large broadcasters clearly offered formal maternity leave arrangements to staff workers which could be relied upon and career paths around which it was more possible to plan. However, in many other ways there was no particular advantage to women's status or career prospects from working for a broadcaster as compared with an independent company. Opportunities for flexibility in working arrangements were offered to some individuals in broadcasters and some working in independents. In both cases it was on the basis of discretion and, more particularly in the case of independent companies, whether it suited the companies' own needs. Bosses could be sympathetic or unsympathetic to mothers and their caring responsibilities in both types of organization. The two women who expressed most satisfaction with their working arrangements over time were working for independent companies run by women. They were able to work part-time continuously, though one (Karen) was concerned that she had not been able to advance her career. Both complimented their employers on their responsiveness to their family responsibilities. There were some female bosses in the BBC who would have taken the same view. However, having a woman boss could at best be thought to be a necessary, but not sufficient, condition for being treated sympathetically, which is a slightly different conclusion to that reached by Baehr (1993) whose study supported the benefit of women bosses in general.

The flexibility injected into organizational structures by the market changes had the good effect, for women, of giving them greater opportunities, but at the same time introduced a new sort of discretionary decision-making. Of lesser significance were the old hierarchical structures in which men's seniority would give them the competitive edge; of more significance were decisions made on the basis of being liked and keeping your nose clean. Not surprisingly, some women felt more vulnerable in this environment and reported cases of sexual harassment. The opening up of more discretion, along with the flexibility which can work against women's status, has been noted in other studies documenting changes over time in British payment systems (IRS, 1992).

The career planning possible in the broadcasting organization also has to be balanced against the fact that the career structures were felt to favor men and to rely on male networks. Measuring commitment and productivity to jobs by visibility, in which long hours counts for higher commitment, was evident in all organizational structures. This, in the end, was the biggest single factor preventing women from combining employment with caring responsibilities. However, it was an assumption which these women challenged. They understood that their male colleagues who were working longer hours were working very inefficiently and that, per hour, their own productivity was considerably greater.

The speed of change in the television industry in the 1990s has had marked effects on working conditions in television and, materially, on the structure and progress of a television career. Those mothers whose job roles had changed or were changing, who found their work downgraded or that increased demands were being made of them, recorded anxiety and stress in their diaries. Changes in technology, or in IT systems for program production management, changes in the culture of the workplace where staff employees might be working in a more competitive environment alongside freelances, who were working very long hours, put extra pressure on respondents. Getting work for freelance workers depends on geography, contacts, networking, information and previous reputation. When they took maternity breaks, these mothers risked getting out of touch with changing commissioning personnel and their new priorities, with heads of departments and with production managers.

The implications for equal opportunities now and in the future are not positive. The changes which workers in television now face have made the chances of getting on and rising up career ladders tougher for everyone. Men as well as women find that new conditions and competition in the workplace generates uncertainty and problems for them. At the same time there is a new measure of flexibility, and gender stereotypes are gone in the cost-cutting, low-budget environment; who will do the job at the price is far more important than whether it is a man or a woman. It is not surprising, therefore, to see a workforce which looks more equal in its gender distribution in the younger age groups, and for some women to have reached top positions in a way that was not thought possible in earlier generations. Equal opportunities for men and women are now fairly harmonized, so long as women are childless, but it is an equality brought about by worsening men's conditions of work, a phenomenon which is apparent in other areas of employment and flexible jobs (Dex and McCulloch, 1997). However, the new climate is probably more intolerant of family or any other responsibilities, or even a life outside of television work.

The mothers who returned after childbirth have all found it hard to sustain their careers in the current working conditions. Those who had been able to establish themselves well in a producer job before the birth of a baby and had staff jobs with an entitlement to maternity leave were in the best position to retain their status and pay across childbirth, although even here at considerable personal cost. Building or consolidating a career was perceived as difficult, if not impossible, as old ladders of career progression had disappeared and the prospects for secure employment reduced. Many sought to ease the situation by accepting a plateau period in their career. Organizational cultures made it difficult for mothers to compete with young but inexperienced visible workers happy to work very long hours. Whether these talented and experienced workers can make it back to senior jobs in television in the future is less than certain. The demand for skilled workers appears to be there. When all respondents in the ITS panel who recruited production staff were asked in November 1997 whether they had experienced any skills shortages in the previous six months, of those responsible for recruitment, more than half said that they had. However, the current modes of production and conditions of work are unlikely to encourage women with children to remain. It is likely that there will continue to be a talent and skills loss of women over forty. The profile of workers in television is likely to increasingly shift toward being young and single, and disproportionately male at the top. The introduction of policies like the Working Time Directive in Britain might help some workers to restrict their working hours to forty-eight per week. However, in the freelance environment of television it is unlikely to have any significant effects on mothers' abilities to combine employment and caring responsibilities.

References

Agassi, J. B. (1982) *Comparing the Work Attitudes of Women and Men*, New Britain, CT: Lexington Books.

Allat, P., Keil, T., Bryman, A. and Bytheway, B. (eds) (1987) *Women and the Life Cycle: Transitions and Turning Points*, London: Macmillan Press.

Almqvist, A. and Boje, T. P. (1998) "Who Cares, Who Pays and How is Care for Children Provided?" Paper presented at *Work, Employment and Society* Conference, Cambridge.

Baehr, H. (1993) *Women in Television*, report commissioned by the Equal Opportunities Unit, DGV, EC, University of Westminster Press.

Bailyn, L. (1993) *Breaking the Mold: Women, Men and Time in the New Corporate World*, New York: Free Press.

Brannen, J. (1987) "The Resumption of Employment after Childbirth: A Turning-Point Within a Life Course Perspective", in *Women and the Life Cycle*, Allat, P. *et al.* (eds), London: Macmillan Press, pp. 164–77.

Brannen, J. and Moss, P. (1988) *New Mothers at Work: Employment and Childcare*, London: Unwin Hyman.

Brannen, J. and Moss, P. (1991) *Managing Mothers: Dual Earner Households After Maternity Leave*, London: Unwin Hyman.

Cockburn, C. (1991) *In the Way of Women*, Basingstoke: Macmillan.

Cooper, C. and Lewis, S. (1995) *Beyond Family Friendly Policies*, London: Demos.

Crompton, R. (1997) *Women and Work in Modern Britain*, Oxford: Oxford University Press.

Crompton, R. and Sanderson, K. (1994) "The Gendered Restructuring of Employment in the Finance Sector," in *Gender, Segregation and Social Change*, MacEwan, Scott A. (ed.), Oxford: Oxford University Press, pp. 271–300.

Dex, S. (1987) *Women's Occupational Mobility: A Lifetime Perspective*, London: Macmillan Press.

Dex, S. (1988) *Women's Attitudes Towards Work*, London: Macmillan Press.

Dex, S., Joshi, H., Macran, S. and McCulloch, A. (1998) "Women's employment transitions around childbearing," *Oxford Bulletin of Economics and Statistics*, 60, 1, 79–98.

Dex, S. and McCulloch, A. (1997) *Flexible Employment: The Future of Britain's Jobs*, Manchester: Equal Opportunities Commission.

Dex, S. and Shaw, L. (1986) *British and American Women at Work: Do Equal Opportunities' Policies Matter?* London: Macmillan Press.

Dex, S., Walters, P. and Alden, D. M. (1993) *French and British Mothers at Work*, London: Macmillan Press.

Ferri, E. and Smith, K. (1996) *Parenting in the 1990s*, London: Family Policy Studies Centre.

Fogarty, M. P., Allen, I. and Walters, P. (1981) *Women in Top Jobs: 1968–1979*, London: Policy Studies Institute, Heinemann Educational Books.

Halford, S., Savage, A. and Witz, A. (1997) *Gender, Careers and Organisations*, London: Macmillan Press.

Hantrais, L. (1990) *Managing Professional and Family Life: A Comparative Study of British and French Women*, Aldershot/Vermont: Dartmouth.

Hantrais, L. and Walters, P. (1994) "Making it in and making out: women in professional occupations in Britain and France," *Gender, Work and Organization*, 1, January, 23–32.

Hardill, I., Green, A. E., Dudleston, A. C. and Owen, D. W. (1997) "Who decides what? Decision making in dual-career households," *Work, Employment and Society*, 11, 2, June, 313–26.

IRS (1992) *Pay and Gender in Britain, 2*, London: Industrial Relations Services.

Jones, J. (1997) "Passion and Commitment: The Difficulties Faced by Working Mothers in the British Television Industry." Paper presented at the University of Manchester Broadcasting Symposium, abridged in Ralph, S., Langham Brown, J. and Lees, T. (eds), *What Price Creativity?* Current Debates in Broadcasting 7, Luton: University of London Press, 1998.

Joshi, H. and Newell, M.-L. (1987) *Family Responsibility and Pay Differentials*, C.E.P.R. Discussion Paper No. 157.

Kanter, R. M. (rev. ed. 1993) *Men and Women of the Corporation*, New York: Basic Books.

Lewis, S. (1997) "'Family friendly' employment policies: a route to changing organizational culture or playing about at the margins," in *Gender, Work and Organization*, 4, 1, January, 13–23.

Lewis, S. and Lewis, J. (eds) (1996) *The Work–Family Challenge: Rethinking Employment*, London: Sage.

Lewis, S. and Taylor, K. (1996) "Evaluating the Impact of Family-Friendly Employer Policies: A Case Study," in *The Work–Family Challenge: Rethinking Employment*, Lewis, S. and Lewis, J. (eds), London: Sage, pp. 112–27.

McDowell, L. (1997) *Capital Culture: Gender at Work in the City*, Oxford: Blackwell.

McRae, S. (1989) *Flexible Working and Family Life: A Review of Changes*, London: Policy Studies Institute.

McRae, S. (ed.) (1990) *Keeping Women In*, London: Policy Studies Institute.

McRae, S. (1991) *Maternity Rights in Britain: The Experience of Women and Employers*, London: Policy Studies Institute.

Martin, J. and Roberts, C. (1984) *Women and Employment: A Lifetime Perspective*, London: HMSO.

Pettigrew, N., Willis, J. and Paterson, R. (1995) *The British Film Institute Television Industry Tracking Study, The First Year: An Interim Report*, London: BFI.

Pettigrew, N., Willis, J., Paterson, R. and Dex, S. (1997) *The British Film Institute Television Tracking Study, Second Interim Report*, London: BFI.

Sheppard, E. and Dex, S. (1998) *Analysis of Attrition in the Longitudinal Television Industry Tracking Survey*, unpublished document, London: BFI.

Smith, R. (1976) "Sex and Occupational Role on Fleet Street," in *Dependence and Exploitation in Work and Marriage*, Barker, D. L. and Allen, S. (eds), New York: Longman, pp. 70–87.

Spencer, A. and Podmore, D. (1987) "Women Lawyers – Marginal Members of a Male-Dominated Profession," in *In a Man's World: Essays on Women in Male-Dominated Professions*, Spencer, A. and Podmore, D. (eds), London: Tavistock, pp. 113–33.

Walters, P. (1987) "Servants of the Crown," in *In a Man's World: Essays on Women in Male-Dominated Professions*, Spencer, A. and Podmore, D. (eds), London: Tavistock, pp. 12–32.

Whitmarsh, A. (1995) *Social Focus on Women*, Central Statistical Office, London: HMSO.

Wilkinson, H. and Mulgan, G. (1995) *Freedom's Children: Work, Relationships and Politics for 18–34-Year Olds in Britain Today*, London: Demos.

Woolf, M. and Holly, S. (1994) *Employment Patterns and Training Needs 1993/4 (Women Freelances)*, London: Skillset.

7

CATASTROPHIC CYCLES

Film and national culture

Sally Hibbin

There are catastrophic cycles in the history of British film. This is how they run: British movies suddenly become internationally popular; the Americans arrive and buy up everything they can; some years later they pull out; our industry collapses in the wake. It happened with *Tom Jones* in 1969 and *Chariots of Fire* in 1982. *The Crying Game* and *Four Weddings and a Funeral* took us to the brink of similar crises. It has almost become a tradition in our industry.

This danger opens up before us time and again: the notion that "the British are coming," the attempt to emulate Hollywood with higher budgets, the eventual self-destruction. The prominent example was the production company Goldcrest: many finely made successes, swelling budgets, and finally the epic *Revolution*, which led to Goldcrest's collapse.

In 1997 everyone was desperate for a successor to *The Full Monty*. Ironically, they were looking for romantic comedies, which *The Full Monty* wasn't; big-budget films, which it obviously wasn't; and star-led vehicles, which it most certainly wasn't, inventing new stars as *Trainspotting* had before it.

Shakespeare in Love and *Notting Hill* once again kick-started the cycle. The success of these high-budget British films has altered the playing field, setting new aspirations for an industry whose previous successes have usually come from low-budget fare. But before we get carried away with the plaudits and the figures, let's consider whether our industry is being encouraged to make films that do not suit its talents and to compete with Hollywood rather than build on its own strengths.

Although there is a lot of investment money around, it is all chasing the same sure-fire hits. Yet simply copying the latest success is a recipe for disaster. Creating a British industry capable of handling big-budget production and distribution is going to take more imagination than the aging American studios. How do we retain the traditional hallmarks of British film – quirkiness, creative risk-taking and originality – on a larger scale?

It is arguable that one of the reasons there is so much investment money around is that America understands our ability to keep originality up and costs down and is desperate to control our product. We should learn that lesson and make sure we keep control of the British film "brand."

Since the 1997 British general election, a new establishment has emerged in the film industry. Lord Puttnam is all-pervasive; Alan Parker chaired the British Film Institute and has now been appointed as the chair of the new British Films Council. Stuart Till of the once-powerful PolyGram headed the government's Film Policy Review Group (whose report created the Films Council) and is now Parker's deputy. These men share a common wavelength and common interests. And the signs are that they are about to make the same age-old mistake, encouraging the industry to spiral into higher and higher budgets while not protecting our core business – the smaller, individually voiced films that have given British films a privileged position in the international marketplace.

In his first year in office (1997–8), Chancellor Gordon Brown announced the introduction of a 100 percent first year tax write-off on production expenditure for British films. To qualify, the film's total budget had to be less than £15 million. It was a very particular ceiling, a quiet way of outlawing the big American films shot at Pinewood or Shepperton from access to tax deduction. Following the Film Policy Review Group's recommendation this ceiling was abolished.

At the same time, the definition of a British movie has changed. There were all sorts of problems attached to the old definition, especially in the case of co-productions or films shot on location abroad, when it was hard to bring British nationals into the production. But now it is defined simply as any film shot in Britain (provided 70 percent of the budget is also spent here), yet another way of giving America access to British benefits. It's galling enough that the profits of the American-financed *The Full Monty* or *Shakespeare in Love* have left these shores but now they have access to our subsidies. These films are interesting because they are undeniably British in their story, casts and crews but not in their finance.

There are also fears that Britain, while chairing the European Union, will back America's fight to get access to European subsidy. The French, attempting to insert a cultural exclusion clause in the GATT agreement, find their arguments for protecting European culture from US predators dismissed by our own film establishment. They are trying to level the playing field between Europe and America. And Labour is clearly reluctant to honor its election pledge to take us back into Eurimages, the only pan-European production subsidy, without which our *Land and Freedom* could not have been made.

Chris Smith, Secretary of State for Sport, Media and Culture in New Labour's first term of office 1997–2001, opened a UK Film Office in Los Angeles. It was intended, he said, to "send a big message to Hollywood that we are not a quaint suburb but a big block on High Street Tinseltown." But the function of this office is not clear: to support the British in Hollywood, or to offer America another easy route to British talent beginning, literally, on its doorstep?

The danger of these decisions is compounded by the threat to the kind of production undertaken in the past by the BFI production board. Despite its minuscule annual budget, the board has managed to launch the careers of Peter Greenaway, Terence Davies, Bill Douglas and more recently Carine Adler. Now the reorganization of the BFI into the Films Council *still* leaves the existence of this kind of support in doubt.

The orthodoxy is the dictum that the higher budget film is the higher ambition film. What exactly does that mean? The desire to make money? To say something to the whole world? Very often it is the low-budget film which is most passionate about what it says, most ambitious to reach the world.

I believe what is meant is higher production values, a larger market share, a product to compete for Oscars, something to put Britain at cinema's top table, that is *Mr Bean* and *Spiceworld*. Yet until recently it has always been the small British films, *Mrs Brown* and *The Full Monty*, which win Oscar nominations, not the costly blockbusters.

So why does our industry want to press for escalating budgets? Nearly every successful British film in the 1980s and 1990s has been low-budget, usually less than £5 million: *The Crying Game*, *Gregory's Girl*, *Trainspotting*, *Four Weddings and a Funeral* and, more recently, *Lock, Stock and Two Smoking Barrels*. These films cost little and succeeded greatly, in terms of money, audience and critical esteem. But it is not to these films that our establishment look to emulate but to *Shakespeare in Love*, *Sliding Doors* and *Notting Hill*.

Financiers, even the BBC and Film Four, seem only to be interested in bigger budgets these days. We are following the American tradition. But in America you make *Titanic* and you know you're going to get your money back tenfold. You spend $50 million; you make half a billion dollars. Never mind the stars, the publicity alone will guarantee a large profit. In Britain you are lucky to have £250,000 to promote a film, which immediately precludes all television advertising. America spends £1 million plugging its slightest movies.

Another dramatic argument against this disastrous cycle is the shift in cinema audiences in the last few years.

It used to be that a film's audience – and hence its potential income – was found 50 percent in America and 50 percent in the rest of the world. That statistic has now been overturned. Europe accounts for half the audience, America and the rest of the world for the other half. Thus the old theory that a film can never make its money back from Europe and will only make a profit in the US has been turned on its head. Ken Loach's *Land and Freedom* and Mike Leigh's *Secrets and Lies* made a profit out of Europe alone. The Americans have been very quick to realize this fact, which is why Miramax,

Fineline and Fox are queuing up to finance and acquire homegrown European films such as *Brassed Off* or *The Snapper*. The crisis of self-confidence that faces the American studio system has exacerbated this with each major studio creating its own "classics" division which is actively engaged in buying up European talent and projects.

But we in Britain have a major empathy with European film-making and finance; it is this, not American affinities, that will create stability within our industry in the end. In France it is very easy to establish what a French film is: it's in French. Britain is culturally dominated by the United States. Sharing a common language with the US makes it harder to carve out a space in our own market for our own films.

The perennial debate which dogs our industry – is it film or television? A peculiarly British anxiety which arises nowhere else – seems to have evolved exactly around such matters. It used to be said that if it had American accents, stars and a tenuous relationship with reality, then it was a film; British accents, people you've never heard of and a core reality – it's television. But *Trainspotting* and *The Full Monty* have changed audience expectations. These films are culturally rooted, one of the characteristics of European cinema.

Think of *Mrs Brown*'s Highlands, *The Full Monty*'s Sheffield, Neil Jordan's Ireland. Consider Ken Loach or Merchant Ivory, perhaps our most enduring successful film-makers. Their work is rooted entirely in class. The opposite – Bond, Disney, *Star Wars*, *Titanic* – may be great cinema, but it is a completely different genre. Where we stumble is when we start to believe we can emulate such films.

So just as we have built a cinematic reputation consolidated for the first time through Europe, and developed an industry independently of America, within our own culture and within our own style, why do we return to the antique notion that what we do next is woo America?

Everyone agrees that the historical problem afflicting British cinema is that we have a cottage industry in which precarious production companies struggle from one film to next. The vertically integrated film franchises set up by the Arts Council with Lottery money allow companies such as our own, the Film Consortium, to unite production, distribution and sales under one roof. This is a clever use of public subsidy because it keeps the profit from our films in Britain. It also helps to establish companies which should be able to stand alone after a few years.

But I fear that the new regime envisages vertical integration on a far larger scale: pan-European studios to compete with Hollywood. Meanwhile the European subsidies, which sustain small national distributors, are also under threat. Without them, none of my films would have been seen in Europe. The drive is toward global monopoly, not national diversity. By moving in this direction are we in danger of defining the audience, reared on *Star Wars* and *Friends*, as too homogeneous, suggesting that every film has to have the potential to "cross-over"? If we sacrifice that healthy diversity in British cinema which speaks to different audiences and recognizes different sub-cultures, are we not cutting off our source of creativity? Some of Europe's greatest movies have only minority appeal, and surely that is worth protecting?

Chris Smith has said that if our film industry is to succeed in the long term, it must be "distribution-led." This is a grave mistake. Our success has always come from being production-led, from making films that people are passionate to make, not products designed to gain the largest audience figures. A distribution-led industry takes you straight down Hollywood Road.

The American system is led by distribution. Before they open a film, studio bosses preview it among sample audiences across the States. On the basis of the cards the audience returns, they will re-cut the film, alter the score, the dialogue and even the ending until they reach an 85 percent positive score.

Smith's idea of a distribution-led cinema is anathema. Market-tested cinema is horribly reminiscent of a market-tested policy, the faith in focus groups as the arbiters of social change. Yet this is a very hard system to counter because it appears to be the essence of democracy. The opposite – that people don't necessarily know what they want, or what's good for them – sounds moralistic and even elitist. But this supposedly democratic form of film-making by tribunal always leads to the blockbuster, never to the small-scale, independently minded movie that has flourished for so long in Britain and which wins audiences despite the odds stacked against it.

My fear is that the small-budget film could end up being categorized as a risk. What we'd get instead is endless Mr Beans and Mr Bonds. Fine movies, but we wouldn't want these and nothing else. This is not an art-versus-commerce argument. It is about recognizing the commercial viability of films with creative integrity.

We have never had the confidence to say that our own culture is attractive, worth protecting and competitive with America in its own right. If we had that confidence we would use subsidies to greater effect, encouraging inner-city multiplexes committed to showing British and European cinema. We would break away from the Hollywood-owned cinema chains and from Hollywood-controlled distribution. Then, by standing against America, we might have a chance to break out of these disastrous cycles.

With all the reviews, reorganizations and recommendations have we actually done anything to shift the balance of power in our industry so that the profit from our films remains in the UK, financing our own films and helping in a serious way to create a stand alone film industry? If we haven't then in the long term we have failed.

8

THE MUSIC INDUSTRY AS WORKPLACE

An approach to analysis

Mike Jones

In his Preface to *Music on Show – Issues of Performance*, Simon Frith (1998) compares and contrasts Film Studies as a "much more firmly established research and teaching area than Popular Music Studies." He goes on to make the point that, in becoming academically established, Film Studies narrowed its focus in two main ways. First, and predominantly, to concentrate on the film as a readable visual narrative at the expense of a consideration of film as, simultaneously, an experience of sound. His second point is that this concentration on film narrative has led to a neglect of research into cinema as an institution. If Frith's judgement is accurate then, for all the dedicated courses and post-graduate research into film, the notion of film production as cultural work appears under-developed.

Consider, then, how under-developed must be the consideration of the manufacture of popular musical products. My purpose here is to suggest a conceptual framework within and through which researchers might begin to analyze popular music production as a site of cultural work. Popular Music is the least considered area of Media and Cultural Studies. Before continuing, it is worth positing some reasons why this is the case. "Pop" is the faint sound of a soap bubble bursting – and pop products are treated, colloquially as well as in academia, as enjoying the same (dubious) qualities as such bubbles – they are short-lived and have gaudy surfaces below which lie hollow centers filled with hot air. "Pop" is now almost a term of abuse – and "pop fans" can be treated with considerable disdain not just by critics of pop but from within the general fields of popular musical consumption and popular cultural studies. Perhaps consequently, when fans want to make a case for their love of a particular style of popular music they tend to give it another name – anything from "Rock" to "Drum 'n' bass."

But, if we set aside, briefly, some of the new complexities of music-making and music-use within club culture, we need to recognize that all pop records are, whatever their style, musical commodities made to be mass consumed. Once we insert the term "commodity" into the debate, and thus re-specify pop as an industrial product as well as a musical activity, a source of pleasure or a source of meaning, it can provoke a kind of reflex response in that debate's participants. "Commodity" is a central, perhaps *the* central, concept in Marxist theory. Theodor Adorno, a leading theoretician of the Marxist Frankfurt School, provided one of the most bitter critiques of popular music. As we know, his work formed an accidental but powerful connection with the mass culturalist critics of popular products – the Leavises. Once again, here we are pitched into an argument that has now been running, almost like a soap opera, for decades. I am inclined to argue that this point of departure into the familiar territory of debates about "popular" versus "mass" culture needs to be resisted if we are to learn more about the phenomenon of popular music. As a new point of departure I think we need to recognize our special dilemma as individuals who are interested in popular cultural products, and especially in popular musical products. This is the fact that we know a great deal about our emotional attachment to the popular music we love, but, simultaneously, next to nothing about how such music is made. Without rehearsing a reading-list of key pop texts (itself a text that would demand deconstruction) all I would argue would be the comparative paucity of dedicated studies of how the music industry works to create popular musical commodities. Further, in the tiny amount of dedicated studies that do consider record-making as an industrial process, what all of the most significant texts have in common (and here I would cite especially the work of Adorno, Hirsch, Frith and Negus) is their neglect of the experiences of pop composers and pop performers within the process of commodification.

In my own researches I attempted to make sense of my own experience of popular music making – one hit single in Britain, but six album releases for various major and independent labels as a consequence of album-chart success in Europe. Despite this "track record," the over-overwhelming sensation I was left with after the money ran out and the plane rides ceased, was one of failure. In trying to make sense of and to theorize this experience I was attracted by a combination of statistics – all of them speculative – which appeared in various accounts of pop music-making. The first of these (derived from Finnegan (1989) but repeated in Cohen (1991)) was that there is one emergent pop act for every one thousand members of the population; the second, from Frith, that only 1 percent of these aspirant pop acts is likely to sign a deal with a major label; and the third, from Negus, a record industry "rule-of-thumb" calculation that, of all the acts signed to a major record label at any one time, only one-in-eight is likely to make a profit. Taken together, this means that only one-eighth of 1 percent of all pop acts extant at any one time enjoys appreciable success – the rest, sooner rather than later, fail. On this basis, it is reasonable to argue that the majority product of the music industry is not success but failure. Once I had made this recognition, I quickly realized that many other people had been through a similar experience to my own. I then needed to find ways of contacting other pop "failures," interviewing them and theorizing the data so generated in order to determine whether there were any significant commonalities in our separate and unique experiences of a general phenomenon.

Industrial conditions

When young people collaborate to play and to create popular music they can be described as aspirant pop musicians – they aspire to pop success. Popular music is what it says it is, music that has become popular, and to become popular music needs to be disseminated and consumed in a mass way. For a musical commodity to be so consumed (in the sense that a record of a musical piece is purchased for the purpose of private listening) then that commodity needs to have been manufactured, marketed, promoted and made available to the general public through distribution to retail outlets, both nationally and internationally. All of this takes investment and organization and the primary agencies for investment and organization on this scale are major record companies (usually through the offices of a series of record labels). It is not only major companies that can make mass selling musical commodities and not all mass selling music is marketed, promoted and sold in identical ways – but, in by far the majority of cases, successful records, "hit" records, are mass selling commodities that are owned by major record companies.

From the above list of what it is that record companies do, it is the idea of "manufacture" that is likely to give most cause for concern – although marketing, promotion and distribution should not be over-looked, for these are not "neutral" stages of "post-manufacture," but can be shown to be intrinsic to a total sense of "manufacture" as "commodification." To attempt to elucidate this rather cryptic point we need to consider Hirsch's contribution to the study of popular music production.

His argument is that records are simply replications of an original artwork and that record companies function as "gate-keepers" in that they choose only certain pieces for replication and ignore others. While this itself hints at the power of record companies to decide which acts are likely to bring what music to our attention, we need to appreciate that what the record industry represents to the aspirant pop act is not simply a gate to somewhere but a series of active relationships dedicated to the transformation of original cultural material into mass selling musical commodities. Commodification, understood in this way, is clearly not a neutral process (a gate that either opens or fails to open); it is an active, transformational one. On this basis, what we need to consider are the types of "active relationships" entered into by aspirant pop acts. Further, we need to see these relationships not as sequential (in a misleading analogy with the industrial manufacture of non-cultural commodities) but as relationships, of varying combinations, that are in continual and continuous engagement.

When pop acts set out to become popular, what each possesses is their own, unique combination of the sounds they make and the way they look, together with the potential for stories to be told about how and why they make the sounds they do. What record companies attempt to create through the process of record manufacture is not simply a "faithful" or even an "enhanced" recording of an original performance; they seek to create a commodity that is marketable as sound, print and vision in order to maximize the chances that the commodity sells as well as everyone involved in its manufacture hopes that it will. For Negus, the goal of record company commodification is the "Total Star Text" and he subsumes the activities that record companies engage in to create such a text under the heading "Artist Development." We will need to consider Negus's designations below (p. 151). Here we need to appreciate why, and with what consequences, "commodification" is a total process that not only impacts on but transforms the combination of the sound, the look and the story of a pop act.

In seeking to maximize the chances that popular musical commodities will sell, record companies need to have access to every dimension of a pop act and its work in order to achieve what it considers to be the prime configuration of those dimensions. In this way, in the creation of a pop commodity, a record company transforms a living entity into a comparatively fixed representation of itself. Before we rush to discuss this as an act of mediation (and, again, begin the rehearsal of familiar debates) we need to be alive to some of the key differences between mediation in pop and mediation in other media industries. Mediation is an inescapable fact of cultural production. Crudely, it brings "production" (in the sense of industrial organization) to the generation of cultural artifacts (understood, in this sense of "culture," as products of the imagination). The music industry clearly exists to create media products in the same way that the print, television and film industries so exist. Where pop music-making differs in a significant way is in the fact that there is a need for all parties to the commodification process to discuss not only music, but music in a "future state" – where each one will offer a version of why the act, and the music that it makes, will go on to make "hit" records. To an extent, this is not unlike other media industries – no one sees a film or a game show or can read a newspaper until each of those artifacts has been edited. Despite this, images on a screen and words on a page have a kind of tangibility that notes in the air lack. Mediation in popular music takes place almost entirely through assertion, and the various parties central to the pop commodification process come from different directions and with very different resources to the Babel of assertion and argument that defines record-making. By identifying who these various "mediators" (or intermediaries) are and by specifying not simply what they do but how they do it in active relationship to, and with, each other, we will be better placed to begin the conceptualization of popular music-making as cultural work – and also to understand why so much of this work results in failed commodities. The strength of Frith's early work (1983) was that he identified the key intermediaries in the pop commodification process. Put simply, pop acts will first have managers whose primary function is to secure a recording contract for the act. Obviously, this contract will be with a record company and, once the connection is made with an interested company, the act and its manager will encounter a fresh set of intermediary figures – in the first instance A&R personnel and (if they sign) Marketing personnel. Frith did not examine in any greater depth the relationships he identified. His subsequent work on pop has been protean, and he has never returned to the industrial conditions of pop as cultural work. Since this early work of Frith, our understanding of how record companies work has been left primarily to mainly quantitative accounts of record company output while the role, function and practice of the pop manager has never been theorized. It was not until Negus's work that any more detailed study of what record company personnel do in their working lives was mounted. In Negus's case, though, there is a marked tendency to allow those particular intermediaries to set the agenda in the description and analysis of the commodification process. Consequently, no sooner are we introduced to the environment of record-making (and to the enormously high casualty rate associated with it) than this latter is disregarded as some unfortunate by-product of "artist development" – as a considered and sympathetic attempt to create successful pop products. Clearly, from the point of view of pop acts as workers in an industry, pop music-making is a particularly dangerous, hazardous job. Viewing pop in this way allows us to proceed by tracing the tensions between the cumulative pain of failure and the ideological representation of pop's industrial process as a benign and "nurturing" one in which the needs of artistic expression are held as sacrosanct.

Artist development

"Artist development" is a delicate "feel good" phrase, but what it masks is a process that is likely to be experienced by the pop act in anything but a pleasant way. It is not simply that the transformation process of pop commodification generates tension but that it is structurally conflictual. Conflicts need not always be disabling or fatal, but they are a continuous feature of commodification. Further, and crucially, within this theater of conflict the pop act is, contrary to popular myth, structurally disempowered.

There is not the space here to explore the entirety of the transformation process of pop manufacture, neither can we explore it fully from the perspective of the pop act, but as a condensed guide to the broad field of the experience we can identify structural conflict in record-making in and through the expression and articulation of differences in perspective,

ambition and definition held by the three contributing parties to pop commodification – the act, its management and the record company.

If we deal with each of these "parties" in turn, then the act can be argued
to hold a conception of itself as, predominantly, a musical entity. On this
basis its perspective on record-making will center on the translation of its
music into a recorded form – an aspirant act is "expert" in its own music-
making but not in record-making. Managers, whether experienced or not,
are not music-makers; their expertise lies in "producing" the act, in the fundamental but non-musical sense of organizing it as an entity that must fulfill
a recording contract – a contract which the manager will have been instrumental in negotiating and securing. In this loose, but important, sense, the
manager's expertise lies in record-making. Finally, the record company's
expertise is an overarching one. Record company personnel are not music-
makers and neither are they record-makers, as such; rather, their expertise
lies in commodity-making. In this very broad way, three entities combine
from three perspectives with a single goal in mind, not a "good" record
(imprecise though this is) but a successful one. Almost inevitably, definitions of what a "successful" record will consist of, and how this might be
brought about, will differ not just from "party" to "party," but often within
the territory of each party.

In the above way, the three parties are united in the ambition of success,
but conjuring success demands the articulation of a strategy, and a strategy
can only be formed through an agreement about not simply the goal of
action but what it is about the act and its work that justifies the development of a strategy in the first place. All parties need to agree a "working
version" of the pop act – what combination of its sound, its look and its
story will be sufficient to invite success. Here the notion of "invitation" is
pivotal. Aspirant acts progress not through their own volition but because
intermediaries create volition through them. In each encounter, in each
spiral twist upwards toward commodification and mass marketing, the
anticipation that success will come needs to be asserted and re-asserted,
defined and re-defined, in order to justify the increasing effort and investment progress demands.

In all of this, all parties will hold and voice opinions about where it is
that the act fits within (and beyond) current patterns of musical–cultural
expression and current patterns of consumer demand. This intense activity is
fuelled by the adrenaline of anticipation but anticipation is, at best, an
extrapolation based on inadequate data – where the term "data" flatters the
information that commodifying teams treat as such: the formal and informal
reactions of journalists and radio producers to the act and its material; the
interpretation of crowd reaction at live shows; the feelings and opinions of
significant others within the "music industry." In short, the data on which
commodification proceeds is captured in the colloquial expression "the
buzz." No one is secure in his or her definition of "the buzz" but the liveli-

hoods of managers and of record company employees alike rest on their ability to divine its condition at any time, at any moment, and to predict the future of an act from that definition.

The irony of all this is, then, that the act is, simultaneously, what "the buzz" is about but it is the commodification party which has least access to its definition (for want of expertise either in record-making or in commodity-making). It is through an exploration of this notion of "least access" that the key elements of a conceptual framework for pop production can begin to be discerned.

Pop acts and pop production

In practice, pop acts are doubly- even triply-mediated: they are represented to the label by a manager, to the company by a team within the label, and to the mass market by the company. Further, the methods of representation made are, in each case, ones that the pop act has little access to or understanding of. When a pop act signs a record contract it signs just that, a contract to record – not one to release, promote, market or distribute a record. Pop acts are powerless to initiate and prosecute these decisive activities – instead, they must rely on the notion that the relationships they enter into with intermediary figures will result in their own successful commodification.

It can be argued that, when they first begin to play together and, especially, when they begin to write original material, the members of aspirant pop acts reproduce the conditions of the experience they have consumed (music that has been commodified as a total of the act, its look and its story). In this way, such pop acts create more than music, they create themselves as a pop act in this comprehensive and thorough way: they "re-invent" themselves as "pop-stars-in-waiting" – artist development begins at home. However, pop acts cannot progress beyond the point of aspiration without mediation – without the support of intermediary figures who can initiate the transformational, commodification process. However, at a local level, pop acts are unlikely to engage any working individuals who will have any more insightful understanding of how pop commodities are made.

Instead, local music industry figures (promoters, local DJs, local journalists, roadies, studio owners, sound engineers, and so on) are likely to be as "unworldly" and inexperienced as aspirant pop acts. Eventually, though, the act will take on a manager of some kind. This individual will already know, or will quickly have to learn, the working methods of the music industry and of the record industry or they, and their acts, will fall at the earliest hurdles. In this way, the act cedes not only a vital degree of control to someone who is or becomes inculcated in the methods of the industry, but they also ensure their own separation from, and ignorance of, the very methods by which commodification takes place.

What managers rapidly learn about how pop works can be understood as a "culture of practice" associated with the methods of popular musical commodification. I have discussed this elsewhere but what it is driven by is the constant need to "second guess" a marketplace for media products in which the fate of those products is decided within days of their release. In other media industries, failures such as *Eldorado*, *Judge Dredd* or *News on Sunday* are rare and notable occurrences. In pop, an average of ninety-seven singles are released every week – but only two of these are likely to reach the top ten. Under these conditions, however close managers and pop acts appear, managers will have their own agendas described by their very different access to the commodification process.

Where record companies are concerned, the notion of an intense "culture of practice" is reinforced by the need for employees to obey company targets and to work within company parameters. Major record companies continuously "hedge their bets" through over-signing acts – as one manager expressed it in an interview I conducted, "record companies back every horse in the race." If we develop this analogy, what record companies do is to sign a number of acts that they anticipate will make hit records. They will establish a budget and a release schedule for each act (strictly within the budgetary limits and international schedules of their parent companies) and they will then expect to process these acts as systematically as possible. However, the marketplace refuses to be systematized – and, often, pop acts will either create problems or experience difficulties. Record company intermediaries are continuously re-assessing the likely fortunes of their signed acts for the very basic reason that they never have sufficient resources to give each act the same degree of support and attention. Consequently, they operate a system of "prioritization," but it is a system largely hidden from the view of the act and, as far as is possible, from the act's manager.

In the above ways, pop acts have little genuine knowledge of their record label's estimation of, and intentions for, them. Further, they have only their manager's account of their overall condition within commodification to rely on. In this way, pop acts are "operationally" disempowered because they are ill-informed and often misinformed. They have little real knowledge of decisions taken about them because they have little real contact with their record companies. All they have to work on is the version of events offered to them by their manager, but managers will always attempt to appear competent and "in control" and acts have no method by which to verify claims made or to monitor actions taken.

For the period of commodification, pop acts, managers and record company personnel assigned to them form a team, a temporary alliance that has been formed to achieve a goal by collective means. In short, a "supraorganization" is called into being with the explicit aim of making a hit record. But there is no equality amongst the components of the organization. As we have seen, the constituent elements of this "supraorganization" are differently resourced. What this means is that, in the search for a "working version" of the pop act and its material, the template from which the commodified representation of the act to the market will be generated, the record company is most likely to achieve the definition it feels appropriate to market conditions. This does not mean that record companies always "get it wrong" (although mostly they do) and neither does it mean that acts are manipulated and exploited (although often they are); rather, there is a "fault line" in the "unity" required to make records, and it widens under pressure. This "fault line" runs through the tension between the record companies' need to create successful commodities and the pop acts" desire for success through record sales, where these are not identical goals.

Pop acts cannot be successful on their own so they need to form working relationships with intermediary figures. From here, what they need to aim at is to be successful on their own terms, but acts rarely attain this, although only partly for the reason of the lack of resources and lack of access to information discussed immediately above. In their, usually short, working lives, pop acts will always be playing "catch-up," "fire-fighting," being reactive rather than pro-active. By the time the axe falls and the record company drops them, they are exhausted and confused and have squabbled amongst themselves, with their managers, and with whatever coterie of friends, relatives and supporters offers them emotional support. Yet this is only part of the story. What makes acts so prone to failure is not simply that they are under-resourced within commodification but that they are rendered vulnerable by their very desire for success, by their need and determination to become pop stars.

New pop acts have to begin as consumers of pop music – there is nowhere else to begin. Further, they are almost entirely likely to have begun as fans of popular music. The actual production processes of popular music are obscure to fans – what we all consume are pop commodities, and these, as we have seen, are not just sounds but total representations of an act – an ideologically-informed representation of the combination of the sound, look and story of an act. Pop consumption is wildly partisan but it is not (or at least not solely) the partisan character of "fandom" that provides an unreliable guide to the social relations of popular musical production; rather, it is that both the successful pop act and its record company will be eager to erase traces of industrial production from the musical commodity. As pop consumers we "know" that "stars" have unique talents, and lead glamorous even dangerous lives in their attempt to capture and express the popular cultural "zeitgeist." Further, we "know" that these stars are threatened constantly by emergent acts who (depending on our tastes) pretend to the definition of the "cutting edge" of pop – where a decisive concomitant of all of this is that everything else which sells or fails to sell is dross. It is fair to assert that the consumption of music is a sensual experience and fans who aspire to become pop stars are perhaps the most sensitized of all pop consumers. Any condition which might detract from the sensuality of the experience will reduce its impact and its pleasure. On this basis, it is in the interests of the pop act and every mediating agency that evidence of an industrial process of mediation is erased. Within the consumerist narrative the pop act is seen as all-powerful – nothing mediates the music and its imaginative and emotional "content." True, there are narratives of "stars" and their careers being destroyed by the "industry" but these are, effectively, reinforcing sub-narratives of the sensually experienced "truth" of the star's unique, imaginative ability to articulate individual (and group and subcultural) aspirations and experiences. It is precisely because this is music's strongest suit that consumers who would be producers are so disarmed when they attempt to enter the music industry.

Pop music is "strong stuff," it is "powerful magic," but pop is also a workplace, and its work is to create pleasure or the conditions of pleasure – pop helps the workforce escape from work. In this way, pop is simultaneously work and pleasure; more accurately, it is work masquerading as leisure. In this sleight-of-hand, the gaze of the audience must be distracted while the trick is performed. Yet it is precisely members of this "distracted audience" who appear at the foot of the pop spiral replete with a sound, a look and a story, begging for a hand-up. Will no one tell them what comes next?

References

Cohen, S. (1991) *Rock Culture in Liverpool: Popular Music in the Making*, Oxford: Clarendon Press.

Finnegan, R. (1989) *The Hidden Musicians: Music Making in an English Town*, Cambridge: Cambridge University Press.

Frith, S. (1983) *Sound Effects: Youth, Leisure and the Politics of Rock*, London: Constable.

Frith, S. (1998) "Preface" in *Music on Show – Issues of Performance*, T. Hautamaki and H. Jarviluoma (eds), Tampere: Tampere University.

Negus, K. (1992) *Producing Pop: Culture and Conflict in the Popular Music Industry*, London: Arnold.

Part IV

REPRESENTATION

The final part of *Cultural Work* looks at key questions of representation. In what sense is it possible or meaningful to talk about "live" performance? How are the workplace, working and social relations, and workplace politics represented in the cinema? How do marketizing forces inform the researching and devising of the content, the location, the look and feel of television drama programs?

Philip Auslander's chapter looks at Walter Benjamin's "The Work of Art in the Age of Mechanical Reproduction" in the context of recent developments in the relationship between live performance and mediatization. While the terms of Benjamin's discussion remain vital, the relationship among them must be rethought for the present historical moment. In Benjamin's analysis, every anti-auratic, mass-reproduced cultural object is preceded by an auratic original: painting comes before lithography, live theater comes before film. Recent developments in live performance have turned this relation on its head, however – pop concerts that recreate music videos and live stage shows that replicate animated cartoons are but two instances among many. Further, there are entire aesthetic discourses based on reproduction. Theodore Gracyk argues, for example, that the primary aesthetic object of rock music is the recording and that live performances typically are re-creations of music originally developed in the studio. What happens to Benjamin's central concepts of aura and authenticity when the mass-reproduced object must be seen as the original of which the seemingly unique object, the live performance, is actually a reproduction?

Yvonne Tasker's chapter explores some contemporary popular cultural discourses about a changing workplace, primarily through an analysis of the film *Disclosure*. She explores the ways in which the movie draws on and re-articulates popular discourses about feminism, female sexuality and new technologies. Our relationship to work (or the lack of it) functions as a key reference point for the constitution of cultural identities. Escaping from work. Escaping to work. Work as something that can entrap or frame social lives. For many people the experience of work involves both these elements,

157

with narratives revolving around work expressing something of this ambivalence. In Hollywood movies, work often tends to be glamorous – or at least thrilling (law enforcement, the military, medicine, performance/showbiz) – typically avoiding (or only briefly alluding to) the more mundane aspects of employment. Yet, like other popular narrative representations, movies use work settings and activities to evoke qualities such as heroism or caring. Work is also portrayed as a contested and, crucially, as a gendered space, one which is constructed in shifting relation to a "domestic" space of relationships, family and the home.

Disclosure draws on a series of figures which recur in discourses to do with gender and work: the construction of a professional working woman in terms of a predatory sexuality; the fear of male redundancy; uncertainties about the role of new technologies, particularly technologies of communication; and a focus on presentation (promotion and advertising, the law) as "feminizing." If, at a superficial level, *Disclosure* suggests a conservative view of a gendered workplace, founded on an opposition between women and men, it can nonetheless be understood, like other films of the 1990s, in terms of an experience increasingly defined by insecurity.

Robin Nelson's chapter closes *Cultural Work* with an analysis of the production and reception of British television drama. He reflects on changing notions of cultural work and raises questions about the "promise" of the contemporary. A number of factors are key to his analysis and reflections. The break-up of the long-established British television industry structure by the 1990 Broadcasting Act paved the way for multi-channeling in the United Kingdom. At the same time, the emphasis on market research – both within the industry and in the academy – quantifies and segments the television audience. A looped market research feedback into production introduces a "television drama by numbers." The combination of a rapidly extended commercialism with a quantifying instrumentalism in "ratings discourse" increasingly constructs privatized consumers in postmodern culture. A communications model that stresses the virtually infinite dispersal of produced meanings further fragments any conception of common culture to the point where Baudrillard and Margaret Thatcher, albeit from different discursive positions, assert the end of society. Having sketched the force field which gave rise to the above detailed circumstances and mindsets, Nelson then raises some questions about the cultural work they have engendered. Is there still a case for retaining a PSB ethos in British television (re-establishing a creative space for writers and directors)? Is a communication model which neither commits to meaninglessness nor abandons wholesale any sense of *Gemeinschaft* or cultural value sustainable?

Nelson describes a British television industry equivalent of the Hollywood pitch. So, just as a movie project is described in the curt one sentence pitch as "*Die Hard* meets *Fatal Attraction* with a *Father of the Bride* twist," so a new British television drama series is characterized as "*Dixon of Dock Green* meets *Juliet Bravo* meets *All Creatures Great and Small* to a 1960s music track."

The almost pathological scrutiny of program ratings manifests itself in the pursuit of the ideal recombinant television program format and a slavish tracking of audience demographics. Although set in the world of art magazine publishing, Wilf Wellingborough, the narrator of Michael Fishwick's 2001 novel *Smashing People*, aspires to work in television. Early in the novel he meets with Humphrey Horsefall, fictitious Controller of BBC2. Taking the notion of high concept, ratings discourse and the recombinant principle to almost absurd extremes Horsefall muses out loud about a new programme:

> We need to [. . .] reinvent the game show. We need to repackage it. All that "Come on down" stuff is fine as far as it goes. And it goes a long way, I admit. I'm not knocking it. It serves its purpose. But there is an audience for something more sophisticated. They have grown out of *The Young Ones,* they like Smith and Jones, but they want something with more bite. What I've got in mind is this. Imagine you've got a couple, and they're thinking about getting married. People are putting it off till much later in life these days, so there are masses of people like that. What we do is take a couple like that and give them an advocate, like a barrister, each. [. . .] and what they do is analyze the couple's relationship, using the brief each partner has given them. They defend their partners, if you see what I mean, against the criticism from the other party, and they make accusations and ask leading questions in their turn.
>
> (Fishwick, 2001: 61)

After Horsefall has described this new gameshow, Wellingborough comes up with a title for it – *Hitch or Ditch*.

Just as Murdock concluded Chapter 1 with the sobering thought that "the aesthetics of selection and recombination look set to become more and more central to cultural practice," so too does Nelson conclude that the marketizing forces anatomized by Murdock and satirized by Fishwick may lead to the dreary prospect of an increasingly recombinant television culture.

Reference

Fishwick, M. (2001) *Smashing People*, London: Vintage.

9

AN ORCHID IN THE LAND OF TECHNOLOGY

Walter Benjamin and live performance

Philip Auslander

In his autobiography (1991), John Densmore, the drummer for the rock group the Doors, recounts an anecdote concerning an early appearance by the group, probably in 1967. Densmore recounts that, having taped an appearance on a variety show, the Doors wanted to be able to watch themselves on television. They therefore requested that a set be placed in their backstage dressing room the night their appearance was to be shown. Because their segment had not come up when they were ready to begin their concert, they took the television set onstage with them, perching it atop an amplifier with the volume turned off. When the Doors finally appeared on the television, they stopped playing mid-song, turned up the television volume, and sat on the floor of the stage watching themselves, their backs to the audience. When their segment was over, they resumed playing.

By staging their relationship to television in this way in 1967, the Doors reveal their prescience concerning what would happen soon thereafter in the relationship between live and mediatized performance. There are several harbingers to be noted, particularly the presentation of a previously recorded event as live; the incorporation of video into the live event; and the precedence of the mediatized over the live even for the performers themselves. Now, over thirty years later, we are well into a period of cultural history in which mediatization has clearly become the experience to which live performance must refer and which it must seek to recreate. This is apparent across a number of cultural realms, from the use of pre-recorded vocal and instrumental tracks in pop concerts to the ubiquity of video in performance art and experimental theater. Television programs are restaged as live performances (*The Real Live Brady Bunch*), animated films as stage musicals (Disney's *Beauty and the Beast*). In 1988 Simon Frith noted in a discussion of music television that "for an increasing number of rock fans the meaning of 'live' performance, the look of music 'in reality' [. . .] comes from its ubiquitous simulation [. . .] a concert feels real only to the extent that it matches its TV reproduction" (1988: 124–5). Theodore Gracyk (1996) takes the position that rock music is a cultural discourse intrinsically based in reproduction; he argues convincingly that the primary aesthetic object of rock is the recording, and that live performances are re-creations of music originally developed for the studio. Steve Wurtzler summarizes the issue in the context of sports: "over time, as the conventions of the televisually posited live come to constitute the way we think of the live, attending the game [. . .] becomes a degraded version of the event's televisual representation" (1992: 92). In all these cases, the traditional assumption that the live performance is the "original" object existing prior to reproduction is undermined and reversed: in what Steve Connor calls an "inversion of the structural dependence of copies upon originals" (1989: 153) live performances are now frequently reproductions of mass-produced, mediatized performances.

Thinking about these phenomena has led me back to Walter Benjamin's crucially important essay "The Work of Art in the Age of Mechanical Reproduction" (1936) and it is my purpose here to offer some comment on the relevance of that essay to the cultural situation I have just described. The focus of Benjamin's analysis in that essay is on the historical progression from unique, auratic art forms to mass-reproduced ones. He does not take note there of the kind of doubling back that I have described, in which the older forms emulate and incorporate the newer ones. Like the Doors, however, Benjamin is remarkably prescient and many of the terms of his analysis shed light on the current situation.

I would begin by noting Benjamin's emphasis on the idea that "human sense perception [. . .] is determined not only by nature but by historical circumstances as well" (1986 [1936]: 31). He describes the mode of perception that characterizes what, for him, was an emergent mass culture in terms of overcoming distance (and therefore banishing aura, which can be understood as a function of distance). He refers to "the desire of contemporary masses to bring things 'closer' spatially and humanly, which is just as ardent as their bent toward overcoming the uniqueness of every reality by accepting its reproduction. Every day the urge grows stronger to get hold of an object at very close range by way of its likeness, its reproduction" (ibid.: 31–2). Benjamin's notion of a mass desire for proximity, and its alliance with a desire for reproduced objects, provides a useful way of understanding the interrelation of live and mediatized forms that I have described. Certainly, the use of giant video screens at sporting events, concerts and other performances is a direct illustration of Benjamin's concept: the desire for the kind of proximity and intimacy we can experience with television – which has become our standard for intimate perception – but that is absent from these performances can be recreated by means of their videation. When a live performance recreates a mass-reproduced one, as in the case of the replication of music video imagery in concerts or cartoon images in theater, an inverted version of the same effect takes place. Because we are already intimately familiar with the images we are seeing from our televisual and filmic experience of them, we see them as proximate no matter how far away we may be in physical distance. If you know what Madonna's videos look like, you can read the images in her concerts as if you were in intimate relation to them, even from the last row. Whether the effect of intimacy results from the videation of the live event or from acquaintance with the live images from their prior reproductions, it has the result of making live performances more like television and thus enables live events to fulfill the desire for reproduction that Benjamin notes. Although my initial examples have been of large-scale performances, the point holds true across the board. Even in the most intimate of performance art projects, in which we are only a few feet away from the performers, we are still frequently offered the opportunity for the even greater intimacy of watching the performers in close-up on the monitors, as if we can only experience true intimacy in televisual terms. This points to another of Benjamin's postulates: that "the quality of [the original's] presence is always depreciated" by reproduction. The ubiquity of reproductions of performances of all kinds in our culture has led to the depreciation of live presence, which can only be compensated for by making the perceptual experience of the live as much as possible like that of the mediatized, even in cases where the live event provides its own brand of intimacy.

I would go so far as to argue that this desire has resulted not just in live performances that are based on or which resemble reproduced ones but also in forms of live performance that are themselves mass-produced. Producers of the genre known as "interactive plays" envision live performances as transportable commodities. Interactive plays are environmental performances that incorporate varying degrees of spectator performance. In *Tamara*, for instance, spectators follow a particular character through a series of rooms, witnessing various scenes of a narrative. In *Tony 'n' Tina's Wedding* and similar performances, spectators actually interact with the performers by eating with them, dancing with them, etc. Barrie Wexler, the California producer of *Tamara*, "franchises [. . .] *Tamara* worldwide, replicating the product in exact and dependable detail. 'It's like staying in the Hilton,' he explains, 'everything is exactly the same no matter where you are'" (Fuchs, 1996: 142). In these cases, live performance takes on the defining characteristics of a mass medium: it makes the same text available simultaneously to a large number of participants distributed widely in space. Ironically, interactive plays like *Tamara* commodify the very aspects of live performance that are said to resist commodification. Because they are designed to offer a different experience at each visit, they can be merchandised as events over and over again: the very evanescence and non-repeatability of the live experience become selling points. One of those selling points is, of course, the intimacy of witnessing the narrative from a particular character's perspective or physically interacting with the characters. Again, the alliance suggested by Benjamin of the desire for intimacy with the desire for reproductions is apparent.

My contention that theater can function as a mass medium leads me to disagree with Noel Carroll, who defines "mass art" in a way that excludes theater and all live performance from that category. Carroll asserts that, "x is a mass artwork if and only 1. x is a multiple instance or type artwork, 2. Produced and distributed by a mass technology, 3. Which artwork is intentionally designed to gravitate in its structural choices [. . .] toward those choices that promise accessibility with minimum effort [. . .] for the largest number of relatively untutored [. . .] audiences" (1998: 196). Although there clearly is much theater and live performance that meets the third condition, Carroll would place such work into the category of "popular art" rather than mass art because it cannot meet his first two criteria. But it seems to me that live performance events like *Tamara* pose difficulties for those parts of Carroll's theory. First of all, if we imagine that the producer of *Tamara* successfully franchises his show so that it is available simultaneously in cities throughout the world, then it seems to me that he would be using theater as a mass technology. Carroll argues that performances of live theater differ from those of films by saying that whereas the performance of a film is generated directly from a template (the print of the film), a theatrical performance of a film is generated from an interpretation of the playtext. He goes on to generalize from this basis that the generation of performances from templates, rather than interpretations, is a crucial ontological characteristic of mass art forms. While it takes no particular artistic or interpretative skill to be a projectionist, "it takes artistry and imagination to embody an interpretation" (ibid.: 213–14). It is for this reason that we recognize theatrical performances as works of art in themselves but do not accord that status to film showings.

The distinction Carroll draws between template and interpretation is sound and useful. But if we take the producer of *Tamara* at his word, and assume that he does succeed in mounting numerous productions of the play that are functionally identical, would it not be fair to say that the interpretation used in all cases functions as a template? (When I refer to the various productions as functionally identical, I am not suggesting that there would be no differences among them, only that such differences would be trivial – differences, but not distinctions that would differentiate one production of *Tamara* from any other in aesthetically significant ways.) While the actors would have to possess a certain amount of craft and skill to replicate the performances established in the template (just as it takes a certain amount of craft and skill to be a good projectionist), individual artistry and imagination would be negative qualities in such a performance as they would tend to work against the success of *Tamara* as a standardized product. (Similarly, we would not want a projectionist to be "creative" in showing a film.)

If this argument seems a bit far-fetched in the context of theater (though I do not believe it to be), we can switch for a moment to another kind of franchised performance. Consider the various live performances of trademark clown character Ronald McDonald which may be undertaken simultaneously at McDonald's restaurants all over the world. It is precisely the point of these performances that they all represent a single, standardized Ronald. All performances of Ronald McDonald are generated from a single interpretation of the character, which functions as a template. (It is significant that our familiarity with this template derives mostly from having seen Ronald on television commercials. The live presentations of Ronald McDonald are further instances of live performance's recreation of the televisual.) If a child was led to make judgements concerning the interpretative quality of the various Ronald McDonalds s/he has seen – such as: "I liked the Ronald at that restaurant in Cleveland better" or "This guy did Ronald better when we were here yesterday" – then the performances would have been dismal failures precisely because they, like interactive plays, are instances where live performance aspires to the condition of mass art. These instances also suggest how live performance may anticipate in the economy of repetition, not just by being recorded and replicated, but through the mass production of the live event itself. As Benjamin notes, "to an even greater degree, the work of art reproduced becomes the work of art designed for reproduction" (1986 [1936]: 33).

I return now to Benjamin's observation on what he called "contemporary perception" and its hunger for reproductions. "To pry an object from its shell," he writes, "to destroy its aura, is the mark of a perception whose 'sense of the universal equality of all things' has increased to such a degree that it extracts it even from a unique object by means of reproduction" (1986 [1936]: 32). I have tried to suggest here that this is exactly the state in which live performance now finds itself: its traditional status as auratic and unique has indeed been wrested from it by an ever accelerating incursion of reproduction into the live event. Following Benjamin, I might argue that live performance has indeed been pried from its shell and that all performance modes, live or mediatized, are now equal – none is perceived as auratic or authentic; the live performance is just one more reproduction of a given text or one more reproducible text. To say that no performance in any medium can be perceived as auratic is not to say that all such performances are experienced in the same way – just that no one of them is experienced as the auratic, authentic original. Live performance could be said to partake of the ontology that Benjamin ascribes to photography: "from a photographic negative [. . .] one can make any number of prints; to ask for the 'authentic' print makes no sense" (ibid.: 33). This situation would represent the historical triumph of mechanical reproduction that Benjamin implies: aura, authenticity, and cult value have been definitively routed, even in live performance, to the very site that seemed the last refuge of the auratic.

I find this argument very tempting, especially as it suggests a possible point of contact between Benjamin and Jean Baudrillard (1983). The cultural landscape I just described, in which no performance of a text has any claim to being auratic or original, is that of Baudrillardian simulation, in which cultural objects and texts are refractions of codes and instantiations of models rather than copies of originals, an account of contemporary culture I find compelling and persuasive. Even so, I must qualify my argument a bit because I'm not really convinced that we are finished with the auratic and everything it entails.

For one thing, it isn't quite the case that we perceive all modes of performance under the sign of universal equality. Live events have cultural value: being able to say that you were physically present at a particular event constitutes valuable symbolic capital – certainly, it is possible to dine out on the cachet of having been at Woodstock, for example. The relationship of this phenomenon to mass reproduction is worth pondering. At first blush, I am tempted to assert that the symbolic capital attached to live performances disdains reproduction: the less an event leaves behind in the way of artifacts and documentation, the more symbolic capital accrues to those who were in attendance (see Cubitt, 1994: 289). But is this the case? Or may it be that having been at the Isle of Wight Festival carries less symbolic capital than having been at Woodstock (at least in the American context) precisely because Woodstock has been so widely reproduced as sound recordings, films, etc.?

However one may answer this question of the relative value of two live events, it is important to observe that even within our hyper-mediatized culture, more symbolic capital is attached to live events than to mediatized ones. For example, in the cultural contexts in which Laurie Anderson matters, I bank far more symbolic capital from having seen her perform *The Nerve Bible* (1995) live than I would from being able to say that I heard it on CD or read the book. The irony of the fact that live performances are still worth more symbolic capital within our culture than mediatized performances, even as live performance loses its identity and becomes more and more like mediatized performance, is clearly illustrated by *The Nerve Bible*, almost all of which was prerecorded and run by computers. During the second half, Anderson wandered on and off stage, as if to suggest that the computerized, audiovisual machine she had set into motion could run itself, and it was the show, with her or without her. Even though Anderson's performance is barely live at all, it still commands greater symbolic capital than fully mediatized forms. If only as a vestigial remnant of an earlier cultural order, live performance retains a measure of cultural value.

Although Benjamin's analysis remains valuable for understanding the relationship of live and mediatized performance forms in our current cultural situation, the cultural value we still attach to live events suggests that the auratic has not been destroyed completely. But I suspect this is a very temporary condition and I think we can begin to imagine a culture in which more prestige would accrue to someone who said she had seen Anderson on videotape or listened to her on CD than to the person who had seen her live. I doubt that having seen the live stage presentation of Disney's *Beauty and the Beast*, for instance, would count for more within the relevant cultural context than owning a copy of the movie on videocassette. Since I'm speaking of children, it might be worth speculating on what it will be like when a generation raised in a culture in which at least some recordings are worth more symbolic capital than the corresponding live shows comes to cultural power. In an essay on Internet romance entitled "Virtual Love," Meghan Daum offers the following confession: "[I] have a constant low-grade fear of the telephone, and I often call people with the intention of getting their answering machines. There is something about the live voice that I have come to find unnervingly organic, as volatile as live television" (1997: 80). Many of us have made calls hoping to get an answering machine, but it is important to note the terms in which Daum describes her anxiety. Daum represents a generation already come of age, brought up in a world increasingly dominated by communications technologies, for whom television represents immediate, live experience (notice that she cites television rather than, say, theater as her model for the live) and live experience of any kind is undesirable and actually distressing.

For the moment, mechanical reproduction's assault on the auratic can be described as thorough but incomplete with respect to live performance. The next age, of which we are on the cusp, will be characterized by the final disappearance of the auratic as a perceptual category, though not of the cultural forms in which it was embodied, and the ascension of a "perception whose 'sense of the universal equality of all things' has increased" exponentially – perhaps even beyond what Benjamin imagined.

References

Baudrillard, J. (1983) *Simulations*, New York: Semiotext(e).

Benjamin, W. (1986 [1936]) "The Work of Art in the Age of Mechanical Reproduction," in *Video Culture: A Critical Investigation*, John G. Hanhardt (ed.), Layton, UT: Peregrine Smith Books.

Carroll, N. (1998) *A Philosophy of Mass Art*, Oxford: Oxford University Press.

Connor, S. (1989) *Postmodernist Culture: An Introduction to Theories of the Contemporary*, Oxford, Cambridge, MA: Basil Blackwell.

Cubitt, S. (1994) "Laurie Anderson: Myth, Management and Platitude," in *Art Has No History! The Making and Unmaking of Modern Art*, John Roberts (ed.), London, New York: Verso.

Daum, M. (1997) "Virtual Love," *The New Yorker*, 25 August and 1 September.

Densmore, J. (1991) *Riders on the Storm: My Life with Jim Morrison and the Doors* (audiobook), n.p. Seven Wolves Publishing.

Frith, S. (1988) "Picking up the Pieces," in *Facing the Music*, Simon Frith (ed.), New York: Pantheon.

Fuchs, E. (1996) *The Death of Character: Perspectives on Theater after Modernism*, Bloomington, IN: Indiana University Press.

Gracyk, T. (1996) *Rhythm and Noise: An Aesthetics of Rock*, Durham, NC: Duke University Press.

Wurtzler, S. (1992) "She Sang Live, But the Microphone Was Turned Off: The Live, the Recorded and the *Subject* of Representation," in *Sound Theory Sound Practice*, Rick Altman (ed.), New York, London: Routledge.

10

OFFICE POLITICS

Masculinity, feminism and the workplace in *Disclosure*

Yvonne Tasker

Our relationship to work (or the lack of it) provides a vital reference point in the constitution of social identity, our sense of who we are. We escape from work; we escape to work; work can frame social lives or alienate. Work has also been an important site for feminist debates and campaigns over equality. Second-wave feminist writers and campaigners not only challenged discriminatory employment laws but also emphasized the ideological work of the organization of gender within capitalism which produced distinctive spaces of public/private, aligned in turn with masculine and feminine. Feminism, then, has long understood inequality as both economically exploitative and cultural or discursive, as in some way expressed and/or produced within popular culture. I'm interested here in the ways in which Hollywood movies represent work, and the ways in which contemporary popular cultural discourses about a changing workplace inform such representations. That is, I am concerned here with aspects of the cultural production of "work."

There have been dramatic changes in American society in terms of patterns of work and employment for men and women. These patterns are familiar in other Western economies, with the rapid expansion of new technologies, part-time employment and a movement away from any notion of the male "breadwinner" or of jobs for life. The development of a small, female, professional middle-class working in areas such as medicine, law, business and education is also a feature of this economic transformation. (Though it is easy to overstate the extent of women's achievements, indeed such overstatement is quite commonplace.) Alongside these economic changes – and their social implications – we can also track the development of popular perceptions about men and women and the work that they do. Such perceptions have the status of a kind of folklore, which feed into our ideas about work: that women are taking "men's jobs," that men either are or would like to be more involved in parenting, that boys are somehow under-achieving in education, that accusations of sexual harassment are or can be (mis)used to political ends, or, to take a final example, that a rigid insistence on equality in work and in culture is stifling anyone of creativity, free expression or entrepreneurial activity (I am, of course, referring to the curious history and seemingly limitless scope of the term "political correctness"). Whether in spurious statistics or rigorous surveys, cinema, television or press features, the circulation of such ideas frames the analysis that follows.

It is partly in this context that the term "post-feminism" has acquired its significance. Since post-feminism is a controversial term, let me be clear what I mean by it here. First, post-feminism signals that certain principles of gender equality are accepted within the legal frameworks of particular Western economies, however patchily this is actually translated into opportunities. Second, post-feminism suggests how discourses of independence and self-definition for women widely inform popular culture, however compromised they might be or are perceived to be. For some writers post-feminism has a straightforward – reactionary – political meaning: it encapsulates an assumption that feminist battles for equality are either already won or no longer relevant. It is in this context that journalist Susan Faludi's 1991 American best-seller *Backlash* explored a contradiction between women's continuing struggles and an equality that is not only perceived to be somehow already achieved, but actually damaging to women. In another book first published in 1991, *Feminism without Women: Culture and Criticism in a "Postfeminist" Age*, Tania Modleski identifies a trend in both mass culture and academic thought – or at least in certain texts of both – which "in proclaiming or assuming the advent of postfeminism, are actually engaged in negating the critiques and undermining the goals of feminism – in effect, delivering us back into a prefeminist world" (1991: 3). As my qualifications indicate, I'm also skeptical about the term. And yet negation is also a response of sorts to achievement. For me, the significance of the appearance of post-feminism at the beginning of the 1990s was not so much a term without a referent, as an indication of both how much and how little had changed. The images that I'll discuss in this chapter are not, I would argue, prefeminist in Modleski's terms, though they are certainly equivocal about feminism.

Representing work

Within popular culture work is portrayed as a contested and, crucially, as a gendered space, one which is constructed in shifting relation to a domestic space of relationships, family and the home. Popular narratives use work to evoke qualities such as heroism or caring, typically avoiding (or only briefly alluding to) the more mundane aspects of making a living. In Hollywood movies work tends to be glamorous, or at least thrilling (law enforcement, the military, medicine and, of course, performance and showbiz). Editing out the dull bits of working life obviously makes sense in terms of the utopian aspects of popular cinema – its escapist role. Workplace settings also make for exciting television, whether work is portrayed as exhausting but ultimately meaningful (typical of police or medical series such as *ER*) or as the vibrant center of alienated lives as in *Ally McBeal's* kooky law office, into which the reality of clients' cases only occasionally intrudes.

Here I'll focus on the film *Disclosure* (US, 1994, *d.* Barry Levinson) to explore further some of these concerns. In particular I'll touch on the ways in which the movie draws on discourses about feminism, female sexuality and technology. Based on a best-selling Michael Crichton novel, the film follows hero Tom Sanders (Michael Douglas) through a nightmare work scenario in which he is passed over for promotion in favor of an old flame, Meredith Johnson (Demi Moore), who proceeds first to demand sex from him and then to accuse him of sexual harassment. The movie was sold as a racy thriller ("Sex is Power") with a powerful woman's harassment of a male employee as its central conceit. Its scenario revolves around the uncertainty of its white, middle-class hero – an everyman who finds himself enmeshed in perplexing circumstances – but, I would suggest, quite guardedly seeks to appeal more broadly to anyone who has been, or perceives themselves to have been, put down at work. *Disclosure* draws on a series of linked figures which recur in popular cultural discourses to do with gender and work, of which I will explore four. First, the construction of a professional woman in terms of predatory sexuality. (In *Working Girls* (1998) I discussed the film in the context of the femme fatale and new film noir, arguing that Moore's Meredith Johnson exemplifies both the power and limitations of an evolving hybrid stereotype produced from a femme fatale defined by sexual power and an independent woman defined largely by professional success. Yet, whilst Johnson is certainly a femme fatale, *Disclosure* is not a film noir (however we define that category) and here I'm framing the film rather differently). Here we have an invocation of one of the perspectives associated with post-feminism and identified above, that of excess: of things having gone "too far," women expecting "too much" and behaving badly as a consequence. Second, anxieties about male redundancy in both the job market and in terms of what Pfeil terms a "protector-provider" understanding of masculinity (1995: 236). Third, uncertainties about the role of new technologies, particularly technologies of communication, in the changing workplace. Such ideas and images build on those commonly expressed in science fiction that machines might replace or transform people, somehow taking away the qualities that make us human. Finally, I'll consider the ways in which arenas which foreground work as presentation (promotion, advertising, the law) rather than production are understood as threatening, and perhaps as "feminizing," in some way.

Of course *Disclosure* is just one instance of the cultural production of work, one which may or may not be read as typical. However, as I hope I've suggested already, it is far from the only movie or set of images to fore-ground these concerns. So, for example the arthouse femme fatale of *The Last Seduction* (1994) whose manipulative use of image is channeled into murder-ous people management; or Demi Moore as FBI secretary turned stripper turned investigator in the comedy thriller *Striptease* (1996); or the heady mix of sexual performance, paternity and unemployment in 1997's surprise British hit *The Full Monty*; or the disturbing and seemingly motiveless con-spiracy to humiliate a female co-worker in *In the Company of Men*, also from 1997. From British national cinema to mainstream Hollywood to niche movies trading off film noir's cultural capital; from comedy to erotic thrillers to US "indie" cinema – distinct spaces in which a supposed transfer of power from men to women becomes the subject of sexual contest. These movies may share certain broad themes, but they are all specific and differ-ent, and it isn't my intention to reductively suggest one dominant reading of the way that popular culture talks about gender and work. Indeed, one point that I'd like to make is that the production of ideas about men and women at work in a film like *Disclosure* can't be easily separated from the film's concerns with technology, for example. One thing we can perhaps generalize about – and this does seem to me to be significant – is that in this cultural economy, power is typically understood as finite: if women gain it, men must surely have lost it. In this the cultural legacy of what was termed in the 1970s the "battle of the sexes" can be seen as staged in the context of the workplace. Whilst I'm not subscribing to this binary model, I think it is important to recognize the continuing purchase of the rhetoric of battle. Equally, I hope to show how *Disclosure* stages, and then qualifies, this defin-ing image of power as "men versus women."

Disclosure resonates with feminist concerns and the cultural production of work as both gendered and meaningful, not only through its lively evocation of a powerful professional woman in the figure of Meredith Johnson, but through the centrality of sexuality and sexual harassment in the workplace. The film's narrative trajectory might seem fairly straightforward: a scenario in which the peace of mind and financial status of a benevolent and success-ful man is unfairly threatened by a younger woman who – it is implied, although we will return to this – has been promoted in part due to her physi-cal appearance, and in part due to her people (rather than technical) skills. And yet even if we focus only on Tom, though the film clearly works to convey the sense of office interactions more broadly, the journey that is mapped for us isn't particularly straightforward.

Following Crichton's novel, *Disclosure* maps anxieties about masculinity and a changing economy onto the figure of a sexually assertive woman. Such a confluence perhaps inevitably recalls the 1987 hit *Fatal Attraction*, a film which sparked the interest of feature writers, and which captured for many feminist scholars both the misogyny (and the contradictions) of Hollywood's version of working women as monstrous. Susan Faludi discusses the film at length and reference to it punctuates the interviews included in her book – with the film cited as a sort of folk evidence that women's independence had got out of hand (and hence, for Faludi, used to suggest the culpability of feminism). Here Faludi touches on a set of questions which have long engaged cultural and film theorists, questions to do with image and influence, reflection and construction. It's certainly the case that *Disclosure* sought to capitalize on a controversial, sexy issue: high-profile cases in the US such as the Clarence Thomas/Anita Hill hearings and the fallout over Tailhook provide one important context. Contemporary reviews and think pieces were also helped by the timing of the release of David Mamet's *Oleanna* (1994) which also explored the implications of a sexual harassment allegation. Further, the film's two stars were both associated to some extent with controversial roles (Douglas in movies including *Fatal Attraction, Basic Instinct* and *Falling Down*; Moore in *Indecent Proposal*). Clearly, then, the movie not only responded to ideas and images circulating in the wider culture but self-consciously courted controversy and debate.

Popular culture is hardly short of images of sexual tension (or even old-fashioned romance) in the workplace: the hierarchical, sometimes eroticized relationship of exploitation and dependence between co-workers, or between managers and assistants, for instance. In turn these tensions form the basis of Neil LaBute's study of corporate misogyny *In the Company of Men* not only in terms of how the two male protagonists treat the woman they woo and reject but also in terms of their shifting relationship to each other and to others at work. As I have argued elsewhere (Tasker, 1998) the location of professional women as threatening in the workplace provides a particular charge to these hierarchies. Neither was *Disclosure* the first film to suggest that women could be just as ruthless as men (or, frequently, more than). Mike Nichols's popular romantic comedy *Working Girl* (1988) trades off this assertion, in the self-centered, cold-hearted boss played by Sigourney Weaver. (For a useful discussion of the film in terms of work and gender see Julia Hallam (1993).) One doesn't have to look far to see that powerful women tend to be inscribed as threatening within popular cinema and culture; this is so clearly spelt out that it can't really be seen as a subtext. Yet we can also interrogate such images further to consider what else might be going on in popular representations of gender and work.

Crichton's novel ends with brief summaries of what happened next to each of the central characters which tells us that "Meredith Johnson was named Vice President for Operations and Planning at IBM's office in Paris. She subsequently married the United States Ambassador to France, Edward Harmon, following his divorce. She has since retired from business" (1994: 454). The scenario thus removes her first from the US and then from the world of business altogether. While Meredith has been fired at the film's end, she speaks with confidence of her future career: "I've had calls from ten head-hunters with job offers in the last hour. Don't be surprised if I'm back in ten years to buy this place." Though at times it is suggested that she has succeeded through exploiting her sexuality, by Mary Ann Hunter for example, more significant is the extent to which Meredith's skills are in communication rather than production (in that the latter has often been coded as masculine). Further, Johnson is not the only powerful woman in the DigiCom workplace – in contrast to, say, the narrative of heroic female struggle against military tradition in *G.I. Jane* (1997, Demi Moore again). Thus, although Davies and Smith are broadly critical of *Disclosure*, they do suggest that the presence of a series of successful women (Cindy Chang, Mary Ann Hunter and Stephanie Kaplan) as key characters "complexifies and somewhat redirects the overtly anti-feminist representation of Moore's character" (1997: 43). Catherine Alvarez (Romi Maffia), the lawyer specializing in sexual harassment cases to whom Sanders turns for help, is both direct and impassioned whilst being a gifted communicator. Both film and book contrast the older figure of Stephanie Kaplan (Rosemary Forsyth) to the aggressively sexual Meredith. However, we might question the terms of the opposition; it is significant that the film is careful not to oppose good women in the home to bad women at work, as *Fatal Attraction* so explicitly had in the past. More significant in terms of the film's preoccupation with new technologies of information and communication is that the final appointment of Kaplan (rather than Sanders) to replace Johnson rewards a powerful woman who is signaled from the start as skilled in both communication and technology.

Masculinity: work, power and populism

Ultimately, for Stella Bruzzi, "*Disclosure* remains a man's film, but an apologetic one constructed around the persistently emphasized weakness of Tom" (1997: 132). What does it mean to say that this is a man's film? Fears of male redundancy are certainly pervasive, expressed in minor characters and in star Michael Douglas's familiar anxious expression, a look of incomprehension that often precedes the face hardening in anger and ultimately resolve. Jude Davies and Carol Smith are not the first to locate the film as one of a series in which the ordinary vulnerability of Douglas's star text is exploited. Douglas, they suggest, has built his star persona "on making explicit some of the contradictions and multivalences in constructions of white masculinity" operating uneasily across "both the traditional spaces of white masculinity and the domestic spaces of the transformed man, staging the difficulties of domestication and some of the frustrations of 'angry white males'" (1997: 25). In the context of a discussion of *Basic Instinct*, Steve Cohan cites J. Hoberman on "Douglas's star persona as 'the heroic, resentful, white-guy, white-collar, heterosexual victim'" (1998: 274), an ordinary man who finds himself attracted to and threatened by an aggressively sexual woman in both *Fatal Attraction* and *Basic Instinct*, or as breaking under stress in *Falling Down*.

Though Sanders protests his powerlessness – "Sexual harassment is about power. When did I have the power? When?" – this is rather undercut, or at least qualified, by, on the one hand, the *mise-en-scène* of a luxurious family home, so lovingly showcased in the opening scene, and, on the other hand, by Tom's learning, through the legal mediation of the sexual harassment case, that his assistant Cindy (Jacqueline Kim) finds his behavior toward her inappropriate. Yet he is also a loser (as Bruzzi puts it) who fails in his attempt to go from rich to really rich. All this is given a mildly populist inflection with the characterization of Tom who, we learn in the opening scene, is both successful and benevolent: his wife affectionately berates him as "the one person I know who sucks up to the people below you." This links the movie to those liberal movies of the 1980s and early 1990s in which Hollywood was both enthralled and appalled by the cult of money and consumerism (in films such as *Other People's Money* or *Pretty Woman*). And given the emphasis that both I and other critics have placed on Douglas's image in making sense of *Disclosure*, there is no small irony in the fact that Douglas, perhaps more than any other star, was associated with this cultural moment in his charismatic "greed is good" turn as Gordon Gekko for Oliver Stone's *Wall Street* (1987).

Fears of job insecurity are, not surprisingly, tied to questions about masculinity and what it means to be a man in work and in the family. As *Disclosure* takes us through the first day of intrigue, Tom moves from a complacent assumption that a promotion is his to the anxiety that he may be out of a job. During his journey to work in the opening sequences, we see Tom talking to an unemployed businessman who comes to underline Tom's own sense of insecurity – and potential fate – as the film progresses. In turn, and echoing the representations of aristocratic men as effete, management is signaled in the film as "feminized," an excessive concern with costume and appearance suggesting here that they cannot be trusted. Phil Blackburn, a key conspirator, is seen early on meticulously manicuring his nails, filmed in close-up as he plots with the well-groomed Garvin via speaker-phone. In this short sequence male senior management are shown to combine deceit (they are plotting), a lack of directness (via the technology) and a concern with personal appearance. After Meredith has humiliated Tom through her sexual demands he goes home to replay the experience in a dream in which he chats to top man Garvin in the lift; Garvin admires Tom's clothes (as Meredith had admired his body) and then makes a pass (using Meredith's words: "Now you have the power. You have something I want"). For Stella Bruzzi this sequence demonstrates "the fragility of Tom's masculine ego [. . .] represented through the rise of the homosexual repressed" (1997: 132), suggesting that what horrifies Tom about the dream is his evident contentment within it, his "ease" with the conversation about clothes and fabrics. Thus the dream showcases Tom's "narcissistic idealization of himself as an expensively dressed man" (ibid.: 133). Such nervous comedy around masculinity, status, and costume is also evident in, for example, Doug Liman's *Swingers* (1996) with the adjusting of costumes in the Las Vegas scene and Trent's repeated insistence that Mikey is "money." However, we can also usefully frame the sequence in terms of the film's broader preoccupation with image and appearance, and with the machinations of management, exploitative arrangements expressed here as sexualized threat.

Tom is defined by his scruffy dress in the film. This aligns him with the other men in his team, engineers and practical people who are working directly with the technology, who are consequently distanced from the management (the suits). His appearance in a suit in the dream is a jolt – a cue that something is not quite right – since throughout the film Tom is shown to have a problem with the signs of power. The toothpaste on his tie in the opening scenes is turned into a joke by Meredith. For Stella Bruzzi the tie functions like "Nick's middle-aged V-neck jumper for the night-club scene in *Basic Instinct* [. . .] as symbols of emasculation, of not belonging, of not understanding the rules of the game" (ibid.: 130). Bruzzi sees such scenes in terms of a "bumbling need to crudely state [. . .] masculinity," an attempt that doesn't work since "[t]his manliness as masquerade is phallic panic, a desperate, embarrassing, hysterical reaction to encroaching insignificance" (ibid.). Yet in *Disclosure* Tom's dress also positions him on the right side, as an honest guy doing battle with the management who provide the money but who don't really understand how things work.

The image of unkempt men has a particular resonance in the popular mythology of the computer business, understood as a sort of new frontier, characterized by a more informal way of doing business which then gets taken over by a corporate attitude alien to the techno-pioneers. (There is a suggestion of this early on in Blackburn's aside to Tom that it was different when they were all together "in the valley.") The film's set design expresses these themes very effectively, constructing an office space that, through its very openness and modernity (glass offices around a central cavernous space), renders Tom vulnerable to surveillance. There is, of course, an irony here in that for a good part of the film Tom doesn't understand why things (that is, the new drives the company are producing and on which the financially lucrative merger rests) don't work. Though it is through solving this problem that Tom is able to defeat Meredith and save his job, it is interesting to note that he is never coded by the film as particularly smart. He is, after all, middle-management, a division head whose role is to manage the work of those in the US and at the plant in Malaysia. It is fitting then that in the aftermath of Meredith's dismissal, it is Stephanie Kaplan (a different kind of suit) who is promoted to the top job – a point I'll return to at the end of this chapter.

New technologies: style and substance

So concerns about appearance and the ability to read signs are central to *Disclosure*. Costume is used to develop our sense of conflict between Tom and Meredith (who, as Bruzzi (1997: 134) notes, breaks the codes which define what working women are supposed to wear) and between Tom and the DigiCom management more broadly. And, of course, as keen viewers we can pick up on some of the signs that Tom seems to miss (we have an advantage over him for most of the movie, after all). In the novel, a frustrated Sanders who has just been humiliated in a key meeting exclaims angrily to Johnson: "You're just talking about appearances. Corporate appearance in a corporate meeting. But in the end someone has to actually build the damn drive" (Crichton, 1994: 142). Later he complains to his mentor Max Dorfman (an important character in the novel, though not in the film) that "she's dangerous. She's one of those MBA image people, focused on image, everything image, never substance" (ibid.: 229).

This kind of opposition between objects and appearances, production versus consumption, is a familiar feature of American populist discourses of the 1980s. The film makes relatively little out of the location of production outside the US, highlighting instead the rise of women professionals and new technologies as the defining features of a changing US capitalism that leaves Sanders vulnerable. Yet evident in the dialogs which take place between the film's Seattle location and the production line in Malaysia is the importance of an economic relationship between West and East. And it is cost-cutting in Malaysia – instituted by Meredith – that is ultimately revealed as the cause of the production problems. For Davies and Smith this is the key subtext of the film, screened by the sexual harassment case, and concerning a "switch away from domestic manufacturing on the one hand, and the globalization of capital and the emergence of Pacific Rim economies on the other" (1997: 39). These themes are more evidently foregrounded in the book which casts Sanders's previous dispute with the narcissistic Phil Blackburn in terms of a desire to retain high-skilled American jobs.

What makes this a little more interesting in *Disclosure* is the particular resonance of the computer business, with the technologies of information and communication that the film showcases. Both novel and film center on technology and its possibilities and implications for working and social relationships. Women and technology are seen to be redefining the workplace – and the role of men within it. As Davies and Smith note, Meredith Johnson is associated not only with sexuality but with a visionary attitude toward new technologies, one that significantly fails to mention money. They quote from her first speech to the Seattle office at some length: "What we're selling here is freedom. We offer through technology what religion and revolution have promised but never delivered. Freedom from the physical body. Freedom from race and gender, from nationality and personality, from place and time. Communicating by cellular phone and hand held computer, PVA and built-in fax modem, we can relate to each other as pure consciousness" (in Davies and Smith, 1997: 40–1). Of course, although this is patently fantasy one can't help but recall a film such as *The Net* (1995) in which freelance computer expert Angela Bennett (Sandra Bullock) is so withdrawn that although she works from home, none of her neighbors can confirm her identity when her existence is erased via computer technology.

Positioning *Disclosure* in relation to what he terms the "yuppie horror film," Barry Keith Grant notes that the film "suggests throughout a fear of the body that culminates [...] in a complete rejection of the body" (1998: 290). (It is worth noting that this is yet another way to generically/thematically frame the film.) It seems to me that Johnson's emphasis on freedom from the body qualifies her portrayal in interesting ways, not least since the audience is so regularly reminded of Moore's star body. As I've argued elsewhere there is a tendency in the film to conflate discourses about gender and about technology, a conflation "literalized in the image of a virtual Meredith Johnson deleting files in cyberspace as Tom Sanders looks on powerless, having been 'locked out' of the system." Despite his exclusion, however, Sanders makes use of "less cutting edge technologies [...] fax, e-mail, video, answerphone and mobile phone all come to his rescue" (Tasker, 1998: 131). These companion fears and fantasies are central to the film – technology as a way of escaping physical proximity, as both threat and aid. Here *Disclosure* expresses something of the ambivalence that many people express about new information and communication technologies, particularly in relation to work. While a mobile phone and home computer can free us from the office, they also signal a process by which work encroaches into other spaces (you can always be reached). *Disclosure* starts and ends with e-mail: in the film's first image Tom's daughter reads a message on the home computer whilst the final matching image is of a loving message sent from his family to the office. Davies and Smith see this as an attempt at an unproblematic ideological closure, with "The Family" as anchor (1997: 46). Although their sentimentality is undeniable, these communications also suggest new channels between home and work, and the blurring of distinctions between these spaces.

Conclusion: the right person for the job?

In conclusion, I'd like to think a little about the movie's end and the appointment of Stephanie Kaplan, who Tom finally realizes is "an extraordinary woman," as Vice President. Addressing the Seattle employees, Garvin suggests that he may have "focused too much on breaking the glass ceiling" instead of looking for "the best person to run things." For Bruzzi, Kaplan is, when compared to Meredith at least, "safe and unthreatening," described as "a middle-aged mother" and "the sort of woman any man would entrust a job to" (1997: 135). Davies and Smith also characterize Kaplan in relation to Johnson, as "less highly sexualized, more hard-working and talented (almost to the point of omniscience) [. . .] with student son in tow" (1997: 40). Whilst the two women are clearly opposed, and it is the case that the film casts Johnson as monstrous in part because of her sexuality, these judgements seem a little problematic to me. Maybe Kaplan is designed to produce a liberal cop-out, but it is one that highlights what is perhaps most interesting about the film – the qualification of the battle of the sexes framework it has initially constructed. And while Kaplan is revealed as the source of anonymous e-mail tips sent to Tom through the course of film, and her speech acknowledges his capabilities, calling on him to act as her "right hand," he still ends the movie not only passed over for a promotion he had simply assumed was his but also genuinely applauding a woman's success. (Crichton's novel has Kaplan tell Sanders that she won't be in the job for long – seeing the chance for a move to new partners Conley-White – and that she sees him as her successor.)

Pam Cook writes about *Disclosure* as a reversal of "the pattern of female victim/male aggressor in what can only be construed as a highly anxious response to the power of women in the workplace." "However," she cautions, "the film highlights with startling clarity the fact that its motivating fantasy of sexual submission and dominance is not gender specific" (1998: 243). I agree that although the narrative is politically loaded, neither the fantasy on offer, nor the experiences addressed, are gender-specific. And I hope to have teased out some of the ways in which *Disclosure*, whilst it is obviously deeply equivocal around sexuality and feminism, has a specificity which repays attention. Tom Sanders is benevolent, but he is also complacent. In the game of office politics with its moves and intrigues, Tom is (almost) always the last to know. In contrast to Stephanie Kaplan, he can't see that the world is changing; he can't read the signs. A final irony: if he wins out in the end, it is by actually grappling with the need to communicate and to listen, to think about images, about how things look as well as how they work.

References

Bruzzi, Stella (1997) *Undressing Cinema: Clothing and Identity in the Movies*, London: Routledge.

Cohan, Steve (1998) "Censorship and Narrative Indeterminacy in *Basic Instinct*: 'You Won't Learn Anything From Me I Don't Want You To Know,'" in *Contemporary Hollywood Cinema*, Steve Neale and Murray Smith (eds), London: Routledge.

Cook, Pam (1998) "No Fixed Address: The Women's Picture From *Outrage* to *Blue Steel*," in *Contemporary Hollywood Cinema*, Steve Neale and Murray Smith (eds), London: Routledge.

Crichton, Michael (1994) *Disclosure*, London: Arrow.

Davies, Jude and Smith, Carol R. (1997) *Gender, Ethnicity and Sexuality in Contemporary American Film*, Edinburgh: Keele University Press.

Faludi, Susan (1992) *Backlash: The Undeclared War Against Women* (revised edition), London: Chatto & Windus.

Grant, Barry Keith (1998) "Rich and Strange: the Yuppie Horror Film," in *Contemporary Hollywood Cinema*, Steve Neale and Murray Smith (eds), London: Routledge.

Hallam, Julia (1993) *"Working Girl:* A Woman's Film for the Eighties," in *Gendering the Reader*, Sara Mills (ed.), London: Harvester Wheatsheaf.

Modleski, Tania (1991) *Feminism without Women: Culture and Criticism in a "Postfeminist" Age*, London: Routledge.

Pfeil, Fred (1995) *White Guys: Studies in Postmodern Domination and Difference*, London: Verso.

Tasker, Yvonne (1998) *Working Girls: Gender, Sexuality and Popular Cinema*, London: Routledge.

Webster, Duncan (1988) *Looka Yonder! The Imaginary America of Populist Culture*, London: Routledge.

11

CITIZEN OR TV BLIP?

The politics and pleasures of a televisual semiotic
democracy

Robin Nelson

Introduction

By reflecting on changes in UK television production over the past decade,
this chapter intends ultimately to point to cultural work to be done and,
indeed, to make a contribution to that work. In the May 1997 British
general election, New Labour achieved a landslide victory. Skeptics doubted
that anything profound had changed in UK political culture, whilst the
more optimistic found just talk of ethics and communitarian values a
welcome corrective to the discourses of aggressive consumerism and individualistic self-reliance typical of the Tory years. The four years between New
Labour's first landslide victory and their second landslide victory of June
2001 have probably done more to confirm rather than dispel the skeptics'
doubts. Nonetheless, how far a cultural shift will be effected still remains to
be seen, but it is important at least to keep open the conversation (in Rorty's
sense, 1989: 318). In Chapter 1 of this book, Graham Murdock does this by
throwing an ethical-political light critically to illuminate the corporatizing
dynamics of today's cultural production. This chapter functions in that
light.

It is ironic, at a cultural moment which speaks so eloquently of choice,
diversity, and pluralism, that "corporatization" (in Murdock's sense of the
privatization of public bodies) denies us a common space in which to debate,
and limits discursive range. In discussing the popular television drama,
Heartbeat, below, I offer an illustration from the television industry. But the
point holds even in higher education – now itself "corporatized" and spoken
of as an industry. Though it was formalized in a directorate memo in one
particular institution, the effective banning of the word "problem" in favor
of "opportunity" will be familiar to many academics as we examine our
"portfolios." My point is that the very discourse of corporate institutions
constructed as businesses frequently talks up choice and opportunity at the
expense of a language of critique.

But it is not just a matter of language. Constraints on openness and creativity are structurally systemic. In Chapter 5, Dina Berkeley, drawing on the Study of Industrial Modes of Production in Television Drama, finds that there are inhibitions to risk-taking and creativity at all levels of contemporary UK television production. The aim in this chapter is more broadly to track the cultural work undertaken in the UK television industry in the wake of Thatcherism and to assess what is at stake practically, in terms of the outcomes of commercial imperatives, and theoretically, in terms of notions of freedom based on consumer choice. For, although television viewing has declined slightly in UK in recent years, it remains the dominant domestic medium of information and entertainment and is thus itself still a powerful force in cultural work.

UKTV goes global

The break up of the long-established British television industry structure by the 1990 Broadcasting Act, that "watershed in the history of British television" (BFI, 1991: 44), paved the way for multi-channeling in the UK. A shake-up was long overdue − in the view of some. Certainly, from the first BBC transmissions in 1936, through the introduction of ITV in 1955, BBC2 in 1964 and Channel 4 in 1982, the pluralizing of television channels in Britain had made limited progress by 1990. The keyword might be "stately," to indicate not just a measured pace but also the BBC's cherished notion of itself as "the voice of the nation" in its semi-autonomy from both government and the market as enshrined in the Corporation's Charter. It was precisely this established situation which Margaret Thatcher's deregulating impulse was destined to explode.

In early 1989, Rupert Murdoch's Sky Television began broadcasting four channels from Luxembourg via the Astra satellite, though the shortage of dishes restricted Sky's audience in the UK mainly to cable users. In 1990, Britain's own official Digital Broadcasting Service (DBS) was awarded two more channels by the IBA, giving it five altogether, but it began hesitantly, postponing its launch until March. The fact was that the viewing public seemed uninterested in satellite, perhaps because the terrestrial broadcasting structure was so entrenched, and indeed genuinely enjoyed a mixture of popularity and prestige. Even Murdoch's vigorous and very expensive advertising campaign had so little effect that Sky and BSB were forced to merge in November 1990, just as the Broadcasting Act received Royal Assent.

Exposure to market forces was, of course, the keynote of Mrs Thatcher's radicalism generally, and the television industry was swiftly unmuffled. To sum up what is now familiar history post-1990: the BBC license fee was effectively frozen by being linked to the retail price index, forcing the Corporation to extend its commercial activities to raise additional income. An auction was set up for ITV "Channel 3" franchises with only a minimal, ill-defined quality criterion secured at the eleventh hour. Channel 4, divorced in its means of funding from ITV, was exposed more directly to the market. A fifth terrestrial channel was facilitated – though it took its time coming into being (Channel 5 in 1997).

Alleged restrictive practices in ITV were under investigation but, in any case, "streamlining" preparations for the 1990 Act reduced staffing levels by approximately 15 percent. In the BBC, an internal market, "Producer Choice," was set up following the Home Office's use of accountants Price Waterhouse to advise on the Corporation's efficiency. A quota requirement was introduced for all channels to import 25 percent of output from independents. The IBA had already relaxed its sponsorship code in 1989 allowing Powergen innovatively to sponsor the weather in its now familiar style (introduced on 11 September 1989). Sponsorship and product placement have since proliferated to the point where nothing is sacred. Boddingtons and Guinness sit alongside Newton and Ridley at the bar of the Rover's Return and *Coronation Street* overall is now Cadbury's chocolate-coated.

In sum, a very significant commercialization of British television has occurred in the last decade of the twentieth century, more than enough to dislodge any residual PSB complacencies. Whilst the penetration of new technologies still accounts for only 10 percent (cable) and 18 percent (satellite) of the UK audience share, it has extended to the point of impact on the schedules, particularly through its purchase of rights to key sporting events but, more recently, for television drama. *ER* devotees are obliged to get dished, or cabled, up to keep up to speed with the next series.

Whilst British television culture remains distinctive amongst national outputs, programming has been directly affected in two particular ways. First, by the reduction of money available for making programs as so much of the relatively fixed income of the industry is dissipated in wasteful pilots commissioned from "independents" for series which never get made, or squandered on franchises and rights-inflation. Between 1990 and 2000 the amount spent on buying rights to sports programs increased tenfold. Second, the programming range has been restricted in response to market forces. As Bourdieu has remarked: "[i]t is very disturbing to see this ratings mindset established [. . .] because it jeopardizes works that may not necessarily meet audience expectations but, in time, can create their own audience" (1998: 29–30).

The history of "quality television" is littered with stories of drama series which became either popular and/or highly acclaimed but were almost cancelled owing to initially poor ratings (see Nelson, 1997: 30–2 and 264n3). The very function of television is at issue here in terms of its capacity to surprise and challenge in contrast with its construction of consumers to accelerate activity in the marketplace through home shopping.

In 1989, at the time of the White Paper anticipating the Broadcasting Act, ITV was reported to have "begun eliminating program strands which advertisers find unhelpful" (BFI, 1989: 19). Where sponsorship or co-production money are needed for relatively big budget drama productions, "safe" twinnings result. Beamish Stout marries with *Inspector Morse* or, in co-production, WGBH Boston hitches up with the BBC on *Middlemarch*. Predictably, stylish medical and detective series and period productions of classic novels have dominated British TV drama output in recent years. Deregulation and privatization do not necessarily entail more choice. As Tony Garnett has remarked, "[a] good rule in life is: look to see who is paying. The ad buyers are the biggest power in television and indirectly control the content of most of it" (1998: 14).

The hard-hitting contemporary dramas of the *Play for Today* and *Wednesday Play* years which – at least in the mythology – established a common space for social debate, may still have their occasional counterparts. But they are more marginal in the schedules, often being relegated to minority or cult slots late night on BBC2 or Channel 4. I shall return to the question of the diffusion of audience below. But to sharpen the focus of my concerns, I turn now to a specific television drama example, *Heartbeat* (YTV for ITV), the first series having been screened in 1991. In ratings terms *Heartbeat* was probably the most successful British drama series of the 1990s, its audience having built from an early 10 million to well in excess of 15 million viewers. I have written up the production history of the series elsewhere (see Nelson, 1997: 73–88) so I shall confine myself here to a summary of points key to my argument.

Under ITV Network's Audience Planning, *Heartbeat* was made and marketed more or less like any other commercial product today. Focus groups were set up to define the product concept and to respond to what effectively became a pilot first episode (as the first shooting was re-made). Viewer-graphics led to target market segments, constructed by Network Planning as "green mums," "EastEnd girls" and "lager lads." A promotional strategy was aimed at these groups, bringing out in a promotional trailer the features attractive to each: soft-hitting, social problem narratives for the "green mums"; maximum exposure of Nick Berry's love interests for the "EastEnd girls"; and vintage vehicles and police stories (apparently) for the "lager lads." Pop songs from the 1960s were shown by the market research to be favored by most, so aspects of each narrative are over-dubbed offering nostalgia to the "green mums" and postmodern "retro" to the younger audience. The second series was modified by product evaluation subsequent to the first. For example, Greengrass, originally conceived as a minor comic role, emerged as a major character; and the popularity of the rural environment led to more frequent, "cinematic," wide-angle shots of the North Yorkshire moors. The point of this sketch is to illustrate looped feedback from market research and evaluation into production to offer, at worst, a kind of "television drama by numbers" in which *Dixon of Dock Green* and *Juliet Bravo* meet *All Creatures Great and Small* to yield *Heartbeat*.

Heartbeat is thus both unremarkable and highly remarkable. In one sense it is an undoubtedly popular, comfortable rural police series for Sunday evening ITV viewing. From another perspective, it inaugurates a new mode of commercialized television drama production privileging a demand-side aesthetic. Extending the instrumentalizing tendencies of "ratings discourse" (Ang, 1991: 50), this approach to making drama feeds the reception information gleaned from the minute-by-minute ratings assessment almost directly back into production. It is the TV drama equivalent of the Benetton economy. The outcome of this mode of production is what I call "commercial postmodernism" (see Nelson, 1997: 84–5). The television text is a kind of bricolage, a reshuffling of "fragments of preexisting texts, the building blocks of older cultural and social production" (Jameson, 1993: 96). Devoid of sense-making frames, the structure of the text is paratactical, the mere juxtaposition of more or less unrelated strands borrowed from a range of other texts. To repeat in plain terms, *Dixon* meets *Bravo* meets *All Creatures* set to 1960s pop music gives us *Heartbeat*. There is little attempt to weave the strands into the organic integrity of a more traditional, authored, television play, let alone to tell, in Garnett's words again, "[s]trong stories about a recognizable contemporary experience; about our own lives and dreams and nightmares" (1998: 15).

Another facet of contemporary cultural production is relevant here: the notion of a dislocation of linguistic signs from referents to yield that "random play of signifiers which we call postmodernism" (Jameson, 1993: 96). The range of meanings and pleasures supposedly constructed by the numerous and various readers of such a fluid text, indicates, according to theorists such as Stanley Fish (see 1980), that there are as many processed texts as there are readers. Such limited models of reception (see also Fiske, 1987: 96) greatly overstress, in my view, the apparent agency of the reader as if s/he were no longer subject to the negotiation of hegemonic social forces, let alone those of textual construction. In a short period of Media Studies history the dominant view appears to have shifted from a 1970s *Screen* conception of the interpellation and fixed positioning of the spectator by the text, to a 2000s semiotic democracy in which everyone is notionally free to be whoever they wish and to read/create textual pleasures and meanings howsoever they like. Borrowing O'Neill's words to summarize the drift of my argument here, "postmodern atomism dislocates individuals from their institutional contexts so that each appears to float freely in an entirely semiotic space" (1995: 7).

At this point, I want to shift another gear to draw attention to an homology between the television industry's extended ratings discourse constructing a segmented audience and the academy's emphasis (in Media Studies particularly) on audience research based on a model of fragmented microcultures rather than a social community. Even in the most carefully structured and self-reflexive ethnography, there is an element of conceptual constructed-ness. Empirical studies, that is to say, are not neutral, they take a discursive position, they are "coming from somewhere." Whilst at once acknowledging the contribution made by television audience studies such as those pioneered by Dave Morley (see 1980 and 1986), I look to bring out here some political implications of models emphasizing difference rather than those shared features of a society, what one might term "citizenship."

Carey has reminded us of the shared roots of the terms "commonness," "communion," "community" and "communication," pointing out that an "intellectual aversion to the idea of [common] culture derives in part from our obsessive individualism, which makes psychological life the permanent reality" (1989: 19). Picking up on Carey's remarks in the light of postmodern notions of textual production, I would suggest that the privileging of the dispersal of meanings and pleasures is imbricated in a rightwards political shift. This is not to deny a proliferation of pleasures genuinely experienced in the contemporary, but it is to suggest a correspondence between textual theory, audience study and a rightward drift in conceiving, and consequently measuring, the pleasures of a semiotic democracy. For, as Carey notes, pleasures are measured almost exclusively in individualized, psychological spaces, exnominating any sense of the value in the commonly-held or collective. As Jenks summarizes:

> The social bond has, it would seem, dispersed into a proliferation of signs and the reality of our being together is fabricated through a series of infinitely reproducible similarities; the simulations of simulacra. History becomes no longer ordained through human desire and purpose but through an apparently semi-autonomous cybernetic technology.
>
> (1993: 125)

Today's cultural questions – perhaps as a result of poststructuralist insights – seem to me, however, to need less "either/or" and more "both/and" thinking. Accordingly, I draw in this chapter on both poststructuralist/ postmodern texts and also on more materially grounded Marxist critics.

I acknowledge some democratic tendencies in the postmodern challenge to traditional hierarchies and the consequent opening up of spaces – of room for maneuver at least – for previously marginalized social groups and individuals. I recognize, too, that quality programs (however they might be defined) may arise in the most commercially-driven production contexts, in the USA for example. However, I attempt here to offer a critique of the political economy of television culture – and of television drama production, circulation and reception in particular – from a standpoint advocating renewed attention to citizenship and common culture. For, unless we perceive the march of history to be either ineluctably progressive or merely ineluctable – and Lyotard (1984), of course, tells us that all the Grand

Narratives of Enlightenment culture are defunct – we need not dismiss such ideals simply as past their sell-by-date.

Attempting, in conclusion then, to relate television culture and television drama to new times, I propose the following. That the multi-channeling impetus of British television should be regarded more circumspectly and that, in the UK, we should be cautious about abandoning our unique Public Service Broadcasting ethos. If the range of programming is narrowed, the proliferation of channels does not present more choice, merely the illusion of choice. A large number of specialist channels may well address the local interests of microcultures, but what is also needed in a pluralist world, as Murdock aptly puts it, is "a collective exploration of difference, not the perpetuation of separate spheres" (Skovmand and Schroder, 1992: 39). The industry structure I have in mind might be more akin to the original Channel 4 remit and funding mechanism than the BBC in its less responsive days. The key point, however, is that some other values besides those of unrestrained commercialism must be kept in play in the context of communications while national governments, working through international agreements, still have the power to restrain transnational corporate giants who increasingly threaten to by-pass them. This last observation brings me finally back to the academy in relation to the industry.

I suffer under no illusions that YTV will stop making *Heartbeat* in the light of my analysis or that Rupert Murdoch will not continue to buy rights on more and more sports to consolidate his virtual satellite monopoly position. So what cultural work might an academic do professionally besides encouraging students to question everything and think for themselves? If the concept of Gramsci's "organic intellectual" is outmoded (and I'm not wholly convinced it is), consider the following. Rorty suggests that if solidarity does not reside in the core self of human beings it may have to be made rather than found (1989). Ien Ang observes that:

> [f]or the academic and professional community of audience researchers [. . .] determining the political context of their work is [. . .] difficult. But this is precisely the reason why it is all the more important to *construct* such aims and purposes, to define the modalities of political intervention which can energize our interest in knowing audiences.
>
> (1996: 79, original emphasis)

Even if, as knowing poststructuralists, we do not recognize the fixity of anything let alone any simple groundedness to truth, we cannot avoid engagement in the construction of values in the world. Collectively, and as individuals, we have interests which should be recognized, acknowledged and mobilized.

My particular plea in conclusion, then, is that the academy abandons its refusal to discuss questions of judgement and cultural value in the fashion-able manner of the past decade and that colleagues be prepared again to get their hands dirty in addressing what O'Neill calls "the life-world claims of everyday knowledge and values" (1995: 6). Matters of ethics, politics and aesthetics, inevitably inseparable in the sphere of television, must be debated if we are to avoid the pseudo-community of "TV blips" offered by Kroker and Cook as the only available substitute for "authentic human solidarities" (1988: 273, 279). If we cannot go the full way with Habermas to assume "communicative rationality" (1979: 3), the very least we can do is to engage in debate "where the hope of agreement is never lost so long as the conversation lasts" (Rorty, 1979: 318).

References

Ang, Ien (1991) *Desperately Seeking the Audience*, London: Routledge.

Ang, Ien (1996) *Looking Glass Wars*, London: Routledge.

British Film Institute (1989) *BFI Film and Television Handbook 1990*, London: British Film Institute.

British Film Institute (1991) *BFI Film and Television Handbook 1992*, London: British Film Institute.

Bourdieu, Pierre (1998) *On Television and Journalism* (first published 1996, trans. Priscilla Parkhurst Ferguson), London: Pluto Press.

Carey, James (1989) *Communication as Culture*, Boston: Unwin Hayman.

Fish, Stanley (1980) *Is There a Text in This Class?: The Authority of Interpretive Communities*, Cambridge, MA and London: Harvard University Press.

Fiske, John (1987) *Television Culture* (Methuen rep. 1989), London: Routledge.

Garnett, T. (1988) "Recipe for a dust-up," *Sight and Sound*, 13–15.

Habermas, Jürgen (1979) "What is Universal Pragmatics?" in *Communication and The Evolution of Society* (first published 1976, trans. Thomas McCarthy), London: Heinemann.

Jameson, Frederic (1993) *Postmodernism or the Cultural Logic of Late Capitalism*, London: Verso.

Jenks, Chris (1993) *Cultural Production*, London: Routledge.

Kroker, A. and Cook, D. (1988) *The Postmodern Scene*, Basingstoke: Macmillan.

Lyotard, J. F. (1984) *The Postmodern Condition. A Report on Knowledge*, Manchester: Manchester University Press.

Morley, D. (1980) *The "Nationwide" Audience*, London: British Film Institute.

Morley, D. (1986) *Family Television: Cultural Power and Domestic Leisure*, London: Comedia.

Murdock, G. (1992) "Citizens, Consumers, Public Culture," in *Media Cultures: Reappraising Transnational Media*, Skovmand, M. and Schroder, K. C. (eds), London: Routledge.

Nelson, Robin (1997) *TV Drama in Transition*, Basingstoke: Macmillan.

O'Neill, John (1995) *The Poverty of Postmodernism*, London: Routledge.

Rorty, Richard (1989) *Contingency, Irony, Solidarity*, Cambridge: Cambridge University Press.

Skovmand, M. and Schroder, K. C. (eds) (1992) *Media Cultures: Reappraising Transnational Media*, London: Routledge.

INDEX